WORLD ON BOARD: NORTH AMERICA

4 Wheels 4 Continents 1 Board 1 World

Written by ADRIAN OH

Edited by ASNAH AHMAD

ISBN
ISBN: 978-1-5437-5313-4 (sc)
ISBN: 978-1-5437-5314-1 (e)

Print information available on the last page.

To order additional copies of this book, contact
Toll Free 800 101 2657 (Singapore)
Toll Free 1 800 81 7340 (Malaysia)
www.partridgepublishing.com/singapore
orders.singapore@partridgepublishing.com

08/22/2019

PARTRIDGE

To my Parents, Stella and William, my Godmother, Irene and my dear Servien who stood by me

Contents

FOREWORD VII

PREFACE IX

WASHINGTON 1

OREGON 11

THE BIRTH OF PUSHIE 13

NORTH CALIFORNIA 23

SOUTH CALIFORNIA 34

NORTH BAJA CALIFORNIA 45

SOUTH BAJA CALIFORNIA 60

MAINLAND MEXICO 75

BELIZE-GUATEMALA 91

EL SALVADOR - HONDURAS 105

NICARAGUA 116

COSTA RICA 123

PANAMA 134

APPENDIX 141

SPECIAL THANKS 143

FOREWORD

I first travelled with Adrian to Hatyai back when he was an impressionable 22. Being the more experienced traveller then, I had planned this short trip for a few of us as Adrian had only been to the neighbouring country, Malaysia. I still remember his excitement in exploring everything Thailand and the picture of him beaming wide after a cabaret show is still vivid in my mind. His thirst for travel and adventure was evident even then. But I certainly did not expect him to take a journey around the world, on a longboard at that! When I found out what he had set out to do those two years, I was filled with pride, like a proud mother (ok, sister maybe). This soft-spoken, quiet, petite young man has decided to take on the world. Like a crazy girlie K-Pop fan, I followed his journey through his social media. I looked forward to each of his post that often came with a short anecdote. His humour is infectious. The pride I felt grew as his journey progressed. So when he was due to return, I was dying to hear all about his experiences. I have travelled over 90 destinations and written about at least 40 countries, but I know I will never experience what Adrian did, given the unconventional journey he undertook.

We met shortly after his return and immediately we spoke about putting his experiences into a book. I knew how avid travellers like me would love to read about his adventures. Many of us would not have the opportunity nor the courage to do the same. Reading some of the entries he made during his travels, I was even more convinced that his story had to be shared. Adrian's sense of humour makes it utterly pleasurable and entertaining to read. I sincerely hope I have done justice to his priceless memories as I co-write and edit the series of books with him. This is just the first of three. There are just too many stories to capture in one book. He is ebullient throughout this whole process and I am delighted he is willing to share his intimate experiences with us. Through his candid journal entries, he takes us along the many unique, unforgettable and uncanny adventures, transporting us to the various cities and travels.

Now as I write this foreword to his captivating book, it is my hope that this book provides a profound inspiration to many travellers out there and spark the inner adventurer in you.

Asnah Ahmad
Travel Writer & Editor

PREFACE

Novelist Nick Burd once wrote, "The world is vast and meant for wandering". That resonated with me throughout my life.

My yearning to travel began since the moment I can start to remember. I grew up in a travelling family. My first few travels with them, like many SIngaporean families, was to Malaysia. Every school vacation, I could recall going on bus tours with my extended family across the causeway. As I grew older, travelling was more reserved for competitions as I represented Singapore in Petanque. The Petanque World Championships took me to France and all over Europe. At first, I was new to travelling without my family. I could recall my mother packed me a carton of instant noodles, worrying that I would not have enough to eat or the French cuisine would not suit my palate.

The moment when I started travelling solo was when I travelled to Kupang, Indonesia, to meet my then girlfriend. I lost my return air ticket and ended up having to travel to Bali alone. There, I realise the joys of travelling alone. I could play arcade games or go wherever I desire. When that relationship ended, I was devastated. To nurse my wounds, I went for my first solo backpacking trip in 2006 to Eastern Europe. Subsequently, I yearn for more adventures to explore.

My history with longboarding began in 2012, when a friend wanted to learn the sport and roped me in. Initially, I was hesitant. The only skateboarding experience I had was during my childhood which left me with bruises. I swore off skateboard since then.

To cut a long story short, I ended up buying a longboard after much convincing. My first longboard was a Lush Machine, from Germany. I fell in love instantly and rode around my block. Soon, it became my main mode of transportation to work. In 2013, I stumbled upon a Youtube video on 3 longboarders skating across South America. This was the video that inspired me to start my own longboard travels. I have been an avid backpacker and my teaching job allowed me the space and time to go on my backpacking trips two weeks to a month at a time. Every year, I would backpack to off-the-beaten destinations like Uganda, Armenia, Georgia, Rwanda and many more. However, after a while, that felt void and empty. After all, sitting in a bus, travelling from city to another, became a prison to me. I found myself yearning to stop and spend some time amidst the wonderful scenery and landscape along the route. But having a fixed bus route meant I couldn't get off as and when I wanted to. Then it dawned on me, why not longboard around the world like those 3 guys I saw on the YouTube video.

Hence, began my journey to the world of Long Distance Skateboarding, where skaters pushed themselves to the limits to conquer various destinations. I researched on longboards that are made specially for long distance pumping and pushing. After tinkering with different setups, I settled for GBomb, a bracket extension for longboard truck to be lowered to the ground, needing less effort to push the longboard. My first trip on the longboard was to Desaru, Malaysia for 2 days. I travelled with a good friend of mine and another longboard buddy. For me, it was a success.

After this short trip, I grew more ambitious and began planning for a longer one. I researched on where long distance skaters have not been. I wanted to be the first. That leaves me to only one region. The Middle East, the region that got people terrified upon hearing its name. This will propel me to international stage. So, I began plotting my route, Jordan-Israel-Egypt seemed to be a safe and beautiful route with Petra, Jerusalem and Pyramids of Giza.

In December 2013, I set off for my first ever major tour on longboard. It panned out to be a disaster. I was not equipped for freak weather anomalies. Once in a century snowstorm hit the region just as I was travelling. I got arrested by the police in Israel for skateboarding in the Dead Sea Highway. I hitchhiked most of the 600 km I planned to skate. The trip was far from a success. But it was a good learning experience. I understood what I needed to do and acquire. Because of the learning points from that trip, my subsequent expeditions to Iceland and Cuba in 2014 was a success.

After several of such trips, I began to desire for something more challenging. Skateboarding one country at a time started to lose its appeal. During my month-long skate vacations, I often had to force myself to skate each day I woke up, even though I didn't want to because eventually, I have a flight home to catch. This eventually got to me.

I started to plan for a bigger challenge to conquer. Every day, after work, I was plotting my route around the world, daydreaming the places I could skate to. Reading the blogs of those who cycled around the world for years inspired me to do something similar but on a longboard.

Come 2016, my grandmother passed away. My father was away travelling in Japan and could not make it in time to her deathbed. That got me thinking. If I don't do this Mega 2-year skate trip around the world while my parents are relatively young and healthy, then when am I going to do this? This was the moment where it all began.

I took a leap of faith and tendered my resignation a few months later once everything is concrete, all ready to set my plans in motion. Only one last task to do. I had to break the news to my family, especially my dear mother. Mother, naturally, was hesitant to let me go. She feared for my safety. Who knows what would happen to me? She understood that my mind was already fixed and there was nothing that could change it. She had her suspicions when I started receiving packages from Amazon and buying other camping equipment. Eventually, she gave me her blessings.

As for my father, he was a photographer and traveling all over the world for photo shoots. He even travelled from Singapore to Europe, entirely overland, no flights. It was easy to convince him how much I wanted to do this. The plan was to set off on February 2017 right after Lunar New Year so I could spend some quality time with my family during the festivities. After that, it was time to chase my rainbows!

I finally returned home on 2 February, 2019, just in time to celebrate the Lunar New Year with my family. Even before my return, I already had in mind to document my journey. The thought of putting my daily entries into a book came naturally. It was too ambitious to put all of it in one single book and so this is one of a three-part series.

I would like to dedicate this book to all the road angels, my support crews and my sponsors, GBomb, Don't Trip, Orangatang Wheels and 1166 Longboard. One couldn't accomplish this feat without the help of others.

The reason for writing this book is to share my first-hand experiences of the kindness I received throughout this long and challenging journey, for it to be a testament that this world isn't so scary after all. If you look beyond the surface, you will find a place filled with compassion and humanity. It has become a mission for me to share this deep, profound knowledge to the whole world and you, my readers.

CHAPTER 1

WASHINGTON

Day 215
Country no. 14: USA
Vancouver, Canada to Blaine, USA
Distance: 50km
Time on board: 5 hours
Average speed: 10km/h
Cumulative distance: 8805 km

It was day 215. I had just completed my Asia and Europe leg of the trip.

I left Vancouver today to officiate the North America Skate down the Pacific coast. Vancouver, just like any North America state, was designed in grid-like roads, making it easy to navigate. It was located in a valley, so there were the downhills and uphill I had to conquer.

I still haven't got rid of my fear for downhill ever since my fateful accident in Spain. If downhill was steep, even at 20km/h speed, I would just get off my board and walk. Wasted time slowly walking downhill. Vancouver roads were shared together with cyclists; there was a dedicated cycle path beside the road making it pleasant to skate through except when I have to cross several Colossal bridges.

My fear of downhill and heights forced me to walk the 3 km suspension bridge. People think I am fearless just because I dare to skate around the world. On the contrary, I do have a long list of fears and phobias. Going on this tour means I have to face my fears all the time. I have learnt not to cower from my fear and walk away but to confront it head on like a bull waiting to charge in a bullfight.

I had to detour to Walmart as my shoes lost its sole, making it almost impossible to brake effectively. The current pair I am wearing has gone through 3 mountain ranges, from Berlin to Santiago, Spain, almost 3000 km distance covered. It has been re-soled twice. At Vancouver, I actually went to several shoe repair shop and they quoted me $70 just to re-sole. That shoe only cost me $17 and I have to spend 4 times the cost to re-sole? I might as well buy a new one. At Walmart, I found a pair for $15 CAD.

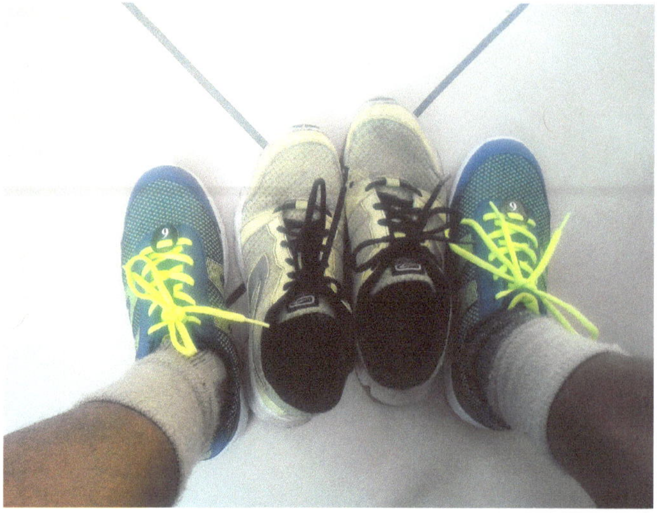

After buying my shoes, I took a break at a food court. Then I heard someone asking, "Where have you been?" I looked behind to find a lady looking all warm and friendly like I was her long-lost friend. Her name was Elen. She was Canadian with a British passport and in the process of getting an Irish one.

She recognized the shell, symbol of the Camino on my backpack. Her daughter completed the Camino de Santiago, the Way of Saint James last month, like I did. Camino Santiago was a pilgrimage leading to the shrine of the apostle Saint James the Great in the cathedral of Santiago de Compostela in Galicia in northwestern Spain, where tradition has it that the remains of the saint were buried. Many follow its routes as a form of spiritual path or retreat for their spiritual growth. Before crossing over to Canada, I completed the Camino on skateboard, as part of my journey across Europe from Germany to Spain.

We chatted for a bit and I was overwhelmed by surprise when she took out $15 CAD from her wallet and handed it to me. What was even more touching was that she even treated me to a hearty lunch. Elen was simply generous. We were total strangers, yet she handed all her cash to me without any hesitation. This was indeed a world without strangers. I am amazed by Canadians' friendly nature. A few I met along the way stopped to ask me about where I have been and what I was doing. They always listened in awe.

I may have lost my sole, but I surely found a new friend.

Soon I was skating on highway 10 towards the USA border. They squeezed a bike path right beside the busy highway, with vehicles zooming past me. There was nothing to separate the bike path from the highway except the white lines. Any crazy driver might swerve to the side and hit me. It was a thin line from fatal accident. But lucky for me, everyone respected their boundaries and kept to their lane.

It wasn't long before the Peace Arch monument came into view. The Peace Arch monument signify the peace and friendship between Canada and USA. Inscripted on the arch were the words, "The Gate never closes". I need to show this to Trump.

There I met a group of tourists from Guangzhou, China. They were intrigued and awed by my story. One lady from the group handed me $100 CAD after I told them how I cooked my pasta while camping in the wild.

That makes it 2 cash handouts in a single day. Unbelievable. Today I am reminded that goodness and humanity still exist.

At the immigration office, I was interrogated as expected. I ended up sharing my life story with them. I even had to show them my Facebook page and Facebook friends in USA. In 15 minutes, immigration officers knew more intimate details about me than my own parents.

I got past the border and entered Blaine, the border town. By then it was already 5 pm, too late to continue on. Since I received generous donations today, I decided to stay comfortably in Anchor Inn Motel. I've only seen Motels in Hollywood movies and have always wondered what it was like to sleep in one. I got the room for $65, with change to spare from my donations. Good thing that I got to stay in a motel tonight, as I realised, I had lost my power bank, meaning I would have empty phone tomorrow if I don't find a place to charge.

Day 216

USA: Blaine to Marysville (50 km skate 70km hitchhike)

Distance: 120 km

Time on board: 4 hours 38 mins

Average speed: 13 km/h

Cumulative distance: 8924 km

I forgot to buy breakfast and toothpaste the night before. Woke up hungry and smelly mouth. I probably stink to high heavens. The motel was comfortable though. It even came with a bathtub. I usually tried to conserve water, but when you pay US $60 for it, you better get your money's worth.

Checked out at 8am to set off along Pacific highway. Stopped by a petrol station to buy my bread. Bread here was much cheaper than in Canada. A loaf in Canada could cost $2 CAD and that was the cheapest in a no-frills supermarket. Filled up my stomach and was energised to go.

I followed the vista drive in Custer, suggested by Google map, it turned out to be a horrible road, like the one in northern France. Switched back to portal way, where I was skating originally.

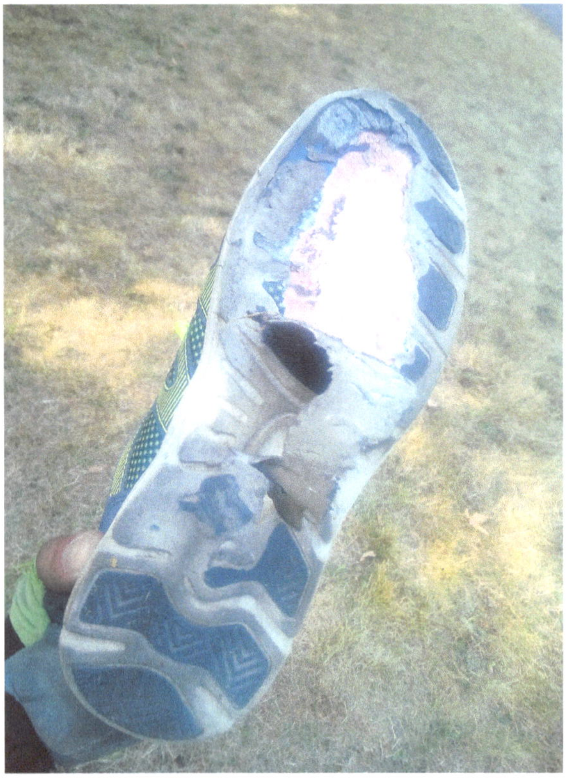

At last, got my USA data sim card at T-mobile in Ferndale. Paid $50 for 10gb data. There were cheaper plans but the offer was if I buy $50 plan, I get the sim card free. Now that I have a 10 GB for a month, I don't have to bother searching for Wi-Fi.

Skating up the Chuckanut hill was a piece of cake after going through the mountain ranges of Camino Santiago in Spain. However, while foot braking during downhill, I felt a lump in foot braking shoe, it turned out that the sole had worn out! I just bought this shoe YESTERDAY. Couldn't even last a shallow downhill. There were more downhills to go, and I couldn't footbrake anymore, so I decided to hitch a ride.

First, was Lauren who drove me 2km to the lookout where cars usually stopped for the view. Toby came next, he was going the opposite direction, but he turned to chat with me and gave me a beer. Everyone else just drove past me. Finally, William came along after his swim at the beach and gave me my ride. William, 63 years of age, was still very active just like my father. He looked more like a 50-year old though.

I needed to get to the nearest Walmart to buy a new pair of shoes. Hopefully this time it could last longer. I cannot afford to spend $15 on shoes every day. So, William drove me to the nearest Walmart that he knew of in Marysville. He wanted to invite me to stay at his home, but he called his wife and was refused. I totally understand having unknown stranger in the house could be quite frightening. Anyway, I was already prepared to camp out. Was really grateful for the ride.

Today's original destination was Burlington, but since I got a ride, I ended up in Marysville just 12km away from Everett, where I would stay with my Warmshower host, Jeff. Tomorrow would be a super short ride.

Shopped at Walmart for another pair. I tried my luck to get a refund but was refused as the shoes were not intended for foot braking. Oh well! I bought another pair for US $12 and got canned hot-dog to put in my pasta for dinner.

Found a stealth camping spot behind Walmart, in case I got hungry in the middle of the night. Pitched my newly bought Black Diamond Spotlight bivy. Bought my bivy in Canada, just in case I cannot find trees, or it gets cold during the night. Only took me a minute to set up. I guess I would be using it more often from now on.

SLEEPLESS IN SEATTLE

with James Peters

Day 218

USA: Everett to Seattle
Distance: 39 km
Time on board: 3 hours 14 mins
Average speed: 11.8 km/h
Cumulative distance: 8962 km

Sleeping in my Black Diamond spotlight bivy was very comfortable. Was hesitant in buying it due to bad reviews. But I was petite in size, hence fitting in the claustrophobic space was fairly easy. All bivy face the issue of condensation. This one wasn't any exception. I close the bug net and left the opening, leaving me to breath better. Hence less condensation. Still my sleeping bag got damp.

Greg picked me up from my camping spot behind Walmart. Went to Walmart to buy toothpaste. Always been forgetting to buy toothpaste and ended up with bad breath. Maybe that was why no one wants to kiss me or get close to me.

Greg, another avid LDP (Long Distance Pushing / Pumping), drove me for breakfast at Denny's and bought me soles for foot braking at motion board shop. Since it was raining, he dropped me off at Everett where I stayed with my Warmshower host Jeff and Maureen. They told me it was the first time it rained since June. I am probably the blessing. The rain quenched the dry season and forest fires, so the air was less hazy. But it would be bad for me. Start of autumn means I must get out here soon into warm California before I freeze to death.

Day 218 left Jeff and Maureen's home. They trusted me to leave the house last while they rushed to work. Maureen was also a special education teacher, just like I was. Had a great chat with her, reminiscing the career I had for the past decade.

The weather was gloomy, and the surface was wet, not ideal but still good to skate though. James Peter and Greg recommended the inter-urban trail route to Seattle. Sometimes the trails goes into a bike path on the highway. A thin line between life and death. Any driver could drive recklessly and hit me, nothing in the bike lane could prevent that.

Arrived at James Peter's home by noon. James was regarded as the Godfather of LDP. He founded the Pavedwave, the website where all aspiring ldpers goes to for advice. It was the mecca for LDP. He was also the man behind the first 24-hours ultraskate and promotes the event to what it is today. It was a great honour to spend some time with him and his family in Seattle.

Day 220
USA: Seattle to Tacoma
Distance: 91 km
Time on board: 6 hours 49 mins
Average speed: 13.4km/h
Cumulative distance: 9064 km

James decided to accompany me through Burke Gilman trail from his home. He mentioned that Bruce Lee studied in Seattle and was buried with his son Brandon here. A Bruce Lee fan, I definitely had to pay homage to the late legend.

Burke Gilman was a pleasant ride, especially when riding with famous pavedwave.org James Peter. We split at the Husky Stadium and I made my way to Bruce Lee 's grave at Lake View cemetery. It was a steep climb, but it was worth to make my pilgrimage to the Legendary martial artist.

Since I skated Seattle yesterday, I don't fancy skating another time with my gigantic backpack through the hectic traffic of Seattle. I took bus 150 to Tukwila where I got on the interurban trail. From there, it was a straight path to Auburn. Cooked my pasta lunch under interstate 5. The hot pasta soup warmed me up in the cold, rainy weather.

Met a Japanese couple at the intersection of West Valley Highway who, like me, were touring Pacific Northwest to Argentina. They wanted to cycle along the freeway interstate 5. I was like 'were they insane or suicidal'?

They were the kamikaze edition of cycle tourers. Tried to convince them by showing them a safer alternative route. But I guess to each his own.

That evening, I met Clark Blumenstein, the maker of Blumenstein audio and stayed with him. He showed me his workshop where he experimented with longboard. He was the maker behind Eric Danger Palmer's 300 mile Ultraskate longboard. Glad to have met him and staying with him that night.

THE RACE

Day 227
USA: Olympia to Chehalis
Distance: 74.5 km
Time on board: 5 hours 24 mins
Average speed: 13.8 km/h
Cumulative distance: 9176 km

Since the Pacific Northwest (PNW) launched its inaugural tri races all over the PNW, I intentionally chose this region as part of my route. The main reason was that my LDP friends were mostly along the west coast, getting them to host me could mean not just great company but would be a great help to my tight budget.

The first of the PNW tri-race was the centennial skate race in Arlington held over 2 days. I stayed with Clark Blumenstein longer than expected as I retrofitted my shoes with braking soles. As Clark owns a workshop, it was easier to fix stuff using his tools. It took a whole 36 hours for the glue to cure. Thanks to Clark's expertise in handicraft, he managed to fix my shoes and gave me his Westssup paddle. At last in this Continent America, I got a paddle to skate with.

On the first day of race, we arrived 15 minutes late. Clark was one of the chilliest guys I have ever met. He could remain so calm in times of stress. Even though the others pushed off way before us, we still participated in the 8.5 miles race, and yes, we came out last.

Angela and Chris Kuhn, the organiser of centennial skate race kindly waived my participation fees, a great gesture by them. Meeting all my newly-found LDP friends once again felt like a family reunion. Especially Ehren, Harrison, Miguel and Conan, who recently got married. After the first race, we gathered at Miguel 's family Mexican restaurant for dinner and camped at the allotted campsite for the races.

The next day, we started with 5 km or 3 miles. I am still confused over imperial measurements system. Apparently, I wasn't a good sprinter. I was going at 25 km/h yet finished quite close at the bottom. Everyone was bursting close to 30km/h. My god, how did they do that. The last race, 14.5 miles or whatever it was in km, I fared much better, finishing 12th place. Though I have a lower max speed than the rest, I could hold it much longer, finishing just over an hour.

After the centennial skate race concluded, Ted Bilderback took over being my personal trip buddy from Clark and drove me to his house in Olympia, Washington. The good thing of the tri series was that it wasn't a final goodbye. I would still meet everyone over next 2 weekends in Portland and Bend.

I suffered a cold over the last few days in Ted 's house. Mary, Ted's wife and his son, Sol, both caught the cold as well. I hope I haven't passed my virus to them. Ted was the only one in the house not to catch a cold. Lucky bastard. Therefore, I spent 2 days sleeping in Ted' s house without stepping out of his house to see Olympia or Lacey.

Portland was only 200 km by skate. I took my time to skate to Cory ' s home in Portland. Ted worked in farms, therefore suggested that I camp in one of his farms in Chehalis. He wrote me a note, giving me permission to camp in the farm in case anyone finds trouble with me, or thinks I am trespassing on private property.

As the morning began, I was going to be the last to leave Ted's house. Ted and Sol both left for work and school respectively. Mary was about to leave for errands. Asked her how I locked the doors afterwards. "Oh, you could close the door, just fine. It was a quiet neighbourhood." I was wowed by the fact nobody locked their house in this neighbourhood. Must be a very safe one. Even in Singapore, one of the safest countries, you would be deemed foolish not to lock your doors. Here, you could simply leave your doors unlocked in this neighbourhood. This was one neighbourhood I want to live in.

Stopped by Wolf Haven, a real sanctuary for wolves. Not even stepping inside, I could hear the wolves howling. Definitely not a good place to camp here. Sat outside to cook my pasta soup lunch. The beef stock cube felt waxy, probably I carried them for a long time since north France. That was ages ago. Better to discard them before I suffered another bout of upset stomach.

Skated into the old highway 99, I couldn't get to skate on the famous Route 66. 99 seems a nice alternative. I stopped at Walmart for grocery shopping and spent $3.55 for the next 3 meals. Walmart was indeed my best friend in the USA.

I continued another 8km to the farm but stopped halfway for mulberry foraging. Since embarking on this tour, I learnt to live off the land and forage as our ancient ancestors did millennials ago. This, my friend, how I get my daily vitamins free and fresh without pesticides.

Arrived at Ted's farm, it was void of any life form except one pussy cat. Supposed everyone knocked off work already. Set camp among the fields of stars. The farm was rural, and far away from any mobile reception tower. I guess it would be a quiet night for the stars. *sounds of crickets*

CHAPTER 2

OREGON

Day 228
USA: Chehalis to Portland
Distance: 73 km / 45 miles
Time on board: 6 hours 4 mins
Average speed: 12.1 km/h / 7.45 mph
Cumulative distance: 9249 km / 5748 miles

I've learned never to assume that I would have a peaceful night's rest. Across the river, lies a railway so the howling of the freight trains had accompanied me all night. Woke up at 6.45 am when the farm workers started scuttling in for work.

I skated back to the trail to connect to highway 603. Man, it was jaw chattering chipseal. I was huffing like an asthmatic old man, struggling below 10km/h. I actually felt orgasmic when I transitioned back to smooth road. It's like releasing your poo after enduring for what feels like hours.

At Napavine, Washington, a lady driver stopped to pass me a note. I was actually hoping for it to be cash. But to my disappointment, it was a prayer booklet. She probably figured I needed a lot of prayers on the road from insane drivers.

Stopped at a road construction. The guy informed me it was going to be unpaved for 3/4 quarter of a mile. In my head, I am scrambling to figure how far 3/4 of a mile was. After 2 weeks in USA, I still couldn't wrap my head around the imperial system. When I see a sign 30 to Seattle, I was like yea, only 30 km to Seattle, just 2 hours of skating. After a while, it dawned on me that 30 miles was 50 km.

By then I calculated the conversation, I would have already reached a mile. By the way, 3/4 mile was 1.2 km. I have to walk 1.2 km through the unpaved road. Fortunately, a lady in a big truck shouted, "Jump in!" I instinctively threw my board and backpack and jumped in to the back of the truck. They drove me to Winlock, apparently where you could find the world's largest egg. I wonder if it's for real. All I could think of was that if the egg was that large, I could eat for weeks.

Skated on Westside highway, till Castle Rock. Should have figured out that it isn't as flat as what Google claimed it to be. I was skating on Pleasant Hill Road. It was far from pleasant. They should change the road name, seriously.

Always had the impression that American cops were brutal, judging from killings of non-white citizens often shown on news. Last night, while camping in a park, a policeman woke me up.

"That was a fancy tent you got there".

After all, I am not supposed to be camping there. But I saw homeless people sleeping in the park, naturally I assumed that it was alright to sleep in parks. However, I pitched a bivy tent in the middle of field, that was super conspicuous, stood out like an elephant in the room. I explained my story once again to the police. He checked my passport and wanted to suggest a decent camping spot for me. In the end, he allowed me to continue sleeping provided I leave at the crack of dawn since he found me cooperative and not causing any trouble. I guess the police aren't so bad after all.

Tried returning to my dreamland but couldn't as I was on alert mode. Once at 6am, when the skies turned greyish blue, I packed up my stuff and squeezed my longboard and backpack into my bivy tent during the night, worrying about theft. After breakfast, rain came pouring down. The weather forecast was accurate over its prediction. It was going to rain the entire day, no alternative but to continue skating to Portland. My consolation was knowing that at the end of the day, I would have a warm shower and a cosy bed awaiting me in Cory's home. Cory Poole had invited me to stay with him in Portland.

As I skated along the boulevard of Longview, a wreckage at the other end caused a massive pileup of cars lining up at the bridge. The shoulder was filled with debris, making it impossible to skate through. Rick and Vince offered me a ride across the bridge. Though walking would probably be quicker, getting a ride beats walking in the cold, biting rain. While waiting for traffic to clear up, we chatted. Rick's son was also a longboard skater and at age 16, he desires to go off the grid; no internet and no smart phone in the wild. That was a 16-year-old I never heard of. Nowadays kids cannot survive without Facebook and other social media, let alone surviving in the wild.

Rick and Vince dropped me off at Rainier. How appropriate, given the pouring rain at this point of time. I was resigned to walking in the rain, but luck was on my side, a car pulled over and Matthew offered me a ride to St Helens. Any distance covered means I could get to warm shower and cosy bed sooner. That was motivation enough for me. The bike lane was mostly filled with stone debris, cautioning me to skate at tortoise pace. I wondered how did James Peter and Clark Blumenstein do their Seattle to Portland in this same road on longboard?

Cory arranged to meet me and accompanied riding with me to his house at St John's bridge. 7 km away from St John's bridge, another car pulled over, offering me a ride. Michael was heading to St John's for work. What a coincidence. Today, I had 3 free rides without me needing to hitchhike. They just pulled over and wanted to give me a ride despite me being drenched, soaked to the bones. I get to know 3 wonderful drivers. I am not into any records since Guinness World Records rejected my claim, so I accepted any ride I could get when road conditions were too dangerous and not conducive to skate.

While waiting for Cory at the bridge, I cooked my noodle pasta for warmth. Cory arrived and we rode 18 km to his house, where warm shower and cosy bed awaits me.

THE BIRTH OF PUSHIE

Day 223
USA: Portland to Salem
Distance: 50.5 km / 31.3 miles
Time on board: 3 hours 24 mins
Average speed: 15km/h
Cumulative distance: 9418 km/ 5853 miles

I was toying with the idea of having a trailer with brakes since my accident in Spain. Cory Poole happens to be the guy who makes them, and I am staying with him in Portland. So I ordered a jogging stroller from Amazon but it didn't work out as the handbrake was hand-locked, meaning it would jam brake, not good at down-hilling at high speed. We looked through Craigslist and got a 2nd hand stroller for $60. The brakes were compatible with bicycles, so I could easily get it replaced.

Push in the Woods, an annual push race in Portland organised by Robin Mcguirk and Cory, was happening that weekend. The race ground was wet and slippery, almost slipped a couple of times, hence I decided to let the guys sprint ahead while I slowed down to enjoy the race. 5 km and 10km race ended pretty fast.

The jogging stroller was a great idea. Initially I was sceptical about the idea. The stroller swerved a different direction from my board. After I got the hang of it, I was on the roll. My back never felt so light and free of burden before. Carrying a 17kg load daily took a toll on my back. Today, my back finally freed from its shackles. The advantages of pushing a stroller were that I could carry more load and water. On my backpack, I could only carry up to 5 litres of water. On the stroller, I could carry more than 20 litres of water, giving me the freedom to skate anywhere I want without having to camp at towns for water supply. 20 litres could last me for 4 days, meaning I could skate through deserted areas without having to worry about water. At last, I am truly free.

Another advantage was that it comes with a hand brake, compatible with bicycle. I could go downhill with ease and reducing my speed without having to burn my soles. Safer than foot-braking. Only pain in the ass was having to tow uphill. Gravity hurts but it was only marginally slower than pushing uphill with my backpack.

Accidentally spilled boiling water on the ground, leaving me no more cooking water as I forgot to top my water supply this morning. Was too hungry to bother saving money, got myself McDonald's meal before shopping at REI Recreational Equipment Inc in Salem. The REI store manager noticed me and was intrigued by my skate stroller. I explained my story. All the whole staff knew my story. Bought a collapsible 20 litres water container so that I could skate for days without searching for water.

Continued my way to Salem, the state capital of Oregon. A couple asked me to take photos for them which I obliged. I explained my story to Dago and his Chinese wife. He gave me $2 for coffee. Wow! The sign I made explaining my travel works. People noticed me and know my adventures without having to explain umpteen times. Next, encountered a homeless on bicycle. Charlie Brown the clown as he called himself. Chatted with him until Larry, the owner of Longboard Larry arrived to pick me up. Had pizza with his family before he showed me his workshop.

Day 234: Master of Improvise

USA: Salem to Shedd
Distance: 49 km/ 30 miles
Time on board: 3 hours 44 mins
Average speed: 13 km/h
Cumulative distance: 9480 km / 5891 miles

Being a special education teacher, you must learn to think on your feet and improvise. There was no one hard rule to teaching each student. Every student was a unique individual. That was how I hone my skills in improvising during my world tour. Switching to pushing the stroller was a good improvisation. Going downhill never felt so safe before.

One of my ex-students always spoke of Oregon USA. He always wrote about the nature and beauty of Oregon and dreamt of visiting Oregon. I dedicate Oregon to him. Since Eugene was more than 120 km away, it was too far for a day ride yet too near for 2 days ride. Helped out at Larry's longboard workshop to kill time and to thank him for hosting me. Larry mentioned to me his clients came mostly from China, Korea, Asia and Europe. Few Americans bought his boards as they rather go for cheap China-made board while the Chinese shunned the cheap China boards and go for USA branded boards. A shift in demographics.

Worked till 10am and bid farewell to Larry. The road was fairly simple, just followed highway 99. Pushing my push trailer was a breeze. Stopped at a state park to cook lunch and nap. Encountered my first steep hill. Pushing up the uphill relatively easy without the weight on my back anymore. Downhill was safer with the brakes too. With the push trailer, I could carry 20 litres of water, granting me freedom to camp anywhere without stopping in towns for water. Now I am free!

Day 235: Hi Eugene!
USA : Shedd to Eugene
Distance: 58 km / 36 miles
Time on board: 4 hours 10 mins
Average speed: 14 km/h
Cumulative distance: 9553 km

The main issue of sleeping in bivy tent was condensation. I tried to improvise by covering my sleeping bag with a trash bag. Apparently, it didn't work. The trash bag got damp, making my sleeping bag even wetter than before. The bitter cold morning reminded me that I should get out of Oregon as soon as possible to sunny California. Skated to Haley city, buying 99 cents loaf of bread for breakfast. Once my stomach filled, pushing gets smoother.

On the flat straight highway 99, I see horizon after horizon. Once I arrived at horizon, the next horizon appears. Never ending horizon. Just like your goals in life. Once you accomplished that goal, immediately another goal appears then you chase after it. Life becomes a series of endless horizon, fulfilling the purpose of life.

Arrived at junction city. Just as I was taking photos, a man walked across the street and came up to ask me about my journey. I was starting to draw attention with longboard and push cart.

Had another round of peanut butter bread for lunch, trying to finish my peanut butter bought from Vancouver last month. Better to finish it before it turns bad. Took my siesta and the opportunity to sun dry my damp sleeping bag.

The push cart was fun. The only issue was I have to watch for debris that could puncture the tires. I have to be more cautious and swerve around debris. Felt like I am riding on a motorcycle. I even pretend to twist my handlebar, just like a biker would.

Followed highway 99 to Eugene before turning to Eugene river bike path. Visited REI camping store. It had become a ritual for me to drop in every REI store in every city. I drool over the latest camping gear like women do for that new handbag.

I passed by a graffiti, "The secret to a fabulous life was to live imperfectly with Great delight." It dawned on me, there was no such thing as a perfect life, to live a perfect life was to actually live an imperfect life the way you want to. Get the irony. Overcoming trials and tribulations in life make living so perfect.

Arrived at my Warmshower host Noah Zitier' s home, the Duma community house. It was co-owned by several people including Noah. All of them were vegans, environment activists and they love biking. It was like a Paradise for cycle tourers. Noah invited me to a monthly city-organized night bike ride. After 58 km, what was another 16 km? So, I joined them for the ride after dinner. It so happened to be the last monthly ride of the year before winter. Just in time.

Final series of Pacific Northwest championship finally concluded in Bend. Bend Beatdown comprised of 3 races 5km, 10km and 25km over the weekend. Colby Cummings and Kyle fought neck to neck over the title and Kyle came out champion and Colby Cummings was the overall champion of the Pacific Northwest series.

The 25 km was rather interesting, rather than the usual flat fast race; competitors had to climb 330 m /1000 ft ascent and descent 330m downhill. I opted to stay alive, paddle braking cautiously. At the end of the race, we gathered at a pizza parlour for the prize presentation ceremony. There was a raffle draw for all participants and I won the longboard from Larry Longboard through the Raffle draw. Would like to keep the board but couldn't carry it with me through the journey. Conan made the exception, allowing me to sell the board to fund my world travel. Managed to sell it to Conan's friend for $100.

It was a rare opportunity to hang out and chill with the homies after the race. Usually, I had to rush off to catch my flight, but now I could spend quality time getting to know the LDP homies better.

Sent off Calleigh Alice for her TransAmerica. Love to join her for the entire journey but it would get really cold in the North. I am not genetically engineered to endure the harsh bitter winter. Miguel, Ehren, Ryan of Subsonic, David and Lance turned up to skate the first km with her.

Going to stay another night in Conan's home before taking the bus to Coos Bay to continue my skate towards South America. Conan would be my last warm bed for weeks before Jack Smith in Morro Bay in South California

Day 241: Pacific 101
USA: Coos Bay to Denmark
Distance: 65 km / 40 miles
Time on board: 5 hours 34 mins
Average speed: 11.8 km/h
Cumulative distance: 9668 km / 6008 miles

Took a bus from Bend to Coos Bay. The view along the route was magnificent. Mountains dominated the view and gigantic trees decorated the mountain. On the bus, there was a passenger, Marc. Let's just say he was rather eccentric. He kept talking to me about aliens, government conspiracy and Jesus 2nd coming. Wait a moment, if he believed in Christ then what about aliens creating us. Contradictory. Not wanting to aggravate him, I nodded in agreement while admiring the view. Gave him my mobile phone number, thinking that I would soon get rid of my T-Mobile number.

Woke up to a rainy morning. Tempted to sleep in and skate the next day. However, I checked the weather forecast, showers over the next 3 days until Saturday. I cannot afford to pay for 3 nights stay in a motel or delay 3 days of my journey. Today was supposed to be best weather among the 3 rainy days. Waited for the window of opportunity for the sun to appear at 10 am. Put on my rain gear and began my Pacific Coast skate.

Though Pacific highway 101 hugs the coast, it isn't flat. Hauling 20 litres plus 17 kg backpack up the slope wasn't the easiest thing ever. Resorted to walk the slope. Heaved a sigh of relief when I reached the peak and descend the hill. Usually, I would opt to walk downhill after my accident. With my pushcart brakes, I had the confidence to skate the downhill, fingers clutching the brake lever, controlling the speed down the hill.

Since I had a late breakfast, I didn't stop to cook my lunch at noon as usual. Stopped at Bandon in search for my data sim card. US cellular, just as Verizon, wants me to buy their phone. They directed me to Bandon IT, another AT&T third party retailer. Mike patiently assisted me to make this work. We tried all options but to no avail. Looks like I am stuck with T-Mobile.

At a highway deli, I grabbed 2 slices of pizza. Strangers kept asking me about my skate journey. I always obliged to share with them however, what irked me was a driver pulling over to take photos of me skating without wanting to chat or enquire about my journey or even ask for permission. Usually, people would chat with me and take photos, but he just ignored me when I say hello. He just drove off. How rude.

My original plan was to skate 90 km to Humbug mountain state park hike bike campsite. Hike and bike campsite were available to hikers and bicycle tourers for a nominal fee of US $5. Rain delayed my progress, so I had to camp along highway 101. The reception was already closed therefore I tried my cheapskate method of not paying and leaving at the first sight of dawn. Camped behind but the owner spotted me. I explained my story to him and he gave me a 50% discount at $15 US. Normally I wouldn't want to pay for campsite since I could do it for free, but it was too dark to skate in search for wild camp spot. Well, at least I got Wi-Fi and hot showers tonight.

Day 242

USA: Denmark to Humbug mountain state park
Distance: 25 km / 16 miles
Time on board: 2 hours 26 mins
Average speed: 10.4 km/h
Cumulative distance: 9694 km / 6024 miles

Pretended to pitch my bivy tent but I was sleeping in the warm cozy recreational lounge. When I was packing to leave, I couldn't find my Anker 26000mah power bank. Searched for hours before giving up the search. Either I misplaced while packing or someone stole it under my nose.

I hardly see any soul around; I like to discount this possibility. The wife of the campground owner returned me $10 since I arrived late and didn't use much of facilities. I only paid $5 for camping. Well, you win some, you lose some.

Wanted to set off early but the rain kept on pounding. Put on my rain gear and left at 9.30am to brave the torrent rain. Stopped at Port Orford, claimed to be the oldest town on the Oregon coast. There lies Battle Rock, natural rock formations off the coast. Reminded me of the twelve apostles in Australia. I stopped many times for a photo, too magnificent to miss the opportunity.

On one of the photo stops, a lady driver pulled over to ask me if I am alright. In my mind, I would like to say no, lady, I am freezing to death in the harsh bitterly rain. In the end, I said I am fine, just admiring the view. Even if I said I am feeling worse, she couldn't give me a ride because of my pushcart. Usually in this weather, I could hitchhike. Now with my pushcart, it becomes impossible for me to hitchhike. No drivers would pull over to load my massive pushcart. In a sense, I am damned to eternity skating on my pushcart throughout. Now I am forced to skate all the way regardless of weather and roads, no more temptation to hitchhike.

I cut short today's skate to seek refuge as torrential rain kept pounding on me. Threw in the towel and surrendered to mother nature. Pushed only 25 km to Humbug mountain state park for hiker/biker campsite. $5 for camping with hot showers. And they couldn't refuse any hiker or bikers even if they were full. They had to accommodate all hikers and bikers.

There wasn't a reception at the campsite, people have to self-check-in, write their particulars on an envelope and place the money inside. I wonder if all Americans were that honest? I skipped the registration, trying to save $5. The handicapped toilet looks spacious enough for me to sleep in for tonight.

The rain finally took a long-awaited break, giving me a window of opportunity to hike. Hiking to battle Rock Beach was like finding a hidden treasure. If I didn't know where I was, I would have thought I was in Iceland; moss-filled mountains and gusty winds blowing the waves to shore. Must thank the rain for forcing me to stop here.

Day 243
USA: Humbug mountain state park to Brookings
Distance: 80 km / 50 miles
Time on board: 7 hours
Average speed: 11.3 km/h
Ascent: 848 m
Descent: 815 m
Cumulative distance: 9773 km / 6074 miles

While admiring the last moment of sun setting down on the horizon, I felt a tinge of loneliness. I wish I could share this moment with someone. Been searching for a companion ever since my last breakup. That someone must be adventurous, willing to accept a tent as home, and not over crazy possessive. My ex-girlfriend was almost the one, but I blew the chance somehow.

Enough said, back to my story. Met a couple at the campsite. First person they thought of when I mentioned I am from Singapore was not our great beloved Lee Kuan Yew nor infamous outspoken Amos Yee. But Joseph Prince, pastor of New Creation church. They were the third Americans who associated Joseph Prince with Singapore. His influence has really grown over the Christian world. Little wonder he was among the top ten richest pastors in the world.

Slept in the handicapped toilet. Showered, shat and slept in the same space. That was how much space I needed. I even ate my breakfast there. After skating in the rain for 2 consecutive days, the rain doesn't bother me anymore.

I dropped by the prehistoric garden for a photo moment. Touring allowed me to visit places that only local tourists would go. Continued on to push into Misty woods and into the coast. Staring into hundred-foot drop cliffs along the road, any wrong move could send me diving to the ocean. The mist engulfed the road like cotton candy.

Finally meet a bicycle tourer Dan from San Francisco, he was making way down south back to San Francisco and invited me to stay in his sailboat. Great. Another place settled.

Every viewpoint was simply spectacular, I have to stop at every few hundred metres to take in the breathtaking views. I rather go slow than to miss the opportunity of admiring the moment. The 101 highway zips up and down, I am starting to detest now. Now it was the reverse. I have to walk uphill hauling my 40kg load and skate downhill, squeezing the brake and footbraking.

Reached Gold Beach just before it showered once more. Sought shelter at the visitor centre with Wi-Fi and area for me to cook lunch. Pushed on the next 45km with more ascent and breathtaking views of the rock formations by the ocean.

Mark Groenenboom, the owner of Gbomb and my sponsor, offered to pay for tonight's motel stay. After suffering in the rain for 2 nights, a hot shower and bed was welcoming. Mark has been a great sponsor and supporter ever since I started my long-distance tours. Gbomb brackets are bracket systems attached on a longboard to provide infinitely adjustable truck angles, ample wheel clearance, modular design for travel, and improved flex distribution for superior strength and lower ground clearance, thus allowing me to expend less effort in pushing. I have been using Gbomb brackets ever since my virgin skate trip to middle East and it never fails me, accompanying me throughout my world tour. Mark also sent me a couple of new bearings in anticipation for wet weather ahead. He has been an amazing support to my world tour. Arrived in Brookings, just in time for sunset. Brookings was the last town in Oregon before entering the California state tomorrow.

CHAPTER 3

NORTH CALIFORNIA

Day 244
USA: Brookings, Oregon to Crescent City, California
Distance: 43 km / 26 miles
Time on board: 2 hours 48 mins
Average speed: 14.3 km/h
Cumulative distance: 9817 km / 6101 miles

I can see clearly now, the rain is gone,
I could see all the obstacles in my way
Gone were the dark clouds that had me blind
It's gonna be a bright (bright), bright (bright) Sun-Shiny day.
It's gonna be a bright (bright), bright (bright) Sun-Shiny day.

Finally, I could get to sing this song by Johnny Nash. After suffering 3 conservative days in the rain, today I could greet Mr Sun. A good omen. Started late as I must wait for AT&T cellular store to open at 10am to get my data sim card. 6 GB for $45. Excellent coverage throughout Pacific west coast. I could surf Facebook while I am skating. Since I have a handlebar mount for my phone on my pushcart, I could literally stare at my phone while skating.

The route was flat, barely uphill or downhill. Shortly after I passed the California state line. Once into warm sunny California, I immediately could feel the sun blazing at me. No wonder it was called the Golden State. Now I could sing Eagle's song Hotel California along the way.

Got a Warmshower host at Crescent city. Skated into Del Norte County with gigantic Redwoods tree surrounding me. 7 km before Crescent city, a cycle tourer caught up with me. He saw me yesterday at Brookings trying to climb the hill. He was making his way down to Baja California.

Highway 101 turns to a Freeway but legal for bicycles to ride on the shoulder. The shoulder lane was wide enough to accommodate two cyclists hence it was pretty safe despite the cars zooming at top speed. Exited the freeway into Walmart where I shopped for groceries. It was going to be my last Walmart store until San Francisco, better stock up on food.

Arrived at St Paul's Episcopal Church where Jeanine welcome me. Katie was the Warmshower host but she was away, so she got the volunteers to aid me. This was the first time an organization was actively supporting cycle tourers in Warmshowers. I got a whole lounge to myself. Spent time watching the sunset and movie Blade Runner 2049 in the cinema.

Day 245
USA: Crescent City to Pairie Creek Redwood state park
Distance: 55 km / 34 miles
Time on board: 5 hours 27 mins
Average speed: 10.2 km/h
Ascent: 722 m
Descent: 726 m
Cumulative distance: 9872 km/ 6135 miles

I had the whole lounge to myself last night. Cleaned up the lounge before the church congregation meet at 9am since they were kind enough to allow me to sleep there.

Immediately upon exiting Crescent city, lies the Del Norte Redwood State Park Hill. A big hill I must say. I had to walk up pushing my pushcart with my longboard. Vehicles must stop at the signal light to allow vehicles from the other direction to pass first. Me being the bottom of the food chain, have to let everyone from my side pass first. Ended up walking for 2 hours before reaching the top of the peak. Met a cycle tourer along the way, decked in green with green panniers. He was going to be my favourite cyclist.

Downhill was steep at 7% grade, further with the sketchy road, I have to combine pushcart brake with footbraking. I pulled over at Demartin Beach to cook my lunch. Dan, the cyclist I met the other day who offered to accommodate me in San Francisco, came speeding down the hill.

Shortly 2km after lunch on the beach, I pulled over at Trees of mystery with museum exhibiting the history on native Indians. The reason why the native Americans were called Indians, was because Christopher Columbus wanted to explore India, instead he went the wrong direction and ended up in America Continent. The first natives he saw were assumed to be the Indians from India.

Diverted from 101 highway to scenic Redwood drive. Redwood trees are the tallest trees in the world, spanning from 100 metres high. Looking at them stresses my neck. I am insignificant compared to these ancient trees.

Once at the top was a 10 km downhill to campsite. At the big tree, James approached me. He was intrigued by my adventure and invited me to his home tomorrow in Arcadia.

Another warm bed tomorrow. For tonight, I had to camp at Pairie Creek Redwood state park with the elks. US $5 for hike/bike campsite.

Day 246

USA: Pairie Creek state park to Arcata
Distance: 67 km / 41.6 miles
Time on board : 6 hours 21 mins
Average speed: 10.6 km/h
Ascent: 548 m
Descent: 572 m
Cumulative distance: 9939 km / 6177 miles

Camping in the wild was literally a 5-million-star hotel experience. Never have I seen so many stars in my entire life. Viewing the milky way galaxy from my bivy tent was indeed a humbling and awe-inspiring experience. Hailing from a city with massive light pollution, I never get to see so many stars. Not that there aren't any stars, in fact stars were ever present, just that we couldn't see them in bright lights. Only time of darkness, that you could see the stars shining. In life, people were like stars. They were around, but you just couldn't see them. Only time of darkness, the stars would shine for you. Today, James and Traci were my stars.

Woke up to Elks herd grazing grass at the field right next to me. Seeing the majestic beasts breathing next to me makes my $5 camping fee more than worthwhile. Best camping experience ever. Rode off into the mist. Continued the downhill where I left off yesterday into Orick.

While skating down a sketchy road with debris all over, my jacket fell from the pushcart. I turned my head to look at where my jacket had dropped and wasn't focussing on the traffic cone ahead. My pushcart tipped over, but I managed to jump off my board safely. Blessing in disguise, I found my lost Anker power bank when everything dropped out from the pushcart. The thing was I already bought another in Walmart. Now I have 3 power banks giving me a total of 56000 mha. I could stay off grid for weeks since I only need to charge my phone and Garmin watch.

A cycle tourer caught up with me in Patrick 's Point right before 101 turns to a freeway. Paul from Germany was riding his way to Argentina as well. Shortly, we were joined by a Canadian father and daughter team, Henry and Hannah. All of them happened to camp in the same campground as me. They noticed my pushcart yesterday but assumed it was a foldie. They wondered why there was a longboard as well. Now, they know why.

Together we diverted to Patrick point scenic drive where I parted ways with them as I was famished, I couldn't go on without food. Furthermore, the roads were rough, couldn't skate fast enough to catch up with them. Stopped at the roadside to cook lunch, same old instant noodles with pasta and hotdogs. Took opportunity to sun dry my sleeping bag, tarp and bivy tent.

Continued on, but the road turn from horrible to abysmal. Potholes, loose gravel, sunken road everywhere. It resembles central America ride rather than the developed first nation USA. Too late to make the change back to 101. At least, the view along the coast make it less miserable.

The scenic drive ended, leaving me skating on freeway 101. Luckily it was legal. Sped off for a short section of freeway before returning to Pacific coast bicycle route. A cyclist asked if I had a pump. Indeed, I do. Pushing my pushcart required me to carry bicycle spare parts, pump, tubes and patch kits. I am becoming more of a cycle tourer than a skateboarder. We pump up his tires and raced on the Pacific coast.

Hammond trail turns to gravel again. I threw in the towel, risking my life to go on freeway 101. Returned to bicycle route and ride along the farmland. Yesterday, James who spotted me on Redwood highway while returning from his surfing trip in Crescent City, had invited me to his home in Arcata. That was the reason why I say James was the star of the day. James and his wife, Traci, welcomed me warmly. They actually made me some curry rice. Apparently, they were cycle tourers as well. They rode across Alaska together. Furthermore, James was also a skateboarder. We had a lot in common to talk about. To top it off, they have a sauna. Sauna to warm me up in cold autumn nights. They were my shining stars indeed.

Day 248

USA: Arcata to Myers Flat
Distance: 96 km/ 62 miles
Time on board: 7 hours 35 mins
Average speed: 12.6 km/h
Cumulative distance: 10,035 km

Found a home for my Westssup paddle. Traci mentioned that she land paddle as well with DIY PVC pipe. To repay their kindness towards me, I present them my paddle since I don't paddle anymore after I got my pushcart. Been searching for a suitable new owner. At last it found a new home. Bid them farewell early in the morning.

I tried catching a bus from Humboldt State University since it was raining. But no bus could accommodate my pushcart and they all refused to take me. Now my pushcart has become my liability. I am stuck with it no matter how bad the road gets. Well, I couldn't 'cheat' anymore.

The road to Eureka was only through a freeway. Skating on a freeway may sound dangerous but actually it was much safer than shoulder-less highway. The freeway shoulder was definitely smoother, just look out for vehicles turning at exits. Eureka was quick, stopped at the last Walmart stop before San Francisco. Stocked up a weeks' worth of food.

Skating through the freeway, I skipped all the towns. Usually I would pass through towns. This time it was just a direct, straight no brainer route. Was famished along the way but nowhere to stop. I pulled over under the freeway bridge to cook my lunch.

10,000 km!! Hit my 10,000 km at Rio Dell. A big milestone for me. 248 days 10,000 km. Felt like a large boulder off shoulder. Was anticipating my 10,000 km and when it arrives, it was like meh. I always emphasise that it was about the journey, rather than the numbers.

Exited the freeway to Avenue of the Giants, the scenic drive through majestic Redwood forest. Then Henry and Hannah, the Canadian father-daughter cyclists arrived. I assume that they would have been a day ahead of me. Apparently, they took a day's rest at Arcata, where I was being hosted by James.

We rode together to the campsite. The avenue of Giants was indeed awe-inspiring. The trees were so tall, they literally blocked the sunlight. We made several stops for photos. Even stopped to hike a trail. It was one thing to ride through the forest, but it's another matter to walk through it. Photos couldn't do justice to the sheer size of these tallest living things on earth.

Approaching the campsite, they sped off. When I arrived, the campground was closed for sewage renovation. I just camped there anyway. Free camping, why not? The Canadian cycle tourers probably continued on 8 km to the next campsite. After doing 96 km, I am not going to skate another 8 km, furthermore, daylight was rapidly disappearing. I thought I was going to be alone tonight, but shortly after Luckie from Toronto, Canada arrived. He was cycling for a cause to raise funds for 5 patients with cancer. He too welcomed the idea of free camping. 3 Finnish female cyclists came by too. Looks like it was going to be a party tonight.

Grant and Melanie, though not cyclists, drove in. They asked us if they could camp as well. After we pitched our tents and got ready to turn in, the ranger came. He was about to let us sleep for the night, since it was already pitch dark. He couldn't possibly ask us to ride another 8km in the dark. But Grant had a car, he could drive us to the next campsite. The ranger got us to pack up and drove us to the next campsite, where I finally met Henry and Hannah and including Dan. It was a big cyclists conference.

Day 249
USA: Myers Flats to Leggett
Distance: 70 km / 43.5 miles
Time on board: 6 hours 41 mins
Average speed: 10.5 km/h
Ascent: 855 m
Descent: 647 m
Cumulative distance: 10105 km

Sleeping in the Redwood forest was a cool experience; viewing the giants from my bivy at night and the trees covering the night stars like skyscrapers. Redwood trees were Earth's natural Skyscrapers. Had a 2nd dinner thanks to Melanie cooking spicy potato's and mushrooms for us, ever-hungry cyclists. Being on tour, we could consume enormous amounts of calories as we burn lot of it daily, especially in my case. Forecasted to rain at 2pm, and with a 1000 m ascent, I woke up extra early to get a headstart, trying to reach Leggett before the rain. The guys were planning to share a motel if it gets wet.

The first hour was smooth, covering 14 km. Pushed on continuously without breaks for 2 hours. Exited 101 to Redway, where the road was closed. The road closure meant having the whole road for us. Then Luckie and the other guy came over. We rode uphill to Redway for a signature coffee. I don't know what it was as I don't drink coffee. Next we continued to Gaberville where I met the rest, Dan, the 2 ladies, Henry and Hannah. While setting off first for a headstart, I went the wrong way. It was the exit for 101 freeway. Turned back to join them. Start of the dreaded hills. The road snakes around the river, looking down at hundred-foot-drop down the cliffs.

I passed the One Log House, where they dug a huge hole on an enormous log, to make a room and a kitchen. Basically, you could live there. The Carver working at the gift shop spotted me, remembered seeing me skating in Fortuna yesterday. He gave me a handshake as he wanted to touch the hands of the guy who skated across the entire America Continent. I feel like a celebrity now.

The weather forecast was so accurate, it really rained at 2pm. After going through Oregon, the sprinkler posed me no threat. Counting down the miles to Leggett campsite or Motel. At last, arrived at the Rock Creek campsite, where there was Dan and Allison. The rest probably went ahead to the motel. The campground got a sheltered recreational area where I could finally set my hammock to sleep in. In the end, it started pouring and I decided to sleep in the toilet once more.

Day 250
USA: Leggett to Fort Bragg
Date of entry: 19 October 2017

Distance: 77.4 km / 48 miles
Time on board: 7 hours 35 mins
Average speed: 10.2km/h
Ascent: 1077 m
Descent: 1371 m
Cumulative distance: 10182 km

'One man's toilet was another man's bedroom'.

Quoted by Dan. I slept comfortably in the toilet last night. Tried persuading Dan and Allison to join me but they prefer sleeping in the cold wet tent. I have grown accustomed to sleeping in toilets, it was warm and comfortable and clean.

People have the perception of toilet being dirty and somehow in their mind, sleeping in toilet was disgusting. I developed this sense of survivor ever since my tour. I would do anything to survive, that includes sleeping in toilet to stay warm and avoid paying camp fees to save money or grab freebies. When you were on a long tour like me, you would resort to anything to survive. I wouldn't claim myself to be an honest man. But I am a survivor. The sky continued dumping rain through the night and morning. Should have slept with other cyclists in a motel 7 km away. Screw it, I am not going to wait till noon for the rain to stop. Regardless of rain, I continued skating. I got acclimated to the wet, chilly rain already. With my rain gear, I am dry and protected from rain. Skated to Leggett's famous drive- through-tree, where cars could literally drive through a tree. However, the park was closed, and signs warned of no trespassing and video surveillance. I better not take the chance, or I would end up in jail.

Prior to going back to the coast, there was a big climb which I spent 2 hours walking up the steep gradient. I could see the hairpin turns from above. After 2 hours of walking and just 15 km, I reached the peak and downhill. Clutching my brakes and footbraking at the same time while swerving the hairpin turns. Had to drastically slow down at the turns, in case any trucks come up to me. Made it down alive in one piece. Thought it was the end of the climb but another climb awaits to torment me.

Unable to go on without food, I stopped at the roadside turnout to cook my lunch. Then the cyclists arrived. I was wondering what took them so long to reach me. First was Dan, he was a fast-strong rider. Next was Allison then Henry and Hannah, followed by Luckie and Leslie. Finally, I got their names right. They were talking about my toilet- sleeping. Arrived at Mackerricher state park only to find the camp fees for hike and bike was $10, double to what I usually pay. Protested to the camp host. She understands, she too took the issue to her superiors but it turned on deaf ears. I didn't pay for yesterday's camping. So, I guess it was karma.

Just as I wanted to pitch my tent, I saw Luckie's message about staying in a motel in Fort Bragg 8 km away. Chipping $19 for a warm bed and shower was way better deal than paying $10 for cold hard camping. I immediately packed up and rushed to camp office to ask for a refund. The lady had already closed her register, but thankfully she was nice enough to reopen her register and do the extra paperwork so I could get my refund. A truck stopped by; the driver claimed to be John Hanson who skated across USA long time ago. I assumed he must be part of Jack Smith's crew who skated across the USA.

With newfound motivation for warm bed, I mustered all my reserve energy, dashed off at the light of speed to Fort Bragg. Got to view the sunset down the horizon while skating. Got to the motel to share the room with 4 cyclists. Finally, a warm shower after 3 days of soaking in sweat and rain.

Day 251: Coasting the rollercoaster in Coast
USA: Fort Bragg to Manchester
Distance: 62 km / 38.5 miles
Time on board: 5 hours 26 mins
Average speed: 11.4 km/h
Ascent: 794 m
Descent: 798 m
Cumulative distance: 10244 km

The hot tub in the motel kept me warm for the cold gloomy morning. Had breakfast with the cyclists in the motel. Set off earlier than them to get a headstart. The road was simply going up and down. Still, the uphill was mellow enough for me to skate smoothly. Push to Mendocino within an hour. Mendocino was a small town hanging by a cliff. I detoured to explore the town as recommended by the cyclists.

Continued the rollercoaster ride up and down. Rinse and repeat. I could skate up most of the hills this time, making much faster than previous days. Spotted a creek after a descent and I pulled over by the road for lunch to watch cars descend down the creek. I tried taking a nap but felt the sprinkler pouring down. Better get moving again. The cyclists caught up with me after 35 km. We rode together to Elk, a tiny town with a population of only 250. They stopped for lunch while I just ate my banana. Only 20 km left to Manchester state park campsite so we took our time and chill out.

Immediately after Elk, there was an outrageous ridiculously steep climb. Even walking up was extremely tenuous for my calves. I had to lean 45 degrees forward to push my cart. Once downhill, I forgot to slow down before the corner and I couldn't stop my pushcart from tipping over the kerb. Note to self, 'Always remember to brake hard before corners.' This I must drill into my head now.

Arrived at Manchester KOA campsite with the cyclists reaching just moments before me. $10 for tent but comes with a hot tub. Totally worth it. As I pitched my bivy tent, Mr Sky dumped its water on me again. This time, I couldn't sleep in a bathroom as they have cleaning scheduled at 12am. Got to try sleeping in the rain.

Day 252

Date of entry: 22 October 2017
USA: Manchester to Salt point state point
Distance: 65 km / 40 miles
Time on board: 5 hours 28 mins
Average speed: 11.8km/h
Ascent: 742 m
Descent: 686 m
Cumulative distance: 10309 km

Yesterday was Karaoke night at the campground. The cyclists invited me to go over to sing as they always hear me singing on the road. They could testify to my prowess, no wonder they were so eager to get as far away from me, avoiding hearing my screeching. Luckily there weren't many audiences at the karaoke to witness my awesome singing.

As I could not sleep in the bathroom last night, had no alternative but to test out the survivability of sleeping in a bivy tent during a rainy night. I managed to keep warm albeit my sleeping bag got damper than usual. Still, it retained its warmth throughout the night. The advantage of bivy tent over conventional tent was it keeps you warm as there was little space for the cold air to circulate inside. The downside was you have to deal with condensation.

Woke up to a wet morning with my stuff and tarp soaking wet. I couldn't wait for them to dry before setting off. The cyclists were aiming to ride 115 km to Bodega Bay. I could do that far if it was flat and smooth like in Europe. But not here in USA. Hilly terrain makes it hard for me to skate above 15 km/h. I suppose today was the day we have to say farewell. I left earlier than them at 9am. The road was rougher than usual here so I struggled a little. The cyclists caught up with me at the 16 km mark. Had our last wefie. Though I travel alone, I was not lonely. I get to meet a lot of people like them. They have accompanied me over the last 4 days. We shared a motel room, camped together and rode together. The company on the road was always pleasant to have.

However, we have different goals and were bound to go our separate ways eventually. San Francisco was their final destination, while I continue my way down south to 'end of the world'.

I gained momentum and started speeding. I wonder if it was the sandwich I received from a kind lady. But then I noticed the grass were pointed towards the direction I was skating to. It was Tailwind that was providing me extra booster. My average speed increased rapidly from

10.8km/h to 12 km/h. Once I crossed to Sonoma County, the road started to smoothen out, adding to my speed.

I pressed on until Stewart Point where I made use of Sun power to dry all my wet stuff. It took mere minutes for my sleeping bag, bivy tent and tarp to dry. As I skated on, a lady driver asked if she could take a photo of me. Of course, I obliged. I never refuse a photo shoot. Judging from her accent, she was from Thailand. She offered me water and asked if I needed anything else. I have food, tent, water. All the necessities to survive, I had it all. That was how sustainable I am. The only other thing I needed was some money and a warm bed.

She was driving to the next campsite at Salt Point and invited me to stay with her. That posed a dilemma for me. Free secure camping with possible Thai food for me or I could take advantage of tailwind and continue skating further. I chose the former. Anyway, I was not in a rush to reach San Francisco.

I arrived at Salt point state park campsite to join Ajchara, if I could get her name correctly. Apparently she was married to an American who was currently working in Australia, so she went on a camping road trip on her own. We hiked to the salt point trail to catch sunset and view waves pounding down on the rocks. Waves reminded me of vanilla milkshake. White foams surrounded the rocks.

I realised that I have the habit to pee at a spot where I could admire the scenery while I pee. It became a ritual for me to do so. Standing there admiring the scene while peeing makes it more memorable as I could really stand still to focus on the image of the view. I suppose that goes the same for dogs peeing to mark their territory.

Day 254: Crossing the Golden Gate
USA: Corte Madera to San Francisco
Distance: 16.9 km/10miles
Time on board: 1 hour 38 mins
Average speed: 10.3 km/h
Cumulative distance: 10326 km

Yesterday, Ajchara invited me to join her for mushroom hunting and stay in her home in Corte Madera, North of San Francisco. The prospect of hunting for mushrooms excites me. There were 3 foods I couldn't resist; eggs, cheese and mushrooms.

We hiked into dense woods where fungus lay around dead trees. Ajchara and her husband were avid mushroom hunters. They hunt many varieties of mushrooms that I am not aware of. She could identify different mushrooms to a variety of tastes. Some taste like beef jerky and some like oysters. It was interesting how mushrooms could have an array of flavours. Must take the opportunity to learn from her so next time, along my route, I could forage for mushrooms.

We couldn't find any mushrooms, she commented we were a week too early. But the hike was interesting. It was the process of foraging for mushrooms and the walk through the woods that makes it exciting. If any consolation, we found US $5 on the ground.

The drive there was spectacular. Viewing the scenery from the passenger seat was rather different from skating through it. Though we went through the view fast, sitting in the passenger seat enabled me to admire the view in a more relaxing way. Skating on the road, I have to stay focus with my eye on the road yet trying to admire the scenery in front of me.

Ajchara was sort of on a long vacation since the winery she works at in Santa Rosa got razed to ground. She offered to drive me to the vista point where I resumed my skate into San Francisco, crossing the famous landmark, the Golden Gate Bridge. Crossing the bridge on a longboard, I was in awe as the towers on both ends enlarged as I approached.

Before crossing the bridge, I had to carry my pushcart up and down the stairs. This was the first time I cursed for having a pushcart. Hopefully I won't get to encounter many stairs ahead.

Some passers-by came to my aid, helping me carry my pushcart up the stairs. I crossed the bridge and officially entered San Francisco. By right, I should have received mobile coverage on my AT&T network. But somehow there was no data or phone signal. Skated through the city in search for AT&T store.

San Francisco was founded on a series of really steep hills. Even my pushcart brakes and footbraking couldn't slow down the speed on the downhill. I just have to walk down. My image of San Francisco was on a tram down to the bay. Today I realised that vision as I followed the tram down the hill into fisherman wharf, then passing through Chinatown, the largest Asian community in North America. I thought I had entered Hong Kong by mistake. Could hear the Cantonese tones along the streets. So surreal. Found the AT&T store but it was busy. I had to make an appointment for the next day.

I navigated the famous steep hills of San Francisco and made it to my Warmshower host, David Helder, for tonight.

As Cascada's song 'San Francisco' goes:
Wake me up in San Francisco
We knew the power was in your head, girl
Party everywhere, girl
I Wake me up in San Francisco
Where the love was in the air
All the people stop and stare
Baby take me back to the city of love
To the place that I've been dreaming of
San Francisco...

CHAPTER 4

SOUTH CALIFORNIA

Day 260: The Skateboard Hall of Fame
USA: San Luis Obipso to Morro Bay
Distance: 23 km / 14 miles
Time on board: 1 hour 44 mins
Average speed: 13.1 km/h
Cumulative distance: 10390 km
Day 255-259

Stayed with my Warmshower host David Helder for 2 days before crashing into Dan's sailboat in Emeryville Marina. I have never slept before in a sailboat. That was an experience and a checklist ticked off. Sailboat was not for anyone, especially those with claustrophobia. Works for me, as I am used to sleeping in toilets. My boat neighbour, Alfredo from Costa Rica, was so generous. He gave me $10 in support of my trip.

Forced to buy another phone since my AT&T sim card strangely doesn't work on my French phone anymore. Only after buying LG Phoenix 3 for US $50, then realised I could have saved the money by renewing my T-Mobile data card. Now I ended up with 2 phones, one to navigate and surf the web, another for photos.

I am going to love central America. Spent days sleeping on sailboat or patronising Barnes and Noble bookstore. Yes, when I do have rest days, you could find me either in REI camp stores or bookstores.

Being a cheapskate, I spent the entire day reading books in the store without ever having to buy one. Finished reading 'South Park and Philosophy'. South Park, on the surface, seems crass, insulting, violent cartoon. If you look deeper, you find it covers socio-economic issues.

REI organized a used gear swap / sale on Saturday, a must go for me. Ever since skating with a pushcart, I could carry more stuff and no longer hesitate to buy more stuff to make my journey more comfortable. Visiting REI was like a kid visiting a toy store. I got myself a 2nd hand MSR dragonfly stove. It wasn't my first choice though as it was heavier and makes lots of noise while burning. But the weight doesn't bother me anymore and as for noise, I am usually by myself, not having to converse with anyone during mealtime.

I needed a multi fuel stove soon as my MSR Pocket Rocket camping stove would be rendered useless due to lack of availability of gas canisters in Mexico and the rest of Latin America.

While in San Francisco, I have to make a tough decision. Though Big Sur was reopened after a massive landslide, further down Mud Creek was still not yet restored. This means there was no through way for me along the coastal road. Alternate route would be an extra 100 km detour up the mountainous terrain, it was going to add 2-3 days to my trip and I have to reach Los Angeles by 9 November to prepare for the Adrenalina race. So, I decided on taking the Amtrak train from Oakland to San Luis Obipso, bypassing 400 km of magnificent coastal big Sur road. A pity, but I don't have any other option. I skated 10 km from Emeryville Marina to Oakland station.

The ticketing agent asked me if my pushcart was a bicycle or not. It has pneumatic wheels and brakes, so I would say it was a hybrid. Ticketing agent wanted me to make a decision as bicycles cost extra $25. Ok, it was a stroller. At the train, initially the conductor won't let me in due to my pushcart. Eventually she relented and gave me the lower level handicapped space.

Arrived at San Luis Obipso by 2.45 pm. Backtracked another 22 km to Morro Bay where the Legendary Jack Smith lives. Jack was the original Transamerica skateboard pioneer, crossing the USA on 4 occasions, 1973, 1984, 2003 and 2013. What was more amazing, he did it on small puny 57mm urethane wheels and anorexic skateboard in the 70s. I did it with the latest technology, massive 80mm Orangatangs wheel and don't trip trucks, Gbomb low lowrider brackets and 1166Longboards quality deck. This was nothing compared to Jack›s journey. Of course, he skated across America with a group of friends in a relay and a van escorting them but given their traditional skateboard, it was a colossal task. Therefore, the backtrack to Morro Bay was a must-do Pilgrimage for all skateboarders. Upon Leaving the San Luis Obipso station, I entered Highway 1, straightforward no brainer route to Morro Bay.

First 5km was surprisingly tedious, was it the rest days in San Francisco that was making me unfit? I gave up, stopped to take a look at my pushcart. Only to realise that I forgot to release my parking brake. Been pushing 5km with resistance.

I passed through California Men Colony. What place calls itself 'men colony'. Upon looking at Google map, realised it was a maximum-security prison. What deceiving name for a prison.

Arrived at Morro Bay and spotted Jack's van. I took a photo with it before paying homage at his skateboard museum. Backtracked to his van, where Jack drove me to his home to stay. We shared our trips and experience. Though I have notched lots of skateboard journey, but hearing his stories was another level altogether. Just in time for Halloween tomorrow.

Since I already skated from San Luis Obispo to Morro Bay, there was little reason for me to do the same route again, so Jack drove me back to San Luis Obispo where I resume my journey once more. Woke up early to bid Cathy, Jack's wife, farewell as she too was a teacher, and had to leave early for school. I fully empathised the hardships of being a teacher, being one myself back in Singapore.

As I tried to skate, my pushcart leaned backwards, doing a wheelie when I applied downwards pressure. The top was filled with stuff together with my 20-litre water container, making it unbalanced. I had to discard half of my water in order to balance the pushcart.

The nearest campground was 150 km away, I could only make it there tomorrow. Hence, I had to wild camp tonight. It was the start of the fall season, meaning shorter daylight. The sun sets at 6pm, leaving me less time to skate. Passed through Guadalupe, reminding me of a French skater Jerome Bevilacqua who lives in the real French territory of Guadalupe. Took a photo of the town and requesting him to accommodate me, which was a joke of course. The French Guadalupe was thousands km away.

Caught on the tailwind and increasing speed. By 5pm, I had to search for a wild camping spot. Ideally, it must be either higher or lower than the road level, so cars couldn't see me at night. Spotted an almost perfect camp spot, right next to Highway 1 where I could immediately resume the skate tomorrow and it was below the road level. Today was the Dia de Muerte, the day of the Dead for Mexicans. Hopefully nothing come and disturb me tonight.

Day 263: Invasion of Ants

USA : Orcutt to El Capitan State park
Distance: 85 km / 53 miles
Time on board: 6 hours 26 mins
Average speed: 13.2 km/h
Ascent : 682 m
Descent : 776 m
Cumulative distance: 10533 km

Surprisingly the night was relatively warm. I didn't have to sleep in my sleeping bag. And the night was relatively bright as well; I could see everything without having to turn on my solar lamp. However, I was invaded by tiny puny ants crawling over my tent and pushcart. Luckily, it was those tiny, black ants and not the ferocious fire ants. On hindsight, I should have checked the wild camp spot for ants.

Woke up early and packed rapid fast as I have already reconfigured my load on pushcart. All camping and cooking stuff and essentials go into my 2 dry sacks whereas those not in use often goes into my backpack so I don't have to unpack to retrieve them. Everything now was very simple and organised.

Set off at the crack of dawn without taking my breakfast as I didn't want to add ants as part of my protein diet. Backtracked to Orcutt main town to connect to 101 highway. In Orcutt, I passed by a Catholic church. I was just in time for the 8am mass. Decided to pop by and attend my Eucharist mass since I haven't done that for a long time. The mass was short and ended in half an hour. Good for me, didn't eat too much into my skating time. Took my breakfast at the church park. Refilled spiritually and physically, I pushed on.

Today's route was fairly simple, just follow highway 101 the entire way and there were only 3 peaks that I have to conquer. A piece of cake for me. The first 2 peaks were just long and gradual, not too steep. Managed to push the entire ascent before descending the way down. Downhill was long and easily controlled. Just clutch my brakes without having to footbrake. As Disney movie Frozen goes, 'Let it go!'. I was zooming at 25 km/h without having to worry about controlling my speed. This was the perfect downhill.

101 alternates between being freeway and highway. I don't really understand the difference. Everyone goes faster in the freeway as the speed limit was raised. That was all. Shoulder lanes was still as wide for me to skate safely in my own bubble.

Left 101 and entered Los Alamos. The town has the old wild west feel with the saloon and tavern. My childhood dream was to be a cowboy. Playing with my play Mobil cowboys when I was a kid and watching the cartoon, the Lone Star, inspired me to dream to be a cowboy one day. Today I skated through wild west town on my trusty Rodeo, Gbomb 1166 longboard like a modern-day cowboy. Helmet replaced the fedora and pushcart replaced the carriage.

Exited Los Alamos and back on 101. 2nd peak began. Conquered with ease and straight downhill to Buelton. By noon, I had already covered more than half of today's distance, a first in American soil.

The Final peak right after Buelton was tough. Not that it was steep, but it was accompanied by the headwind, transforming into an Everest for me. Walked up the hill with gusty wind blowing against me. Victory was sweet upon reaching the peak. It was the last climb of the day. Now I could savour the downhill and flat roads onwards.

Arrived at El Capitan State Beach campground. The hike and bike camping were an extortion at $10. Oh well, at least it came with a beautiful view of the sea, and the sounds of the ocean waves crashing.

Day 264: Ace Ventura
USA : El Capitan to Ventura
Distance: 77 km / 48 miles
Time on board: 5 hours 58 mins
Average speed: 12.9 km/h
Cumulative distance: 10609 km

Had my peanut butter breakfast as usual before setting off at 8 am. Entered freeway 101 and skated 33 km nonstop to Santa Barbara. Prior to Santa Barbara, Goleta, a passer-by commented that I was carrying too much load. Well, I was going for self-sustainability. The main bulk of my load was actually water. Of course, I could carry less water and stop at every town to refill. But finding places for free refill was tough too. Shops scorn at you for free tap water. So, I'd rather just carry large amounts of water with me. I could go light like I used with my backpack. But that also means I have to find a place to stay in towns and cities. That cost money. With my pushcart carrying loads, I have absolute freedom to go wherever I want.

After months of skating 10,000 km, I would expect my legs to be iron strong. Today, felt tightness and aches on my legs. Each push was sluggish. Arrived at Santa Barbara at 11 am, later than I would expect. Dropped by the REI store to fix my camp fuel. Two sales rep tried their full might to open the could but to no avail. They had to get their hulkiest sales rep to assist. Even he was having difficulty opening it. I am glad cos that means I am not weak. In the end, they replaced it for me. This time I managed to open the new one.

Visited their bicycle section to ask the mechanic if there was any way to upgrade and strengthen my braking power on my pushcart. I have to get new calipers and stuff. It would take time to install hence they just tighten the brake cable and it worked much better now. Outside REI, I made peanut butter sandwich for a quick energy boost and to wait for a cycle tourer. I am always interested to meet new cycle tourers and enquire about their journey.

Santa Barbara has the Mexican town feel, as seen in their architecture. Skated along the beach bike path. Wished I could stay in Santa Barbara longer for its beach. But hostel bed costs $60, as much as a motel room I had paid before. So I had to move on elsewhere.

It was already 2pm, I was too lazy to cook. Stopped at 7-11 along the way to get a microwaved Burrito for $2. Continued on pacific coast bike lane, which then led me to a bike path next to 101. On one side lies the mountains and on the other side lies the pacific coast. I could only marvel at the road ahead of me as I pushed on.

Close to Ventura, I met Badara from Sierra Leone. He makes jewellery in Malibu. The reason that he stopped me was to ask if I got any marijuana. Dude, I am from Singapore where taking drugs was heavily punished. Maybe I looked homeless with my loads on pushcart. Anyway, explained my story to him, earned myself another fan.

I decided not to skate to LA tomorrow. Firstly, hostels would cost a lot during the weekends. Secondly, I wanted to drop by Orangatang headquarters. They wanted to see how the Kegel wheels they sponsored look like after 11,000 km. They were only open on weekdays, of course.

Emma Beach State Park wasn't on my list of campgrounds so it come as a surprise. Anyway, decided to stop there so I had more time to admire the sunset. It was a self-register kiosk. Cost was $10 for hike and bike but I only placed $5 into the envelope since I strongly feel that would be a fair price to pay. $10 for a simple small tent space was extortion, once again I have to reiterate this point.

Pitched my tent and off to view the sunset. When I got back, the camp host suggested that I should move to a spot next to his trailer as homeless people wander around the hike and bike area to steal unwary traveller's belongings.

The camp ranger found me later at night and asked me how much I paid. Since I was the only camper on site, he probably knew how much I paid. I responded I paid what I think was a fair price. Anyway, I paid up the remaining $4 cos I have either $20 bills or 4 $1 bills. He accepted the $4, saving the hassle to find change.

Tomorrow would be a short day, hopefully I could arrive early to enjoy the Malibu beach.

Day 265: Malibu Dream
USA: Ventura to Malibu
Distance: 54 km/ 33.5 miles
Time on board: 3 hours 58 mins
Average speed: 13.6 km/h
Cumulative distance: 106663 km

'How was it going?' The first phrase all Americans use to greet. Even if the stranger was meeting you for the first time, they would go, 'How was it going?'. No one says 'Hello'. Only the foreigners do. The scenario going in my head was played out in supermarket. When checking out my groceries, cashier would greet 'How was it going?'. Naturally I would just reply "Great and you?".

But let's say I decided to reply, "I've been skating for months, thousands of miles going through hot desert sun and torrential rain, cold bitter nights and mountainous terrains. What do you think? Everyday sucks."

The cashier would then reply, "Oh I am stuck in a minimum wage job, struggling to pay the rent and feed my kids. Life sucks too". Then we both would start wailing.

Woke up late since I decided to skate halfway to Malibu, not reaching Santa Monica, L.A. today. Since it was the weekend, hostels were probably occupied by drunken teenagers or too expensive. Skated to Ventura downtown to buy bread for breakfast and grabbed a couple of stuff for dinner.

Followed the Pacific coast bike route sign and led me to Oxnard. Straightforward route, Google map suggested to stay on Harbour Boulevard for 10 km. No brainer. Then another long stretch of road out of the Oxnard, skirting around Point Mugu naval base. Passed by Point Mugu missile park. Displaying the F-14 planes and missiles. Stopped there for lunch. The gusty wind, close to a gale, I would say, affected my igniting the MSR pocket rocket. After countless attempts to ignite my rocket, waiting for a break in the wind, I finally launched my Pocket Rocket. How ironic? I am in a rocket park trying to blow up my mini rocket for lunch.

Continued on freeway 1, this time there was a sign that says bicycles and pedestrians were prohibited but Google map suggested this was the only route I could go. Ignoring the sign, I made my way. If patrol highway caught me, I would just lay the blame on Google map. And I am not a cyclist, I am on a skateboard. No sign prohibiting skateboarders on freeway, right?

Entered the coastal highway. Santa Monica mountains on my left and Pacific Ocean on my right. My favourite type of ride. Flat with mountain and ocean view. I could go on skating like this forever, never having to stop. Not eager to reach my destination, I skated, pushing one at a time, hoping there was no end. Paused at the viewpoint to clear my mind. Arrived at Leo Caprillo Campsite by 3 pm, leaving me plenty of time to sit on the beach in Malibu. If only there was Malibu Dream cocktail for me.

Tomorrow, on to L.A!

Day 266: Holy Hollywood and city of angels

USA: Malibu to Santa Monica, Los Angeles
Distance: 44 km / 27 miles
Time on board: 3 hours 11 mins
Average speed: 13.9 km/h
Cumulative distance: 10,707 km

6.30 am. Oh no! It's so bright! The sun usually rises at 7.30 am. Why was it daylight so early? I double checked my watch and mobile phone. I recalled today was the beginning of daylight savings. The clock set backward by one hour. Doesn't make much difference to me as I still have the same amount of daylight hours to skate. Just that now I start at 6.30 am and stopped by 4 or 5 pm. I have longer hours psychologically to skate till 12 noon for lunch and shorter hours afterwards to arrive at my destination.

Upon exiting the campground into Highway 1, the sign says, "Lane closed. Special Event". I wondered if they were anticipating my coming to Los Angeles city and closed the road to welcome me into L.A.

The only time I received such hero welcome was in Cuba 2014. I skated from Santiago Cuba to Havana 750 km. In the city of Cienfuegos, the police blocked the traffic on one lane and personally escorted me skating into the city. Either they got nothing to do or they were really intrigued by me. It was not to be today.

Today was the Malibu Marathon. The city closed one lane for runners. That means I don't have to jostle for space with traffic. I only have to push my way through hordes of runners dashing towards me. I quickly set up my rudimentary cardboard sign reading, "Skateboarding America to Argentina", so runners knew why I am skating in their lane in the opposite direction. I cheered the runners on as I passed them.

Finally, the road closure ended once I skated away from the racecourse. Back to jostling with cars once more. Pushed through Malibu luxurious residences where houses were right by the beach. Residents could literally jump out of their home straight into the ocean. They must be filthy wealthy and famous. Hoping to bump into some Hollywood's stars however I saw none.

By noon, I have arrived in Would Rogers beach, the beginning of bike path along the beaches of L.A. Skated leisurely along the bike path while admiring the beach view or more like the bikini girls. The final hurdle was to haul my pushcart up the stairs of Santa Monica pier. Made several trips up and down the stairs to carry my load separately. There lies the Route 66 marker. Though I didn't skate the famous Route 66 running from Chicago to LA, I did transverse nearly the entire Pacific coast highway 101. A group was offering free hugs there. They didn't mind I haven't showered or washed my clothes for 5 days. I earned their hugs with lots of sweat.

Booked myself in HI Santa Monica hostel. I have been to L.A before in 2014 to participate in Adrenalina skate marathon and skate Cuba. Therefore, Santa Monica isn't an unfamiliar place to me. In fact, Santa Monica was my favourite part of L.A. Now I am back again for Adrenalina next weekend. This was nostalgic for me.

Day 274: Light at the end of the Tunnel

USA: San Clemente to Encinitas, California
Distance: 55 km/ 34 miles
Time on board: 4 hours 1 mins
Average speed: 13.7 km/h
Cumulative distance:10875 km

Day 268 – 273

Skating fast in 42 km Adrenalina Skateboard marathon race in San Diego was tougher than touring 80 km daily. Touring was skating at a leisurely pace with plenty of breaks whereas in a marathon, you have to push as fast as you could, trying to beat your time and others. I pushed my muscles to the limits, trying to beat the sub 2 hours barrier. In the end I fell 28 seconds short of sub 2 hours. I could achieve sub 2 hours if I could turn around fast enough for the hairpin turnaround at each lap and if the volunteer could fix my Tailwind Nutrition. He didn't understand what was pouring the powder into the bottle and mixing with water.

Anyway, I could only blame myself for that. Still, I finished 3rd in my age division 30-39. What a way to end the IDSA race season and end of USA and meeting my LDP skate family for the last time before exiting USA. However, I lost to my buddy DeeJay Pascua by a minute. I accounted it to the vegan food he has been force feeding me in the days I stayed with him.

The following day after the race, DeeJay took me and his friend, Guvitiar, hiking up Echo mountain. My legs were sore after the race.

Left DeeJay's home in Fontana on day 273 to continue my way. Skated to San Bernardino to catch a train to San Clemente. I didn't know the last direct train to San Clemente was at 12 pm and I missed it by seconds. Took longer train to los Angeles before transferring to San Clemente. By then, it was already dark at 5pm.

Skated in the dark to my Warmshower host Ken Meade. He has the most amazing house.

From his balcony, I could see the sunset and the Pacific Ocean. I was lucky to get hold of him as he would be returning back to South Africa soon.

Left Ken's home at 8.30 am. He was probably my last Warmshower host for USA. I was just 130 km away from Mexico border. I was not in a hurry to get out of USA as I still wanted to catch the movie 'Justice League' before I leave for Mexico. Justice League premiers on 16 November therefore I have lots of time to hang around in San Diego. Hence, I split the skate to San Diego into 2 days instead, stopping at Encinitas today.

The skate was fairly straightforward until I entered a military base. The gate was unmanned with a sign warning 'Trespassers would be prosecuted'. There was an opening for bicycles to go through. I entered the military base but didn't take any photos in case the US military thinks I was a North Korean spy. Happened to me once in Malaysia.

Back then in 2015, I was skating with Flo, from Germany, from Malaysia down to Singapore. We were stopped at a military checkpoint near Port Dickson. They wouldn't let us skate through the base but turning back would mean a 15 km detour. We decided to walk along the beach at the perimeter of the base. When we finally spotted a road, we immediately jumped on it, not knowing we had entered the military base. Which military base would leave an unmanned area without fences?

Once we realized we were in the base, we made a mad dash to get out. As we were exiting the checkpoint, the sentry stopped us, wondering how we got into the base. The guards interrogated us, checking our passports and made us explain our stories. A Singaporean and a German nazi spy? Kidding right. In the end, we were let off with a warning. That was a memory of a lifetime.

Day 275: Hello Sweety my life Navigator
USA: Encinitas to San Diego
Distance: 43 km / 26.5 miles
Time on board: 3 hours 27 mins
Average speed: 12.5 km/h
Cumulative distance: 10,917 km

By 3pm, I arrived at San Eijo state beach campground but I was too early, they only allowed hikers and bikers in at 4 pm. With an hour to spare, I entered the camp store. There, the owner spotted me skating along the highway 101 when he was driving. He immediately made me burritos and gave me a can of beer too. As I checked in, Paul cycled in. I met Paul while skating down the Pacific coast a month ago. I thought with his pace, he would have to reach Mexico by now. Apparently, he took a long break.

Paul managed to arrange a Warmshower host for both of us in San Diego. Another night of accommodation saved though I would be hanging around in San Diego for a few days to catch the Justice League movie. Watching movies was my only luxury. Ironically, back in Singapore, I didn't get to catch as many movies as I'd like due to a busy work schedule.

Only 40 km left to San Diego. Sleeping in the campsite was a constant nightmare. Though the ocean view was magnificent, but we slept opposite Amtrak train rails. Trains kept zooming throughout the night. Next time before camping, always check whether it was near a train rail or not.

Initially, I started fresh and vigorous, chasing after Paul at 20 km/h. Looks like we could make it in 2 hours. 7 km after the first hill looms and Paul sped ahead of me, leaving me struggling with the hill. Hills was my biggest nightmare now. I thought it was the end of it at the downhill. I was so wrong, the next hill before La Jolla was higher than the previous. Thankfully, it was the last big one of the day.

Besides my new companion, Paul, it dawned on me, I do have a companion all the time. Her sweet, robotic voice guided me throughout my journey. She directs me to turn whenever I should and tells me the estimated distance to the next point. She never screams at me when I go the wrong way, and exhibit patience with me when I scream at her for leading me to off road paths. Unveiling my all-time companion, Google map voice navigation. I should give her a name right. Sweety was my first childhood crush and rhymes with Apple's Siri. Sweety shall be her name.

As depicted in the movie Blade Runner 2049, K has an unusual obsession with his Holographic female companion whom you would not classify her as human yet her concerns for K made her more human than most of us actual humans. Wonder if Sweety could one day exhibit human consciousness while navigating my journey. Wouldn't it be great?

Paul waited for me at the bottom of the final hill. We rode together until Sweety led us to a construction site. Lambasted at her for making us lost.

While turning, my longboard wheel jammed on a tiny stone, I didn't fall, thanks to my pushcart. I tipped over my pushcart and my longboard went backwards and hit a car. No scratches and damage to the car. The owner was alright and just warned me to be careful next time.

I lost Paul, as he sped off in his usual bike pace. Just me and Sweety to guide me. Pushed along the grid-like streets of San Diego. Last obstacle was the steep climb up few blocks. San Diego was just as hilly as San Francisco. Made it to our next stop, Judd and Victoria 's home, 5 minutes before noon. My timing estimation was impeccable. Given the distance and elevation, I could estimate the time of arrival. Waited for Victoria till 2 pm to finish her work in College, as she was a professor. Would be spending my last few days in USA before leaving for Mexico Baja California. We celebrated Paul's last day in USA before he heads to Baja, California tomorrow over Thai food.

Day 281 : Adios USA! Hola Country no. 15 Mexico
San Diego, USA to Tijuana, Mexico
Distance: 32 km / 20 miles
Time on board: 2 hours 51 mins
Average speed: 11.5 km/h
Cumulative distance: 10953 km

Day 276-280

Worked in ITH Adventure hostel for free accommodation to save costs. Spent 4 hours of cleaning the dormitories and toilets daily and I am free for the day. Back home, I never ever clean my room. My mom must be proud upon hearing this. Best of all, the hostel provides free breakfast and dinner for guests. Truly a cost saver for me.

Watched Justice League. Rather disappointed that DC chose to compress the movie into 2 hours, rather short considering they have to introduce all heroes. DC should follow Marvel's formula of taking time to introduce standalone movies of all the heroes first before rolling out Justice League. Rest of the days spent binge watching Netflix in the hostel. Finished the entire Punisher series. Thanks to my sponsor Mark from GBomb, he sent me another GBOMB t-shirt, collected from Pablo in Adrenalina Skateboard store. Explored La Jolla and got really close to seals and sea lions. I could literally touch them and smell their breath. During my stay in Hostel, made many friends. One stood out for me, Joey from China. We were roommates during the entire stay. Since we both spoke the same language, Mandarin, we clicked rather well.

Day 281

Finally mustered my will to leave San Diego, USA for my country no. 15, Mexico. Had my last hearty breakfast in the hostel and bidding farewell to my hostel mates. Skating to the Mexico border Tijuana was very straightforward and flat. Just 30 km away from San Diego, and arrived in San Ysdiro, the border town shortly.

Exchanged my remaining US dollars to Mexico pesos. Exiting USA and entering Mexico was the simplest border crossing ever. I never had to go through USA exit checkpoint, in fact there was none. Exiting USA was easy, it was like they want you to leave. Of course, entering the USA was a different story, it was what I would describe as a pain in the ass. USA - Tijuana was one of the world's busiest border crossings. Entering Mexico was another simple affair. No queue or whatever. Walked straight into custom and paid 500 pesos or US $27 for 180 days Visa. Enquired about Singapore visa free entry but it was only applicable to air travel, not for land border crossing. My Singapore's Ministry of Foreign Affairs never mentioned this fact, they should update this important information. Thankfully, getting my visa to Mexico takes only a matter of minutes, as compared to all the other border crossing, I've encountered so far.

It was evident when you arrive in Mexico. The whole world immediately changes upon leaving the developed USA. From relatively calm USA, entered into the chaotic Tijuana. I have been pampered by the Western civilization in Canada and USA over the last 2 months. Now I felt I was back in Asia. Mexico was like Vietnam and Thailand where chaotic cars ruled the lawless roads.

Received loads of birthday greetings from my friends though technically my birthday was tomorrow 22 November. Since Singapore was a day ahead of USA, it was already 22 November Singapore time. All my Singaporean friends and family started leaving me greetings on Facebook. Since today was considered my birthday in Singapore time, I treated myself to a hotel stay. US $60 for a queen room which would have bankrupted me in USA. Heard of Tijuana 's notorious reputation for crime, therefore I researched for the safe areas in Tijuana and found this hotel with many good reviews.

Finding my way to the hotel was absolute chaos. Unlike typical grid like system in USA which makes it a no-brainer to navigate, the Tijuana roads swerve whenever they feel like it. Facing the behemoth mazes of Tijuana, getting lost was a common occurrence despite my hotel was only 2 km from the border crossing. I cannot follow Google map navigation for bicycle anymore. Surrendered trying to skate in the right direction, I skated in the direction towards the oncoming traffic as it was the direct route to the hotel. Do as when you were in Rome. I followed the Mexicanos cyclists riding against the traffic. Finally arrived in my hotel after an hour of navigation through the maze.

Incoming journey through Baja California would be a very simple affair. Once out of Tijuana I would be riding on highway 1 throughout, entire way till la Paz, 1000 km away. There would be days without any civilisation or towns as I would be riding through the desert. Therefore, don't panic if you haven't read my posts in a month. Only panic if u haven't heard from me in January when I should be back in Miami for the Ultraskate.

CHAPTER 5

NORTH BAJA CALIFORNIA

Day 282: Birthday in Baja
Mexico: Tijuana to Campo Lopez
Distance: 53 km
Time on board: 5 hours
Average speed: 10.6 km/h
Cumulative distance: 11,006 km

Exactly on this day 22 November, 35 years ago, I was evicted from my mother's womb. Yesterday was my birthday in Singapore time, today was still my birthday in Pacific West Coast time. All my American friends started wishing me on Facebook this morning. Great, get to celebrate my birthday twice. This was the first time I spend my birthday on the road. The first birthday of the journey.

In my opinion, birthdays should be celebrated by thanking my mother, instead of making a special entitled day for me. After all, on this day, my mother had to endure great pains equivalent of multiple fractures to get me out. That was why the process was called 'labour'. Therefore, my birthday should be a tribute to my mother.

Best thing staying in a hotel was the sumptuous breakfast. I had 10 slices of bread spread with peanut butter and plates of scrambled egg and lots of fruits. Planned on setting off at 8 am, instead spent lots of time stocking up my calories for my first day in Mexico. I chose this hotel because it was directly on Highway 1. Basically, I have to ride all the way on Highway 1 to La paz, South tip of Baja California. Made my first blunder. I carelessly forgot I am no longer in USA or Europe where I could drink water straight from the tap.

Staying in USA and Europe for too long, I forgot how it was like touring through developing nations. If I got sick, you would know what happened. I took out my Steripen, UV light water filter which has been left in cold storage at the bottom of my backpack. At last, my SteriPEN comes to good use once again and would be an essential component to surviving my journey if I want to make it out alive.

My first 11 km was a long gradual uphill. Though not steep by my standard, I got fatigued after just 5 km. Funny how upon entering a new country, everything changes as well.

In USA, my 1.5 litres Camelbak hydration pack could last me at least 30 km including ascent. Here only 5 km up less than an hour, I already finished my pack and have to refill. I have to make my first pit stop at just 5 km. Baja California was indeed drier. Road also differ significantly from USA. Massive traffic squeezed on two lanes. Drivers u-turn whenever they want. Road has little or no shoulder at all, leaving me at the mercy of Mexican drivers. A saying goes, in Mexico the driver was your God. I have to agree. It seems they like to get an inch closer to me. An inch away from disaster. Now I really miss USA drivers. USA drivers were angels compared to Mexicans. My American friends, do not complain about your comrade driving ability. Wait till you skate in Mexico and Latin America, you would understand what

I mean. I really have to forget the western society's standard way of living and got back to rugged life back in Asia.

At last, 11 km of walking and skating, arrived at downhill. Don't assume downhill was relaxing. Road shoulder was filled with debris like a war zone. Have to brake hard to navigate down safely in one piece. After that, it was all relatively flat land.

Since I had an extremely heavy breakfast, I didn't feel hungry. I went on all the way to Puente Nouve and stopped at OXXO, Mexican version of 7-11 convenience store. It was the equivalent of 7-eleven in USA except it was way cheaper. 2 hotdogs and a soft drink only cost 37 pesos which was around US $2. I couldn't buy a hot dog for US $2 back in the states. I am back in cheap land like in Asia, I could afford more comfort items for a fraction of the cost in USA. But why did I have to bring my cooking stove since eating out costs almost nothing? Oh ya, there were days I would be skating without encountering any civilisation.

Uphill and headwind was mild by my standard but however chafing on my groin was a painful affair. I never have abrasion on my groin till now, I discarded my chamois cream back in Asia. Now I regret the decision. Each mongo push, it was agony on my balls. Making the push uphill with the headwind was even more daunting. What a birthday skate.

I was planning to skate halfway point between Ensenada without knowing where to sleep. Just as I skated with agony, I passed Carlos who was watering the lawn outside an estate community. I stopped to chat with him and had a photo session, explaining my story to him. I asked if there was any hotels or campground nearby. He invited me to camp in his estate. It turns out he managed the gated community. It was better than camping out in the wild where it could be risky for me. Inside the estate, there were security guards so I am certainly much safer there. Since it was my birthday, I was planning to stay in a hotel with some comfort. But the offer to camp inside for free was very tempting. Of course, I accepted his invitation. Apparently, he had invited cyclists on this route to camp inside his estate too. What a nice guy. Mexicans were great. I have never cooked rice before, today would be my first attempt since I got MSR Dragonfly stove with the ability to simmer. Might as well use it rather than eating pasta every day. I would let you know how it goes tomorrow.

For now, thank you my mother and dad for popping me out 35 years ago.

Day 283: Thanksgiving in Ensenada
Mexico: Campo Lopez to Ensenada
Distance: 51 km
Time on board: 4 hours 41 mins
Average speed: 10.7 km/h
Cumulative distance: 11, 056 km

My attempt to cook rice last night was a mixed result. Too much water and my rice turned out to be wet. Well, not bad for the first attempt to cook rice on a camping stove. Cooking rice was another game changer. 1 cup of rice could make into a huge plate providing heaps of calories as compared to macaroni which requires 8 fistfuls in order to make a filling meal. I could carry less amount to get more calories now.

Slept in the toilet as I was lazy to pitch my bivy tent and didn't want to get my sleeping bag damp. Set off without any breakfast. Sought to find food in the next km before I faint. At 4 km in Alistio, there was another OXXO store, so I grabbed 2 hot dogs.

There were two highways 1 paralleling each other. One was the toll road, Cuota and another was the free road, Libre which I took earlier. The toll-road was way quieter and smoother and comes with wider shoulder, safer for me to skate on. Today I decided to go on the toll road. Indeed, I was faster on the toll road. Should have made the switch earlier. Another factor was the free road diverts inland, with higher ascent. The toll road parallel the Pacific Ocean, making it more scenic.

Approaching the downhill section, the road curved and was completely filled with the popup barriers. I don't know what to call it thus 'popup barriers'. Descending on pop ups made the ride extremely bumpy thus I still had to walk downhill. My water bottle fell off from my rear pouch and rolled on to the other side of the road. I ran across to retrieve it. Meanwhile, my pushcart toppled to its side as I accidentally parked it angled, not flat. All my stuff spilled out onto the road. A lady driver pulled over to ask if I needed help. On hindsight, should have asked her for a lift to Ensenada.

I gathered and packed my stuff onto the pushcart once more, only to find my underwear flying away. This time, I didn't want to risk my life trying to pick up my pair of purple underwear. So, I let it go.

Since the beginning of Mexico, the colour of my urine had become very yellow meaning I was dehydrated even though I drank loads of water. The climate in Baja was really hotter and drier than in California. Had to readjust my water supply usage. Carrying 20 litres might only last me 2 days through the desert.

Stopped for lunch at a rest stop. Lunch was a much simpler affair, just boiling water for my pasta and instant noodles mix. Shortly, I reached the end of the toll road. The guard stared at me. I used the most common blur tourist ruse to get away. Pretended not to understand Spanish and pretended that I am not supposed to ride on the toll road. He surrendered and wave me off to continue my way. Back on the free road, the shoulder got narrower and rougher with significantly busier traffic. Given a choice, I'd rather pay to ride on the toll road.

Pushed on to Ensenada by 3 pm. The only hostel Ensenada backpackers was fully occupied until Saturday. Probably due to the Thanksgiving weekend, the Americans traveled here for a cheap vacation. US $20 for dorm bed though cheaper than the ones in USA, was still expensive by Mexico standards. Found a motel for 400 pesos or US $22 per night. I thought I got a good deal. I was gutted to find more motels offering 240 pesos or US $14 down the road. Should have skated further to search for better deals. At least I get the sense what was the standard rate for motels in Mexico.

Since it was thanksgiving, the equivalent of Chinese Lunar reunion dinner, I had Japanese ramen dinner. I miss ramen noodles. Viewed the night light show to finish the day.

Day 288: Wine Road
Mexico: Ensenada to Santo Tomas
Distance: 46 km
Time on board: 4 hours 15 mins
Average speed: 10.8 km/h
Cumulative distance: 11,106 km

My Warmshower host Jorge and his family totally caught me off guard when he presented a birthday cake to me in his home. Though my birthday had passed 3 days ago, and I never told anyone about it, he found out through my Facebook and his family got me a cake when having dinner. I have never been this surprised on my birthday as it was always expected that your family and friends would always present you something. I only get to know Jorge couple of days ago through warmshower hospitality site and he really take the effort to get a cake topped with peach for me. In fact, I nearly missed staying with Jorge as he only contacted me on my 2nd day in Ensenada when I already got a motel but I extended few more days to stay with him and his family. There in his home, I stayed with another of his warmshower guest Christen from Switzerland in his guest room. Christen was also cycling to Argentina. From 1 day, I kept extending to stay with Jorge. Ended up staying for 3 more days. Jorge in his free time, drove us to Bufudora, the blowhole or underwater geyser and drinking with his friends. His university schedules were oddly in the evening. Nevertheless, he drove us around.

Realised my Spanish has improved by leaps and bounds when I could understand what his parents were speaking in Spanish, though they took effort to speak really slow for me to understand.

Today morning, Jorge made us a sumptuous breakfast. Rancheros. Tacos with eggs to get me and Christen going for our ride. Christen was taking route 3 across the Baja divide to San Felipe. Obviously, it would be mountainous for me and sections of it would be off road. Therefore I am sticking to highway 1. We would meet one day when his route merge back to highway 1. We split off and mine route was way simple. Once turn into highway 1, it was all way straight on.

Leaving Ensenada was a challenge with the hectic traffic. Buses kept cutting into my lane to collect passengers yet they provide me protection from other traffic. At the traffic stops, a longboarder skated past me. He was chasing me when he saw me on the road. Apparently he knew my journey from Orangatang Wheels Instagram. I could see that he really put his Orangatang kegels to good use. The 85 mm wheels was reduced to its core.

The first section was flat thus pushing at fast pace. Until the start of the climb, a touring cyclist passed me without saying hello. Guess he was in a hurry. Slowly pushes on after some kms, spotted the same cyclist by the roadside fixing his flat tyre. Offered my help, though I don't know much on fixing a flat. He was from Italy and cycling to la paz as well though he has to rush.

He has to return back home to Italy on 17 December, leaving him only 20 days to reach LA paz. I probably take my time to reach in 30 days. After fixing his flat, we rode together for a short section before he sped off.

Seeing the silhouette of the mountains bring me to reality that I am going to have a tough time ahead. Roads were rough, real rough. Thanks to Orangatang wheels for sponsoring me new 85 mm prototype wheels, which made the rough road a lot manageable. No more smooth roads of USA and Europe, I have to expect more of these conditions as I head south to Argentina. My daily mileage has to tone down. No more than 100 km per day in this condition. In fact, 80 km would be an excellent distance for me now as daylight was shortened to only 10 hours. By 4.30 pm the sun sets, leaving me to set camp by 3-4 pm.

Passed by a military checkpoint. The guard inspected my passport and my pushcart. Had to explain my story this time in Spanish. I don't know whether he understood my broken Spanish or not, he waved me off to continue my way.

Spotted a sign advertising crab burritos. I have never tried burrito with crab. Though the tiny burrito cost 45 peso or US $2.5, I got to try their local speciality. Burritos in Mexico was way smaller or anorexic than their counterparts in USA. Americans like their food upsize. After lunch, I am only left with 12 km to Santo Tomas campsite. At 40 km, arrived at the peak and was 6 km downhill to the El Palomar campsite. It was currently off season, seeing none other campers. The owner charged me a mere 100 pesos or US $5.50. The campground was completely desolate and without water. They turned water supply as it was off season. In this sense, this was more expensive than campsite in USA. Thankfully I carry loads of water, enough to survive for 3 days. Could have wild camp somewhere but prefer to pay for security. Heard horror stories of cyclists being robbed on the roadside. Rather not take the risk of losing my possessions.

Day 289: Amazing people of the road
Mexico: Santo Tomas to Colonet (then got a ride to Camalu 30km away)
Distance: 77 km
Time on board: 6 hours 13 mins
Average speed: 11.8 km/h
Ascent: 770 m
Descent : 879 m
Cumulative distance: 11, 213 km

You realise when you have left USA and Europe when dogs start chasing you. The memory of horrible dogs chasing me everywhere in Asia was back again. Unleashed and stray dogs chased me once again In Mexico. I am suspecting this would persist on all the way till Argentina. To deal with dogs, I carried small rocks in my pocket to scare them off when they get too close for comfort. At yesterday's campsite, the 2 resident dogs kept harassing me for food. One even peed on my longboard to mark his territory. Be sure to check for dogs at every campground before paying.

Last night's attempt to cook rice was a success. Put less water for cooking. The rice finally tasted like rice. Even fried an egg. The first ever. My parents would be so proud. I am becoming a master chef. Increasing my repertoire of food means I no longer have to eat pasta soup with instant noodles every day.

Today's destination was estimated to be 80 km. With shortened daylight hours, sun setting at 4.30 pm, leaving me less time to skate before dark. To make it worse, today's route isn't flat. I am passing through San Quintin Valley which gives you an idea of the terrain. Woke up real early at 5.30 am. Planning to set off right at the moment of daybreak. However, I forgot to account for the time taken to push up my loaded pushcart the steep slope in the campground. My wheels got stuck in gravel and toppled over to the side. I had to pick pieces by pieces and bring each piece to the other side of the road to reassemble. Found the screw on the left side of my pushcart missing. Returned to the site of carnage to search for screw. Finally, ready to go at 7 am.

First 7 km was long gradual uphill which I never noticed until I started to push with some resistance. Next 5 km or so, I have to walk up which takes me an hour or so. I studied the elevation chart the night before. This was the one big hill I must conquer. Bid my time to conserve energy, knowing once this was over, I would have massive downhill to make up for lost time. Just like in life, don't frown if you were slow in the beginning. Once past the summit, you could make up for lost time.

Indeed at 12 km, a long downhill awaits me. A 15 km long subtle downhill that I need not to control much with brakes. I was cruising down at 22 km/h, easily making up for lost time. Only at 27 km, I have my first break, preparing for the next climb. Back to cruising mode, till San Vicente at 38 km where I had to stop at Oxxo store for food. I never know when I would see the next Oxxo store on the road. Target was to hit 50 km by noon. I was way on target. 38 km at 10.30 am.

While having my hot dogs outside Oxxo, Frank on his dirt scrambler pulled over to chat with me. He was heading to the mountains for some adrenaline downhill biking off-road action. Though Baja 1000 rally was over last weekend, the action still persists.

Checked the elevation chart, I am expecting 3 remaining summits. I figured out how to tackle the hills. On the downhill before the climb, gather as much momentum, before I start to lose energy going up, I started pushing as fast as possible catching the momentum to ascend as high as possible.

On the last hill, I stopped for another break. Spotted a figure looming near on the horizon, it was Pietr the Italian cyclist I met yesterday. I expected him to be way ahead. This time, he didn't have any flat tires to slow him down. He made his way up the hill way faster than I could walk. Along the way up, spotted a water slide in the middle of nowhere. Who would have thought to build a water theme park there?

At 67 km, while having a pee stop, a motorcycle with side wagon pulled over and the rider started waving at me. I wondered why would anyone be interested to watch me pee. Apparently, they met Jack Smith in Morro Bay and he told them about me. They were the girls from Ride4love travel. Stephanie and her companion were riding on motorcycle to Argentina.

While chatting on the road side, we could feel the dangerous situation we place ourselves into when monstrous trailers truck came zooming. We could feel a gust of wind and hear the roaring thunder made by these monsters of the road. Surprisingly, I don't feel the threat when skating on the road. They usually gave lots of leeway for me cos I occupied the entire lane, forcing the traffic to divert to the next lane to overtake me.

Arrived at Colonet, a dusty town. Sought to find accommodation for the night, either camping or a motel. There isn't a hotel I could afford. The only hotel was rather expensive looking. An old rusty Volkswagen pulled over. Daniel and Perla asked me if they could be of any assistance to me. I asked if they knew any place to camp or cheap hotels in this town. They immediately offered to invite me to their home in Camalu 30 km away.

With only 1 hour before sunset, I knew I could not make it for sure. They wanted to give me a ride but fitting my pushcart was an issue. That was why I never bothered to ask for a ride. Furthermore, theirs was a tiny rusty Volkswagen from the 70s. But to my bewilderment, my pushcart did manage to fit in their car. So ya, for the first time since Ajchara in San Francisco, I got a ride.

Before driving me back to their home, they had to settle some matters. Daniel's parents were pastors in Camalu. They were helping the church in running a project constructing a day centre for kids and single mothers. From the top of the hill, I could see the shanty built town. It was amazing how Daniel's old Volkswagen could easily manoeuvre up the hill.

Once at his home, his parents made me a typical Mexican dinner. Rice with mole, cactus, beans. Amazing people. If I persist on completing my record, I wouldn't have to meet all these amazing people. I would have just bulldozed my way through, missing all the adventures and stories I could experience. Tonight, I could sleep soundly in the house of God. Thanks to Daniel and Perla.

Day 290: Tortoise shell road
Mexico: Camalu to San Quintin
Distance: 36 km
Time on board: 3 hours 1 min
Average speed: 12 km/h
Cumulative distance: 11,249 km

One thing about staying with Mexican family was they would torture you. They would force feed you with Mexican delicacies that you couldn't simply refuse stuffing your stomach. If I stayed with Mexican families often, I would end up becoming unrecognizable due to weight gain from eating all the Mexican goodies.

In the morning, Perla made me Cochilo, eggs, beans. Breakfast fit for a king. Ate together with the family. Since my distance to San Quintin today was cut to mere 36 km, I could afford to set off later and spend more time with Daniel's family. They showed me around the church and the flags of the world. What's missing was my country flag Singapore. I promised to mail them a Singapore flag when I return home.

To end it all, we had a prayer garnering, blessing me a safe journey. Daniel gave me a plastic bag of tea which could last me for months and a pair of shorts, as he saw a hole in my pants. He also gave me lots of burritos. Soon, I need to get a more spacious pushcart to carry more gifts that the Mexicans keep giving me.

Though a brief moment of time we spent together, it remains eternally etched in our stories we wrote of our lives. I only spend a night staying with them, yet they would remain in my memory as part of my journey. So do many others I've encountered previously. You all were part of my story to tell in years to come.

Daniel and Perla walked me off to Highway 1 where I continued my way. Today was a cool day, never having to see the Sun yet I was sweating buckets. The road was cracked open like tortoise shells, making the short 36 km seemed double its distance. Adding to my agony, was the hectic traffic squeezing on two lane road. When there isn't any traffic on the other side, vehicles could simply divert on to other lane to overtake. If not, there were long trains of vehicles trailing behind me. Some vehicles really take their time to trail behind me to take videos and photos and shielding me from the traffic.

Several pulled over to offer me water and food. I accepted the first. The driver gave me a litre of water which I accepted. Subsequently, I had to refuse accepting goodwill of others as I am running out of space on my pushcart. Initially, I bought the pushcart to carry more load. But it still wasn't enough in Mexico given the generosity of its people.

I wasn't paying attention to the terrain and scenery that I was skating today. Mainly, because I was focusing on staying alive on bumpy rough tortoise shells road and looking on my side mirror for raging traffic behind me. Anyway, the terrain was lined with dusty, dilapidated buildings. Rustic travel in a sense. Vendors parked in their lorries selling all sorts of goods from corn to hardwares dotted the sides of the road.

Filled with the Mexican breakfast enough to sustain me 36 km to San Quintin without having to stop at Oxxo store for food. Highway 1 was the only paved road. The rest of the roads in the town were all off-road. Made it to my Warmshower host Gabino in San Quintin where he took me to Taqueria, a Tacos stand. Mexican cuisine was not limited to tacos and burritos. Gabino was anticipating few more cyclists tomorrow. I might hang around for another day to meet them.

Day 292: The Great Cyclists migration
Mexico: San Quintin to El Socorrito
Distance: 30 km
Time on board: 2hours 3 mins
Average speed : 13.5 km/h
Cumulative distance: 11,277 km

A good decision to extend my stay with Gabino. 3 more cyclists, a couple from France and Scott from England arrived at Gabino's house. It was fast turning into a party. Gabino was the only Warmshower host in San Quintin and last one in North Baja California before the great desert. Naturally, all those on cycling tour heading southward would stop at his place. And now it was the season where the temperature was cool and dry, optimal for touring.

Those who start from Alaska in June, would probably be around the precinct by now. This was the Great touring migration of America Continent. I guess I would keep on meeting lots of cyclists along the way. After all there was only one road in Baja. Gabino had hosted over 350 cyclists from 65 countries over 4 years. I was his first longboard tourer and from Singapore. I am the first on longboard to many hosts as well. Scott mentioned that Alison was a day ride behind him. I met Alison with the herd of cyclists that I travelled in the Pacific coast highway. She got injured with cuts on her during the trip, therefore she had to stop for a day and recuperate in her home in Santa Rosa. We would have a chance to reunite once again.

I spent my rest day binge watching Big Bang Theory sitcom series and watched a mind blending boggling movie Predestination. Without giving much spoiler, it was about time travel and time travel paradox. An Agent time travels to prevent major crimes from happening. However, altering the past has its consequences. That was why whatever mistakes we made in the past, should not be altered or changed. We just have to live with our mistakes and regrets to make us a better person. The movie literally give meaning to the phrase 'Go F yourself'. Predestination haunts my mind so much that I couldn't sleep during the night. It wasn't scary but the mind blending twist in the show kept lingering in my head and looks like it was going to wander in my thoughts for a long time. Go watch it.

Gabino took us to his favourite taco stand, Matia, and I loaded up with 2 tacos and 2 sopes. The French couple took a bus from Tijuana to San Quintin to avoid the chaotic traffic. The next 400 km would be really tranquil. The next morning, I bid farewell to Gabino to set off for El Socorrito, another short 30 km. Jorge, my warmshower in Ensenada introduced me to his friend Paco, whose family owns a ranch in El Socorrito and invited me to stay there. Since the next 350 km after Rosario would be desert and sparsely populated, I figured I better take as much opportunity to sleep with comfort and shelter while I still could.

I set off from highway 1. The road was much smoother than the section arriving into San Quintin the other day. The road in Baja was Hyde and Jekyll. Some segments smooth as ice and other rough as cracked up tortoise shells.

Today's terrain was completely flat and smooth. As Gabino mentioned, 10 km after San Quintin, it would trickle to few cars every hour. Indeed, he was spot on.

Spotted an interesting taco restaurant with the skeleton of a whale as deco. As I stopped to take photo, 3 ladies stepped out to offer me water. More water in the dry desert, yes please. I obliged with wefies and Facebook account exchange. 15 km after, Gabino's nephew drove past and pulled over. More Wefies and chatting.

By 1 pm, I arrived at El Socorrito. To enter the town, I exited the main Highway 1 and went off-road. Sand was soft thus my loaded pushcart sunk under the weight in the sand. Had to push my cart with all my might for the next 1 km. Paco couldn't send me an exact address cos there isn't any. Just a pin on Google map indicating its location. Then Rodriguez cycled to me. Obviously, I was out of place here. Being a small town where everybody knows everyone, I asked Rodriguez where was Aurelio Ruiz's house. He directed me but there isn't anyone at home. Thus, he brought me around to approach other Ruiz family members. There, I got the keys to the house. The whole house to myself. Mexicans were so trusting.

Day 293: Baja Cactus

Mexico: El Socorrito to El Rosario
Distance: 35 km
Time on board: 3 hours 14 mins
Average speed: 11 km/h
Cumulative distance: 11, 313 km

Another short skate to El Rosario before spending 4-7 days in 350 km long stretch of Baja Desert. Better enjoy some comfort of civilisation before spending alone time with me and myself.

Though it was a short skate for the day, I had to transverse through the desert terrain up and down before encountering a long steep hill. Thanks to Paco's family for accommodating me in their family weekend home. They aren't at home, leaving their entire home to me. There isn't any grocery store in the vicinity, I am left with whatever provision in their refrigerator. Used my limited cooking creativity to make dinner and breakfast. I finished their eggs, bread and water. Set off at 9.30 am. Received a message from Scott and the other French cyclists that they have already set off from San Quintin an hour before. Figured out they would catch up with me soon.

Started off with rolling hills, skating up and down. Took my time to enjoy the vast desert. I could see the road leading all the way to the horizon. That was how vast the terrain was. Along the road were scrubs and cactus. It was amazing how cactus was that hardy and possess the ability to survive in dry desert.

While I was taking a break, Scott cycled up. The other French cyclists were much slower and taking their time while Scott intended to ride further after El Rosario to finish the series of hills in the desert.

Continued to walk my way up after Scott left me biting dust. Had to stop once more to grab some biscuits for energy. I thought I had arrived at the peak, but no, it was a false peak. I saw a further climb. Held my breath and persevered to make my way up.

At last, on the peak, I spotted a building and it turned out to be another military checkpoint. I pretended not to understand Spanish, but there was someone who could speak English. I explained my story to them. Without further ado, they waved me off.

After 6 km of descent, made it to El Rosario, my last stop before venturing into the great Baja desert for days.

Enquired the price for a room in two motels side by side. Baja Cactus appeared more luxurious yet was cheaper at 350 pesos. I moved on in search of a cheaper room. There, I found Scott having lunch at a restaurant. I joined him and had a hamburger and fries. Hamburger actually cost less than having 4 tacos required to fill my stomach. Scott rode further on while I decided to stop here for the night.

Another hotel further down offered 350 pesos yet it appeared shabbier and without any television. I turned back to settle for Baja Cactus. After paying, I realised that their Wi-Fi isn't working. Luckily, I got 6 GB of data from AT&T to write this post.

Tomorrow I shall venture into the 350 km stretch of desert. I got my 20 litres of water and food supplies enough to last me 5 days. Therefore, I am completely self-sufficient. It was expected that there isn't any cell signal. Don't panic if you haven't read my updates on social media in a week.

Date of entry: 4 December 2017
Day 294: Into the Desert
Distance: 123 km (42 km skate/ 81 km ride)

Mexico: El Rosario to Catavina

Day one into Great Baja Desert began. As I exit my motel, passed by a room. The guest immediately recognized me. He saw me skating on the road yesterday and thought I am cool. The guest was on a motorcycle ride trip with his wife and friends. They were riding to La Paz.

I passed by the food stall that I had dinner yesterday. The owner actually gave me a discount yesterday after I told everyone my story. Instead of paying 70 pesos, I only paid 50 pesos. Though not much of a discount, but it was a nice gesture from her. The perks of touring on a longboard. Waved goodbye to the food stall owner. They wanted to invite me for breakfast and coffee but I already had my peanut butter breakfast and had to rush off as I got a big climbing day. My target was to finish 36 km long steep uphill climb in 4 and a half hours by 12 pm. Then I could slowly relax to skate remaining 15 -23 km flat roads in 3 -4 hours before sunset. Hoping to reach a roadside restaurant and camp there.

As I start my arduous climb, 2 cyclists passed me. They were from USA and England. I couldn't remember their names though. I have been meeting so many cyclists, it was tough for me to remember their names, especially when they all sport a beard, trademark for male touring cyclists. They were aiming for Catavina 122 km away. Judging from the elevation gain, I doubt I could make it to Catavina today.

Why didn't I choose to tour on bicycles? Answer was I simply love the challenge of touring on longboard. I like achieving the mere impossible.

Slowly I made my way to the top. As estimated, I arrived at the top by 12 noon. Stopped for lunch, decided to go for peanut butter bread again. Cooking and eating a meal would take at least an hour. Making peanut butter bread was much simpler only requires 30 minutes to finish 10 slices of peanut butter spread bread.

As I start to move off for my second half, a pickup pulled over, asking if I wanted a ride. Why not, if they were willing to help me fit my loaded pushcart to the back of the pickup. It was rare for me to get a ride with my loaded pushcart. Since they offered, why not enjoy the opportunity. The journey was not particularly interesting as well. It was all the same vast barren desert terrain with gigantic cactus. I didn't know that cactus could grow that high and there were so many varieties of cactus.

Al, Guy and Rick were from Canada. Guy and Rick were here visiting Al who was 80 years of age and going strong. In fact, Guy and Al participated in Baja 1000 off-road rally. They shared their experiences with me. Baja 1000 was not just a race, was a race to make it out alive. There were some idiots who set up booby traps on the roads so that they could watch racers crash. How sadistic.

Al was inspired by my journey and added travelling the world on a motorcycle to his bucket list. Soon, the pickup passed the 2 cyclists and now I am ahead of them to Catavina. They would be shocked to see me there.

They dropped me off at Catavinaz. Now I had saved a day of travel through the desert. Instead of estimated 4 days more, I would probably take 3 more days to complete the desert segment. The guys drove on to Bahia los Angeles, bay of the Angels. I turned back 3 km to visit a prehistoric cave painting since I had lots of time to spare.

When I returned to the town Catavina, I stopped at the police station to ask if I could camp there. Before I could try to explain my story in Spanish, the officer immediately understood what I wanted and led me to a multipurpose hall to camp for the night. Perfect, it's sheltered.

As I went out to look for grocery, 3 cyclists on fatbike passed by, I invited them to camp with me in the police station. I might come out rather creepy that they would rather sleep over at the luxury hotel. I am trying to look for company. Back at the station, I saw the 2 other cyclists I met earlier on. I explained to them how I got here faster than them. They too opted for a motel. I am becoming harder core than cycle tourers now, choosing to forgo showers and comfy bed to sleep in a police station.

Made my dinner. Steamed egg with mushrooms, chicken pasta soup and rice. The steamed eggs were intended to be fried eggs with mushrooms. Somehow, I messed up, making steamed eggs instead. Need more practice to be a Master Chef. For now, I am proud enough that I could cook.

Date of entry: 5 December 2017
Day 295: 3 nemesis of skate
Mexico: Catavina to Chapala
Distance: 56 km
Time on board: 5 hours 52 mins
Average speed: 9.5 km/h
Ascent: 631 m
Decent: 548 m
Cumulative distance: 11,498 km

The sleep at the police station hall was a nightmare. The wind kept howling throughout the night. The zinc roof kept flapping and the door, no matter how I closed it, the wind kept slamming the door. Should have shared the motel room with other cyclists. The vast hall was so empty that I could hear a pin drop.

Woke up to a bad omen. I could hear the horrifying wind blowing to bend the trees against their will and it was blowing against my direction of travel today. Massive headwind. At least I get to view the red sky in the morning when the sun begins to rise. Ate my usual peanut butter breakfast. I met a Dutch guy who was sleeping at the police station as well. He was travelling across Mexico on his Volkswagen beetle. Dropped by the cyclist's motel. Their 500 pesos motel room doesn't look any better than my stay at police station. That makes me feel better. At least I don't have to pay for my stay there.

Began my agonising skate today. Usually I could estimate how far and fast I could skate by analysing the elevation chart and distance on Google map. However, I could never predict the wind conditions. Today was the day where all my 3-nemesis appeared in cahoot to give me a hard time. Uphill, headwind and my number 1 villain, rough roads. Usually I could cope with two of these at the same time but all three together, I need all the prayers I could get.

I had to walk most of the time today. The headwind was not normal wind, almost a gale force. The brutal wind relentlessly blowing against me added much resistance to each push as if someone was constantly pulling me backwards. Temperature was 18 degrees celsius yet felt like 0 degrees due to the wind chill factor. I had to put 3 layers to keep warm. My rain jacket on top of my sweat hoodie on top of my tee shirt. Still, snot kept dripping from my nose like a water fountain.

Today's elevation wasn't as steep as yesterday climb, however with the gale wind pulling me, it was like climbing Everest. I could only manage to skate 30 km from 7 am to 12 noon, averaging 8 km/h. The road was laden with potholes. The traffic had to dance to avoid the potholes. So did I. At times, I had to divert to the opposite lane while watching my side mirror for traffic. Most of the time, I simply walk.

Cooking lunch in the midst of gale wind was another tough chore. I couldn't light a fire as the wind kept extinguishing the flames. I could have resort to having peanut butter with tortillas. No need to make fire. However, with the plummeting temperature, I needed warmth. I developed an ingenious method. I found a discarded car tires and placed my MSR Dragonfly inside. The car tire helped to block the wind, protecting the flames. Desperate situations require desperate measures. In times of disaster, I have to adapt and evolve accordingly. I could finally make a hot meal of spaghetti soup. I am so proud of myself that I could manage to cook despite the force of nature. After cooking my warm meal, a car pulled over and the ladies handed me a bar of chocolate. Just what I needed the most.

According to the information drawn out by cyclists who transverse across Baja, there was a roadside restaurant at 55 km where I could camp if I patronize their restaurant. Wild camping tonight isn't a good idea with the wind adding to freezing temperature. I needed to camp behind a building from the wind. Therefore, I had soup and rice with chicken for dinner. And camped behind the restaurant tonight.

Date of entry: 6 Dec 2017
Day 296: Chasing Rainbow
Mexico: Chapala to Rosarito
Distance: 100 km
Time on board: 7 hours
Average speed: 14.3 km/h
Cumulative distance: 11, 598 km

I woke up early at 5.15 am when it was still dark and packed my gear while having peanut butter tortillas breakfast with my headlight on. The dogs kept on pestering me. They somehow ate my chocolate bar left on the ground sheet.

Once at the first light, I was ready to set off. The wind isn't as intensive as yesterday. But I had to get over the first hill before the downhill. First hour was slow at 12 km/h. Once after I passed the first hill, I thought "Yeah, it was speedy Gonzalez time". But it was not to be. It was a flat plateau with really rough roads.

If this persists, I would never reach Rosarito today. Horizon after horizon, I kept on pushing in hope and belief that at the end of the horizon lies the smooth road. Each time I was disappointed. But I kept pushing. Without hope and belief, life was meaningless. Even if that was nothing, I must believe in order to keep moving forward. And I was rewarded with newly freshly paved tarmac road and the most optimum downhill gradient. The gradient isn't steep for super-fast speed downhillers but very gradual that I could cruise at a nice comfortable speed for a long time without having to brake. That was the optimum downhill for me and long-distance skaters.

Indeed, the rainbow appeared for me because I kept believing and never stop moving. The moral was to keep believing that the worst would be over and the rainbow was over the horizon. I guess that goes the same for religion. We have to believe in something, God or even just humanity. Because without that belief, moving on would be hard.

Cactus dominated the scenery along the highway. If the giant redwood trees symbolise California, then these giant cacti were the mascot of Baja California. Cactus could grow to many metres tall. Though it was not as gigantic as the redwood tree, but it was still as impressive.

By 3 hours, I already hit 48 km and still increasing. I was pumping on the smooth road with one hand steering the pushcart. One of the rare occasions that I could pump on my pushcart. And pushing the pushcart was assisted by the downhill. I was belting all my songs all the way. However, all good things must come to an end. The fresh paved road returned to its original rough state, but it isn't as bad. I had my bar of snickers to replenish my energy before continuing.

By 11.45 am, I already hit 70 km, with just 30 km to go. It was a good time to stop and cook my lunch. Found a huge cactus to block the wind from extinguishing the flames so I cooked a quick spaghetti mixed with instant noodles soup and was back on the road by 1 pm. I cannot afford to be complacent though I had only 30 km to go with 3-4 hours of daylight. I could never predict what lay ahead of me.

I was right. It wasn't the road condition this time. I felt my pushcart to be very bumpy, even though the road was very smooth. I stopped to check; everything seems in place. Then I saw my right tyre sunk under. It was a puncture. Of all the days, it chooses to go flat when I am on a rush. This was the first time I had to change a tyre. I was prepared and I got all the necessary spares and equipment to replace my inner tube. There's one issue though. I don't know to replace the inner tube. In my defence, I did ask the bicycle shop to demonstrate to me when I bought the spares but they brushed me off, claiming that it was idiot proof to do so.

Right! I have been a skateboarder all my life, our wheels don't get punctured, thus I never learn to replace it. I was struggling to get the punctured inner tube from the tyre. At this rate, I was never going to make to Rosarito or maybe get stuck in the desert for eternal life. An Irish motorcyclist pulled over and asked me if I needed any assistance. That was God-sent. The bearded Irish motorcyclist was riding from Alaska to Argentina like me. He pulled out the inner tube like in an instant. That simple? How come I was struggling for eternity. We managed to replace the punctured tube with my only spare left. Let's pray that doesn't happen anymore as nobody sells 16-inch wheel tube in Baja. Thank God for another Angel. Otherwise, I would really have to hitch a ride.

Upcoming was the uphill. I ran uphill pushing my pushcart with all my might. Back to the downhill, this time it was really steep, thus I had to brake hard on the corners. While cruising, 2 cyclists sneaked up on me. They were from Quebec and cycling from British Columbia to Guatemala. They too were heading to Rosarito today. Great, I got company to camp with tonight. They slowed down to keep pace with me so that we could ride together.

At one downhill, the road was laden with enormous potholes. One cyclist was riding abreast with me and straight ahead was that pothole. I had to make a choice. Either to crash into the pothole or swerve to crash into him. I chose the latter. I did give him a warning about the imminent crash about to happen. He braked hard to reduce the impact of my pushcart crashing on to his fatbike. My pushcart banged on his front wheel, upon impact I swerved to the side leaving my pushcart behind while I skated on to run off that fast speed. Luckily, nothing was damaged. No injuries or damages to the bike and pushcart. We continued on our way. This time, they either ride in front of me or behind.

Riding with companions was refreshing. I am really motivated to keep up with them thus I found the energy to go fast. 2 km from Rosarito, one of them pulled over and realised that his camera was missing. He must have dropped it while taking photos of me. They had to backtrack at least 17 km when we first met in search of his camera. I cannot go back uphill again so we split our ways. Hopefully, they would return back before the sun sets.

I hit my 100 km by 3.50 pm and stopped at Mauricio restaurant for dinner and camping. Tried their local speciality Machuga. Basically, shredded beef with rice. Tomorrow I would be out of the desert.

Felt the roar of the wind through the night. Woke up to realise it was towards my direction of travel today. That placed me in a jubilant mood. Haven't seen the Canadian duo cyclists yet. They probably were still searching for their camera. The downhill continues. After passing up the first climb, it was mostly the perfect gradient for downhill. Negative 1% gradient or maybe even less. Aided by the massive tailwind, I was roaring through the way. Occasional segment of rough road but other than that, the road was smooth. Not silky smooth but smooth enough to keep me pushing at 15 km/h.

I realised the tailwind was really the main factor of my speed today. Arriving at Valley of Jesus Maria, I broke my momentum and stopped for tacos. Finally, the taco restaurant had Wi-Fi. First contact with the outside world or aka Facebook ever since I skated into the desert stretch 4 days ago. Notifications kept ringing nonstop. The owner and the guests were intrigued by me skating. Though I had only one fish tacos, they offered to refill my water bottles and Camelbak.

After the valley of Jesus Maria, the wind intensifies, I could see the sand flying. Good thing I am not facing the wind. Couldn't imagine the wind blowing against me together with the desert sand burying my face. Encountered two female cyclists from the opposite direction. They were heading towards USA. I don't have to imagine what they were facing right now. Another two cyclists from Mexico passed me. They were supported by one car driving and carrying all their load. The wife was the driver.

The road was the longest straight road I ever skated. Though not as long as the world's longest straight road in Australia, it certainly holds its weight. I estimated the straight road to be at least 30 km long. The wind was like a push from God since I was in the valley of Jesus and Mary. What a divine intervention. I was speeding at 20 km/h or even more. I was skating nonstop for 30 km since my taco break. I don't need to stop for breaks as I wasn't pushing much. Not even wanting to stop for lunch.

By 1 pm, I passed the Baja California south border. Immediately, my phone finally got reception. The days to check facebook while skating was back. More distraction for me I suppose. I noticed the time has changed. Baja south was on a different time zone; 1 hour ahead. Weird, it was on the same latitude yet the time zone has changed. This I couldn't comprehend. Same goes with Indonesia and Singapore. We were on the same latitude yet different time zone. This illustrates that time was an invention of men. Now I have to readjust my waking time and time to rest for the day.

Shortly, I passed a sign Ojo de Lieber (eye of the hare) to welcome cyclists and motorcyclists to free camping. The word 'Free Camping' immediately caught my eye. Decided to check it out. The restaurant owner welcomes cyclists on touring. We could camp in the backyard and there was a hot shower. I haven't had a shower for 4 days. There were 3 cyclists camping already. One of them was Christian, my co- Warmshower guest in Ensenada. Finally our path converged as he went on route 5 across the mountain range. The other couple was Yves and Frederique. Initially, I assumed that Yves was the female since Yves in French sound like Eve to me. Frederique sounded like Fred to me, thus I assumed she was the male. Thus, the joke was that I addressed them wrongly. They laughed it off and explained that they often got the mistakes from strangers, I wasn't the first and won't be the last. Silly French pronunciation.

Since the restaurant offer free camping, it was only right that I should have a meal there to patronize them. The amiable owner chatted with me and even notified the local newspaper Guerrero de Sal. The reporter immediately came down to interview me. My celebrity status continues to grow.

6 more cyclists eventually arrived throughout the day. 2 Canadian duos, the French couple whom I stayed with Gabino in San Quintin. There was also another French couple Oceanie and David who was a day behind me. This was turning to a Francophile place. The owner allows us to use their kitchen to cook our own meals. This restaurant was by far most touring-friendly place.

CHAPTER 6

SOUTH BAJA CALIFORNIA

Day 299: Wind couldn't break me
Mexico: Guerrero Negro to Vizcanio
Distance: 76 km
Time on board: 6 hours 36 mins
Average speed: 11.4 km/h
Cumulative distance: 11,759 km

Forced to take a rest day yesterday as when I woke up, I was gutted to see my pushcart's left wheel suffered another puncture. I already used my spare tube previous day. Luckily, I was camping with lots of cyclists. Christian assisted me. Well he did most of the job. First, I had to remove the inner tube which I was still grasping to learn the technique while Christian effortlessly removed the tube in a blink of the eye. Next, we had to find the leak and patch it up. Unfortunately, it was a slow leak. We had to apply soap and water to the tube to search for the puncture. The air would escape from the puncture and create a bubble from the applied soap. It was still searching for a needle in the haystack. Meanwhile, we easily found the puncture leak in my previous tube. Now, the process of patching up. I had the task of making sure the patch sticks well to the leak. By the time, we fixed my tyre, it was already 10 am. Too late to make 76 km journey as I couldn't predict whether I will be skating fast or slow. Better to take another rest day and go into town to buy a proper pump and patch kit. Christian and the other French couple left for Vizcanio while 2 other French couple and the Canadian duo still stayed behind to take a rest day with me.

Ojo de Liebre translates to Eye of the hare. Rocco, the restaurant owner explained the story. Guerrero Negro was famous for the lagoon where whales come here to mate. Every year, the Japanese would come to hunt for whales in the name of scientific research, instead it was a cover for meat consumption. Every year, the lagoon was filled with blood of innocent whales. From an aerial view, it looks like blood red eyes of rabbit hence the name Eye of the Hare. My Japanese friends, if you were reading this, you got to protest this senseless cruel act against nature. Hunting whales using the name of scientific research was bullshit, an insult to Mother Nature.

Today I checked to make sure that my wheels were all good to ride. The French couple Oceanie and David, together with Canadian duo set off with me to Vizcanio though I started 30 minutes ahead of them. The first 20 km was great, smooth roads and nice wind. Until the road headed south east, colluding with side wind blowing from the north. Massive side wind, equally as bad as a head wind. I could see the gulf of sand migrating from the left side of the road to the other side, crossing my path. I was literally eating sand entire time. My speed drastically fell below 9 km/h and effort pushing doubles. As I have my break, Oceanie and David caught up with me. Together we rode, suffering in the wind. I simply kept my head down, kept pushing. Surprisingly, I was faster than the French cyclists. My pace merely increased to 10-11 km/h. I switched to the rhythm of two kicks on each side. A short push followed by a long push. It sorts of worked for me. Several long pushes simply fatigued my muscle. Short series of push worked for tough conditions like this as I wasn't going for speed rather than the conservation of energy to survive.

The stretch of road was flat and straight. I could see the mountain 80 km away, which means tomorrow I not only have to fight the wind, uphill as well. But a day at one time first. A car pulled over, it was the Canadian duo sitting in the car with a young attractive American lady driver. Apparently, they threw in the towel and opt for a ride. The lady wanted to give us a lift as well but her van was stuffed with other cyclists gear. She would drive them into Vizcanio 20 km away and return for us. We continued pushing on. Indeed, at 60 km, she returned to pick us up. However, she asked the French couple ahead of me. They wanted to continue riding. But I was dying for a ride. The lady assumed I wanted to continue as well and drove off. No, there goes my ride. Now I have no choice but to continue skating the next 16 km against the wind. Thanks to the French couple, they pushed me to my limits. I could have thrown in the towel as well. But riding together motivated me as well to keep up with them. I would have stopped and try to hitchhike. Instead, they motivated me to beat the wind. The wind could break my body but it couldn't break my will and spirit.

I yelled in joy when I spotted the first sign of town. The struggle was finally over. We high-five each other as we beat the wind together. The Canadian duo and the lady were camping in a church 6 km away. I am not riding another 6 km, not today. We settled for Hotel Kadekaman, which has a campground. The French couple probably felt bad for refusing the ride for me or just impressed by my tenacity to skate that far in the wind, paid for my camp fee of 7 US. Another free stay for me. It comes with Wi-Fi and hot shower. To end the night, we celebrated today victory against nature with hamburger in the restaurant. Tomorrow would be another tough day. Rest well and fight another day.

Day 300: When life hands you a cactus, you make tequila
Mexico: Vizcanio to San Ignacio
Distance: 69 km
Time on board: 5 hours 32 mins
Average speed: 12.5 km/h
Cumulative distance: 11,827 km

My body ached badly in the morning after yesterday's battle with the wind. I'm expecting another tough battle with uphill and wind. Opt to wake up early to have a head start against nature. Instead, took a long shower. In the end, set off at 8.19 am. The wind somehow trickled to a breeze. Without the wind pulling me back, I skate a cruising pace at 13 km/h with one or stops for 40 km. Noticed the flies were following and sticking to me. No matter how fast I skate, I just couldn't shake them off. They settled on my pushcart. Without the strong wind to shake them off, they were persistent. So, either the wind or flies. Well, I would choose the latter though they looked disgusting, better than being shagged by the wind. At 40 km, stopped for lunch as Oceanie and David caught up with me. I was wondering when they were going to catch up with me. We had our lunch together before the start of the climb. The next 30 km was hilly.

We rode together again and leapfrogged each other when we stopped to take photos. I stopped by to take some photos with cactus. I observed once out of Vizcanio, the terrain become greener, more variety of trees rather than dominating Cactus.

Soon we encounter our first of the many steep climbs. One thing about uphill was that you know it would end and downhill awaits. As for the wind, you could never predict when it would ever end or which direction. After 2 or 3 hills, it was finally downhill. At the end of downhill, lies the military checkpoint. This was the first time they check our baggage. And only one soldier was checking our bags while the rest of the soldiers was just eye watching. The soldier checked every single pannier belonging to French couple. When it comes to mine, it was too messy. Packing load on my pushcart was like solving a jigsaw puzzle. Everything must fit together. After 15 minutes, they let us off. I wondered what were they checking for. Another 4 km at 3 pm, we arrived at La casa Del Ciclista, a private residence allowing cyclists to camp with showers and wifi for 100 pesos. We got reunited with Christian and another French Couple Yves and Frederique. They took a rest day to recuperate from the outrageous wind and to wait for us as well. Now we could make our way together to La Paz.

Joined forces to make a taco dinner. Using all our camping stoves. 2 MSR and 2 primus camping stove, cooking all at once. I thought I would be the first Singaporean to stay here. Apparently, I wasn't. I saw the writing on the wall by Marcus Seng last October. He rode his motorbike across Mexico. At least I was the first to arrive here on longboard. If today was easy mode, yesterday was only medium mode. Tomorrow would be the hard mode.

Day 301: Entering into three virgins
Mexico: San Ignacio to Santa Rosalia
Distance: 73 km
Time on board: 6 hours 56 mins
Average speed: 10.6 km/h
Cumulative distance: 11,901 km

Last night sky appeared ominous therefore I employed my back up emergency plan for camping in the rain. Tied my tarp to my pushcart and secure the remaining 3 ends. It turned out to be a dry night yet again. At least I had some practice in setting my rain tarp when it really rains. Had to yell out loud when the dog came snatching my bivy tent in the wee morning, disturbing my sleep. What was with the matter with dogs? Knowing today's ride would be a hell of a climb so I opted to wake up early to have an early head start to slowly walk up the hills. Instead, I spent time having breakfast with the cyclists and chatting with Casa Del Ciclista owner. Every morning, the cyclists would prepare a hearty breakfast. Eggs bacon, toasts. For me, just simple peanut butter spread on tortilla. I am too lazy to lit up my MSR Dragonfly in the morning. End up leaving at 8.30 am. Anyway, I calculated the uphill climb would last 38 km then would be downhill all the way. I have to bid my time to climb the hill before enjoying the downhill. Upon leaving San Ignacio, another french touring cyclist turned back to chat with me. He was heading northwards towards USA, starting from Ushuaia, Argentina. That were a lot of headwinds.

Soon after, the cyclists caught up with me. It was great to have companions riding with me through the journey. I never felt alone in the way. Like the pacific coast, people on the same route would form camderies to ride, camp together.

Apparently, I was climbing the mountain range known as 'The Three Virgins'. What if the Mexican dug a tunnel through the three virgins, could I say I entered the holes of the virgins. Then if everyone entered the holes of the three virgins. Wouldn't it be called 3 whores? You see such random thought process kept on entertaining in my mind as I slogged through the days. The gradients weren't that steep, but it stretched a long distance to drain your legs. Each section of uphill slope came with a flatter segment where I could rest my legs and get some pace before going up again and walk. I know this would end eventually thus I patiently struggled up. I placed a packet of crackers in my pushcart pouch. After every km, I would have a cracker, motivating myself to go fast so I could have the next cracker.

At 60 km, the cyclists waited for me at the top. The guys wanted to try skating. Naturally they struggled balancing on my board, let alone trying to align my pushcart with my board. It could be said that Skating 12, 000 km was quite a feat. At last, I could see the sea of Cortes from the top, signalling that we were going down. Really steep down. The road plunged into the sea that I couldn't see the road ahead of me. It was like taking a rollercoaster, I tightened my balls and braked hard together with footbraking. I thought It was the end of my nightmare. The flat road was along the industrial area with heavy trailers destroying the road, breaking the surfaces into tortoise like shell patterns. Further impeded by the dogs, I couldn't outskate them in this type of road condition. Each time, they chased me, I would have to stop and get off my board and chase them back. Either that or throw rocks.

Arrived at the Santa Rosalia's fire station or Bomberos in Spanish with the cyclists. to settle for the night.

Day 302: Wheels of puncture
Mexico: Santa Rosalia to Mulege
Distance: 65 km
Time on board: 6 hours 6 mins
Average speed: 10.6 km/h
Cumulative distance: 11,966 km

First time sleeping in a fire station. So far, I have slept in police stations, churches, temples, mosques and petrol stations. We slept side by side on our sleeping mats, behind a fire truck. One thing about me is that I get up to pee a lot during the night. Only to find out the firemen locked the doors to the toilet. So, I had to rush outside the station to pee on a puddle. Woke up when the fire truck drove off, signalling it was time to leave. I settled for eggs and bacon breakfast at a food stall while the cyclists went for bread at Panderia El Boleo. By the time I finished breakfast, it was already 9 am. Today was only 65 km to Mulege. Even if I were to take my sweet time at 10km/h, the latest I would arrive was 5pm.

Though Google map plotted a flatter elevation after the first climb, if you zoom in further, the elevation isn't that flat. The cyclists caught up with me while I slogged, feeling aches on my legs. Making less than 10 km/h by 2 hours, just 19 km in 2 hours. A large truck pulled over to gift me a brand-new polarizing sunglass. That was really thoughtful, as it really would be useful in protecting my sights from the glazing sun. I got a shock when my camera screen went blank while taking photos. Only then I realised my sunglasses couldn't see the screen on landscape mode. The explanation was that phones have a polarizing filter that helps to cut glare and reflections, ironically to make it easier to see in bright sunlight. The problem was, so do polarized sunglasses. When your phone and sunglass filters were aligned in opposite directions, all the light from your screen was cut out so you cannot see anything.

At 30 km, I stopped to cook lunch. Instead of opting for a quick simple peanut butter, I cooked macaroni with instant noodles. After that, my stomach felt queasy and have the need to purge its contents in the middle of the desert. Hid behind a rock to shit. I came prepared with toilet paper. This roll of toilet paper was actually salvaged from the road in USA.

After finishing my big business, I continued on my way. I was facing a tailwind and all of a sudden, the pushcart became bumpy once again. This time it was my right tyre to be punctured and go flat. No cyclists to help me this time. I had to rely on myself to fix the tyres. After observing Christian removing my inner tube the other day in Guerrero Negro, at last my eureka moment arrived. Removing the inner tube became so simple. An achievement unlocked. My first tyre replacement. After that, I harnessed the power of the wind blowing from North, giving me a tailwind to gain speed and made up for lost time. I was expecting to arrive in Mulege by 2 pm, given the so called relatively flat elevation. There's always a new challenge or obstacle thrown at me daily.

After fixing my flat tyre, I raced with the wind on my back, my average speed rapidly increased. I raced to the bottom of the second climb. That was why I called today's "skate the Devil's horn". There would be 2 climbs. One at the start, another at the end. Resembling a devil's head. Now on my final climb before descending to Mulege. As usual, I walked up. Only 2-3 km walk. At the downhill section, my pushcart started to wobble again. Another flat tire. This time I just give it a pump and raced my way down to Mulege. On the foothills, there was a procession. One of many Feast days in Catholic Mexico. Men riding horses accompanying the procession to the church. I continued my way as I was running out of daylight. The last 2 km to the Casa de Poncho Villa where we agreed to meet and camp, was horrendous. Mud laden road. Even walking and pushing my pushcart was a challenge. The wheels kept getting stuck in the mud. Not mentioning the flat tyre. It was a miracle that I made it all the way through. Yolanda, the owner of the restaurant right next to the beach and view to the lighthouse welcomed me with open arms. The cyclists waited for me since 1 pm and I arrived at 5 pm. We camped at the restaurant and had our big hamburger dinner to replenish the lost calories. Tomorrow would be a rest day to explore Mulege and find a solution to my flat tyres.

Date of entry: 16 December 2017
Day 306: Oh Crab, Crepes
Mexico: Mulege to Km 68 marker Mulege - Loreto
Distance: 70 km
Time on board: 7 hours 12 mins
Average speed: 9.8 km/h
Ascent: 923 m
Descent: 708 m
Cumulative distance: 12, 049 km

Spent 3 days chilling in Yolanda's Poncho Villa restaurant in Mulege. It was located right next to the beach and lighthouse. A great place to rest for 3 days before making our way to La Paz. The gang planned to reach La Paz in time for Christmas which gives us roughly 7 days of riding. Therefore, we took our time here to enjoy Mulege while I fix my tyre issue. We thought it was just going to be the 6 of us. The next day, another couple arrived. Lester from Venezuela and Stephanie from Switzerland rode their bikes with trailers carrying Surfboard. They started from Argentina and heading northwards in search for the best waves to surf. Lester gave the true meaning of 'ride and surf'.

I tried patching both my punctured tubes but to no avail. One had an enormous leak and another had several tiny leaks. Then I recalled my buddy, Deejay, handing me a bottle of slime to solidify the tubes, making them more puncture resistance. Christian and Yves's bicycle-repair expertise were put to use. Even so, the tubes were still unsalvageable. Plus, my tyres were too worn out after 3000 km. The pushcart was meant to use for jogging with toddlers, not to carry heavy loads and skate around the world. Yolanda's brother happened to run a bicycle shop and sold me a 2 16-inch inner tubes. However, the width 2.125 were too wide for my 1.75. Still, I have to do with it. As for the worn-out tyre, Lester managed to search. And found a pair of 16-inch tyres in a second hand store Segunda Martinez. I quickly dashed to the town on Yolanda's old worn but green bicycle. However, I ran out of pesos and ATM doesn't accept my card. Same issue encountered in USA where my visa debit card only works with certain banks. Had to use my emergency US to buy the tyres. Mexicans love US and you could widely use it in Baja. The going rate in most stores was 18 pesos to US $1, better rates than money exchangers after Ensenada. They returned the change in pesos. This way, I managed to get more pesos. While at the store, I bought another new 16-inch wheel rim. Though mine currently was still useable, but I could never know. Better err to caution. Couldn't get stuck in the middle of nowhere without any spares, especially the pushcart parts were hard to come by. Yves and Lester managed to squeeze the wider tube into the narrow tyre and apply slime to the tube. It should work for now. The remaining days we explored the Mulege town. Since the town was 4 km away from Yolanda's restaurant and I was too lazy to skate to town with mud laden road. Borrowed Yolanda's green yet antique bike to ride with the gang to town. Cycling after a long hiatus, was ass hurting. Prefer skating to cycling. I guess to each his own. Mulege has an interesting ancient church dated back to 18 century where the Spanish mission began spreading Christianity in American continent.

A funny anecdote was the gang wanted to prepare a crepes dinner but I misheard their heavy French Pronunciation as crabs. They asked me if in Singapore, locals love crepes. I told them we Singaporeans love crabs especially with chilli. Chili crab was our specialty. Of course, they misunderstood as chili crepes. Oceanie and David managed to go fishing hence deepening the misunderstanding as I assumed, they were hunting crabs for our dinner. It was until dinner; I saw everyone preparing pancakes. Where was the crabs? I thought we were having crabs party. I even gestured the crabs sign by having my hands pinching in the air. Then I realised it was crepes, not crabs. We all have a good laugh. Such fun only happens when you were touring with people from different cultures and backgrounds.

The rest of the day was spent on the beach or Yolanda's restaurant binge watching my YouTube videos and Big Bang Theory sitcom. The day finally arrived when we had to start going, otherwise we would never make it to la Paz. The distance from Mulege to Loreto was 138 km. Had to split into 2 days of riding. The gang opted to have a short 38 km ride to the beach to camp before riding 100 km to Loreto the next day. I couldn't ride 100 km judging from the elevation climb. Therefore, I have to temporarily split from the gang and ride at least halfway today and another 70 km to Loreto to meet them. We arranged to gather in El Banjo Restaurant in Loreto the next day, supposedly well-known place to host cyclists. And so today, I started on my own, trying to skate as far as I could.

Starting, I had to walk through the 2 km mud laden road. Once back to main highway, I began the proper skate. Km markers indicating the km remaining to Loreto were placed accurately on every km. Therefore, I used these markers as a gauge for tomorrow's distance to Loreto and served as a motivator for me. The more I skated today, the less I have to for tomorrow. Initially, it was demoralizing to see the km markers still at 130 odd km. As I grinded the distance down, the distance gets smaller and smaller, motivating me more.

A car pulled over and handed me some snacks and 1.5 litres of water. Should have stored it in my water bank as later on, it somehow fell off from my bottom food pouch on my pushcart. Now I have to ration my 11 litres water for 2 days. It should suffice but it was always better to have more than less. Better Err to Caution. The road followed the coast, going up the hills before plunging to the beach. The turquoise water at the beaches and outlying islands were common sights on this road, tempting me to join the gang for the short ride today. But I would rather suffer more today so that I could enjoy a shorter more relaxing ride the next day. That was my mentality. I rather suffer now and to relax later. That was why I tend to finish my projects real early and then relax till I realised the deadline was looming and rushing to complete the deadline in time.

Another cyclists couple spotted riding my way, from far I assumed they should be my gang but it was not. They were from USA, trying to escape the cold winter. I supposed my gang were taking their own sweet time to set off since only 38 km for today. As usual, I walked up the steep uphill. Facing the headwind now, doesn't bother me much as I was walking. The headwind doesn't slow me that much to my already slow walking pace. The headwind acts as a natural brake for me during the descents so headwind isn't that bad for me. Only when it comes to flat land, it really matters.

Stopped for peanut butter tortillas lunch at the roadside. Got to ration my water, thus having peanut butter tortillas was the best alternative since I don't require water to cook it. 5 pieces of tortillas spread with peanut butter provide me 1500 calories. Fast and simple with more Calories.

The countdown to km markers began as I passed the 90 km marker. Grinding down the distance as I could physically see the distance to Loreto getting shorter and shorter every km. Target was at least getting pass 79 km marker, leaving me 70 km to skate tomorrow while searching for a suitable camping spot in the wild as there wasn't any town in between. The cutoff time to stop was decided at 5 pm, well I could push it to 5.30 pm, 10 minutes before the sun sets. As I left the bay area, entered the hilly terrains, began to walk more than skating. Good thing I have already grinded pass 70 km marker. Any distance I passed was a bonus. As I rode by, spotted several suitable perfect camping spots, however it was still early, I could have pushed more to get less distance for tomorrow. After all, I am on a hill, any distance skated up was less the distance skating up for tomorrow. I realised I was close to the top of the hill but it was close to 5 pm and opted to stop at 68 km marker where there was relatively secluded spot by the roadside. I couldn't take the risk to skate further and not having to find a good camp spot while there was still light. I thought nobody could spot me but the drivers as they drove up, waved at me. I guessed I still am easily visible to the traffic but I couldn't be bothered to set camp elsewhere. I supposed no robbers would patrol along the road during the night with a remote possibility of robbing a penniless stinky skateboarder. I still have faith in humanity. Good night to sleeping with gazillions of stars

Day 307: Loretooooooo!
Mexico: Km 68 marker to Loreto
Distance: 68 km
Time on board: 6 hours 21 mins
Average speed: 11 km/h
Cumulative distance: 12,118 km

Of all nights, the sky chose to rain when I am camping in the middle of the highway roadside. Woke up abruptly by droplets, hastily brought all my stuff and squeeze them together in my claustrophobic bivy tent. Amazingly, everything fitted perfectly into the head compartment. Couldn't be bothered to set up the rain tarp in the dark, simply zip up the bivy, leaving my pushcart, water bank and backpack out in the rain. Continued sleeping while the wind kept howling and blasting at my black diamond spotlight bivy, putting my bivy to the test. Well I must say my bivy was able to truly withstand the powers of wind. The rain turned out to be a few droplets as the wind rapidly blow the rain clouds away from me.

Barely caught a few winks's sleep. Woke up at 6 am and pack up my stuff and breakfast. Despite getting ready so early, Still I have to wait till 7.30 am for the sun to shine on the road for traffic to see me. Since I have climbed almost to the top yesterday, leaving me to walk up just 500 metres before descending down. If only I knew the top was near, I would have to skate further yesterday. Along the way down, found many more suitable camping spots. If only I knew. In the midst of the dark clouds above the mountains, there lies the rainbow. What a sight. However, I don't know if that was a good thing for me or not. It could signal that rain was coming and I better hurry my way.

Each time I pass the km marker, getting closer to Loreto, I would announce aloud "mas XX km a Loretoooooo!" Imitating those south American football commentators shouting gooooooooalllllll! Practised reciting the numbers in Spanish from 68 km to 20 km as the km markers seems to stop appearing at 20 km prior to Loreto.

The couple I met yesterday appeared behind me. They were from North Carolina, USA and camped somewhere in the mountains like me. I continued skating up and down the hilly terrain. As I spent long hours skating slowly, by 11 am i have already skated 38 km. Ready to push some more, but felt my pushcart wobbling. This time, Puncture on my left rear wheel. Puncture could't stop happening to me. Pumped it up and continued my way. Stopped by Llantera, car tyre workshop to see if I could buy more water. The hot desert makes me consume more water like a leaking tap. Even carrying 12 litres yesterday wasn't enough. The water bank was running dry. I could survive with the remaining amount to Loreto if I don't cook. I approached the workshop to try my luck. The guy only sells coke and beer. But he had gallons of potable water for me to fill up my water bank. I asked if how much do I need to pay. The owner gladly said it was free. I thanked him for the water. Extra water meant I don't have to ration for water and could cook lunch. The wobbling wheel meant it was time to stop for lunch and fix my tyre. Cooked my lunch before settling my tyre. After learning from experts on repairing tyre, it took me no time in removing the inner tube and replacing with wider inner tube and slime sealing it. All it takes only 15 minutes. Becoming an expert myself. Few days ago, I was completely clueless on repairing bicycle tyres. By observing and learning from the experts, I managed to figured out. One of many things I learnt during my tour. Cooking and this were just one of many survival skills I learnt during my journey. Never think something was too hard to learn.

Only 26 km left to go. Should be easy peasy and done in 2-3 hours. Was wrong. The hills got steeper. Plus, I spent a considerable time at the military checkpoint. The diligent soldiers checked thoroughly the bus in front of me. When it was my turn, they checked through all my stuff for drugs. If I am skating through the world, why I would want to get high through drugs. They made me unpack and pack my stuff on pushcart. It was much of a hassle for me to pack perfectly into my pushcart. After they have their fun with me, they waved me off to continue my way.

By 3.45 pm, I had arrived at Loreto. Made my way to the first missionary church built in 1697 for landmark photo. Skated to El Bajon restaurant where the gang have arranged to meet. The gang have to cycle 100 km while I only did 68 km. Naturally, I arrived way ahead of them. El Bajon, ran by Sandra and Lalo, was a good friend of Gabino whom I stayed with in San Quentin. Sandra and Lalo warmly welcomed and hosted cyclists just as many in Baja. About 4.30 pm, Christian, Yves and Fred arrived. Together, Sandra showed us our room which all 6 of us have to squeeze in. We have slept together in Fire station therefore it was nothing new to us. When people kindly welcome you, you have to appreciate their gestures. Shortly, Oceanie and David arrived. The gang was once again reunited. To show our appreciation to Sandra, we had dinner at her restaurant. Have Papa Rellenas, mashed potatoes with beef cubes and cheeses.

Day 308: Last Big Climb before La Paz
Mexico: Loreto to Km 63 marker Loreto - Ciudad Insurgent
Distance: 56 km
Time on board: 5 hours 35 mins
Average speed: 10 km/h
Ascent: 714 m
Descent: 360 m
Cumulative distance: 12,174 km

Realising that squeezing in a tiny room with 5 other cyclists wasn't such a good idea. First, I tend to run to the toilet often in the middle of the night. Secondly, I wake up really early to start my day. I slept on a couch just the right size for me while Christian, Oceanie and David slept on the floor with their sleeping mat. Perks of being petite.

Once again, had to split from the gang as they were planning to ride to Liguii beach 37 km away then 80 km to Ciudad Insurgent. Looks doable. However, I analyzed the elevation chart. After Liguii, there was the mother of all Hills to climb. I couldn't make it to Ciudad Insurgent 80 km with that much climb. Therefore, I had to pass Liguii and climb as high as possible today. Next day, would be a sweet long descent to Ciudad Insurgent. If possible, I could actually reach Ciudad Constitution 93 km from the downhill. That was the plan.

The gang wanted to explore Loreto before heading to Liguii while I spared no time in starting off at 8am. Entering back to the main highway was freshly paved smooth tarmac for a couple of km before reverting back to usual not so smooth yet not that rough asphalt road. First hour I started off real fast with that smooth tarmac. Better to get over the flat area fast so that I could have more time walking up the big mountain pass later on.

Google map suggested it would be flat for 37 km to Liguii. But I checked it together with the big climb. Therefore, the route seems very flat in comparison to steep elevation gain. But I was wrong. It wasn't flat. There were many steep slopes awaiting to torture me. Just that I couldn't detect over Google map since it was masked by the high elevation later on. The route to Liguii was going up and down after the first hour. At Mirador, a viewpoint to one of many seaview, a car pulled over and the family handed me Gatorate Energy drink and snacks. That sure would come in handy later on. Another car pulled over, they mentioned that they passed by me skating on the road few days ago and wanted to buy me a beer in Loreto. Beer in the middle of a skate. Nah. Drink and skate doesn't bode well for me. At a resort, met a touring cyclist but he was trying to hitch a ride to Cabo as his family would be arriving tomorrow to spend Christmas.

Pushed on towards Liguii where I stopped to buy eggs and just in time for lunch before the big climb. This time, I carried way too much water. In Loreto, I bought 3 gallons of water. I assumed a gallon was only 3 litres so 9 litres plus 5 litres in my water should suffice for the next 2 days. A gallon is 3.78 litres. Why was it so funny the conversion? I ended filling up 11 litres together with 5 litres. The top-heavy water bank bears down on my pushcart, making it susceptible to toppling. I had to rearrange my load before starting my day. Cooked lunch; Fideo pasta with instant noodles and eggs and hot dogs. Enough to fill me for the upcoming climb.

Immediately resumed after lunch with the commencement of the mountain pass. I could judge how steep the climb was by looking at my walking speed on my Garmin GPS Fenix 3 Watch. Anything faster than 4.6 km/h was mellow. 4.3 km/h was very steep. Thus, my benchmark was 4.3 km/h. Anything than 4.3 km/h was insanely steep. Today I was walking up the mountain at 3.6 km/h, which was extremely steep. The road winds around the curvature of the mountain. If only they could build a tunnel through the mountain, it would be a godsend gift to me. Instead I navigated through the hairpin turns, indirect long route. Nevertheless, I spent almost 2 hours walking up the 6 km long mountain pass. That wasn't the end yet. It only meant the road now was less steep but still have to walk yet at a slightly faster pace. I allocated 3-4 hours to navigate the remaining 20 km climb, therefore I am not in a rush. Entered less steep segment of the mountain and could finally skate a little and walk. The terrain started to be going up and down. At last, I could skate more. By 48 km, it started to go more downhill. My average speed gradually picked up. Stopped after 63 km marker at 4 pm. Though I could continue to cover more ground since I have finished the ascent and descent already continue but I choose to stop at a restaurant to camp for the night. The restaurant wasn't really a restaurant, just a store for snack and drink. Asked the owner if I could camp in her backyard. She kindly welcomed me. In return, I bought some snacks and drink from her. Tomorrow would be a long distance yet it could be fast as I would be mostly descending just as in El Rosario. If my calculations were right, I would arrive in La Paz 4 days' time.

Day 309: Momentum momentum
Mexico: Km 63 marker to Ciudad Constitucion
Distance: 92 km
Time on board: 5 hours 48 mins
Average speed: 16 km/h
Ascent: 238 m
Descent: 525 m
Cumulative distance: 12,266 km

Usually I am too lazy to boil water to make tea in the morning. It was too much of a hassle to set up my MSR Dragonfly in the morning. Last night I didn't disassemble my MSR and left it outside my bivy tent so when I wake up in the morning, I just have to light up the stove to boil water. Sleeping in this restaurant was extra safe, they locked up the gate at night and the owner opened it up for me when I want to leave.

I thought yesterday was the end of the uphill, once again I was wrong. For the next 18 km and 1.5 hours, I was skating up and down. Before the start of long descent, I climbed the last hill, it seems never ending. At the last turn of the hill, my eyes gleamed at the paradise ahead of me. Long straight gradual descent lies ahead of me. The descent was optimal for me, cruising at 24 km/h without having to put a foot down to push for the next hour. I was belting songs after songs. Simply paradise.

As descent gradually flatten out, I was still having so much momentum from the long descent, I was pushing at 20 km/h with minimal pushing. Short pushes to maintain speed. I didn't want to pause for breaks or photo, not wanting to disrupt the momentum. A rare opportunity that I could keep going at such speed. If I have to pause and restart, I might not regain that speed again or exert more effort to gain that speed. Thus, I kept going on and on without any breaks. Not even for interesting photo moment. For next 2 hours, I already covered 40 km and by 11.30 am, I skated 63 km to Ciudad Insurgent. Insurgent sounds like a dystopian city in some Sci-fi movies. Had lunch at a restaurant. Has been ages since I have Fried chicken. It tastes so juicy and oily. Yummy. Took my time to enjoy it until 1.30 pm. Since I got lots of time and momentum, decided to continue skating another 30 km to Ciudad Constitucion. The road was literally flat and smooth that I was easily pushing at 16-18 km/h without ever stopping.

Skating fast was actually less exhausting than skating slowly. Once I get to cruising speed more than 15 km/h, it actually takes less effort to maintain pace. Just few kicks at a time to continue coasting. In no time, under 2 hours, I arrived at Constitution. It was much larger than its counterpart Insurgent. Stopped at Santander bank to withdraw cash. Running low on cash, better to withdraw money before I am stuck in nowhere again. Santander bank seem to be the only bank in Mexico to accept my visa debit card.

Approached the Red Cross first to camp but they refused me. I asked where was the nearest fire station. They directed me to the Bomberos a block away. Immediately, the firemen welcomed me with open arms. Before I could finish my sentence to ask, they pointed to the floor which I could camp. "Mi casa su casa" My house was your house. I was made at home.

No signs of the gang by 5 pm, I presumed that they were not going to arrive here tonight. After all, they have to ride 115 km with really insane hills. I went out for dinner. When I returned, I saw the station filled with tents. The gang had arrived. This time, I beat them to it. Now only 200 km to La Paz.

Day 310: Berserker mode
Mexico: Ciudad Constitucion to Las Pocitas
Distance: 97 km
Time on board: 6 hours
Average speed: 16.1 km/h
Cumulative distance: 12,363 km

If you think yesterday's 92 km was fast and far, wait until you see me today. Yesterday, I was fast due to long downhill, but today's journey was almost flat. I did 97 km with 16.1 km/h average pushing on flat roads. If the road was any smoother, I could easily do even more. Though 97 km was not the furthest I ever skated in a day, I did 150 km in Germany with the long 15 daylight hours but I did this 97 km with a short 10 hours of daylight. That was an accomplishment. Of course, I ever did 97 km in Cambodia, ending by 2 pm, fastest average speed 17 km/h with silky smooth paved road. In other words, as long as I have flat smooth road, the distance isn't any issue, 150 km was easily attainable for me. I could easily cruise at speed of 16-20 km/h on flat smooth land.

Woke up early in Bomberos or fire station to set off early. The guys lit up their camping stove for breakfast in the fire station. Ironic, they were setting fire in a fire station.

I was expecting flat land most of the way but I wouldn't predict the road condition which was a major factor to my speed. Bid farewell to the amiable firemen in Constitucion and had a head start from my gang. Once on the highway, I was easily pushing above 16 km/h. Since it was a long flat road, there isn't much to stop for photos except the Cross shrines laid along the roadside for those who perished in road accidents, reminding me the perils of being on the road. I am aware of the risks and I am willing to accept whatever consequences. The reward was living Life.

By 2 hours, I had done 32 km. Time for a short break. The gang finally caught up with me. We rode together, even my fastest couldn't match their cycling speed. Christian offered to tow me along. He tied a rope on his bike and I held on to the rope while he pulled me along. I did my part to make his life easier as well by pushing fast. Together we were speeding 20 km/h for next 8 km until Christian threw in the towel. Pulling a 55 kg guy with probably 40 kg loaded pushcart was exhausting. I am back pushing on my own. I found my 'Berserker mode', a state in which I was in a zone of focus. In psychology sense, it is better described as a flow state or as being in the zone. It is the mental state of operation in which a person performing an activity is fully immersed in a feeling of energized focus, full involvement, and enjoyment in the process of the activity. In essence, flow is characterized by complete absorption in what one does, and a resulting loss in one's sense of space and time. I was pushing with much gusto, belting songs after songs while catching my breath though I forgot most lyrics. And announcing the km to la Paz as I passed the km marker. I was pushing like 18 - 21 km/h for next 10 km like a mad man. Soon I overtook Oceanie and David and caught up with the faster Christian, Yves and Frederique in Santa Rita at 53 km where we stopped for lunch. We gathered at a seemingly desolate sport ground. While they had their sandwich, I cooked my pasta. Got to finish my food supply somehow.

Resumed at 1.30 pm. 3 km after, Christian has passed his 10,000 km mark in this tour. He celebrated with a jump and snack. This 53 km was considered flat, next 44 km was relatively hilly with rolling hills. My speed declined. Took my strawberry cake snack and motivated and energized myself every 10 km with the snack. Though with tiny hills, I am still able to maintain my average 16 km/h speed.

A pickup carrying loads of oranges passed me and offered me to take an orange from his truck. I obliged. At 80 km, I had to stop to change my pants. As my pants kept rubbing on my left thigh when I pushed Mongo, the rubbing became an irritating pain for me. Once I've changed to my new pants given by Montana Perlo in Camalu, pushing become more comfortable.

Left 16 km more to Las Pocitas, I pushed with even more gusto trying to reach my destination as soon as possible. By 4 pm, I arrived at Las Pocitas. Found the gang at Los Dolores restaurant to camp for the night. We celebrated our days riding together and Christian's 10, 000 km milestone over beer. Our ride together would come to an end soon as we were only 110 km to La Paz. If only it was flat, I might attempt a day ride to La paz, but it was not. 600 m elevation over 110 km would definitely hamper my speed. Have to contend with 60/50 km split over 2 days to La Paz.

Day 311: Sleeping among Cactus

Mexico: Las Pocitas to Km 49 marker to La Paz
Distance: 60 km
Time on board: 5 hours 7 mins
Average speed: 11.8 km/h
Ascent: 609 m
Descent: 420m
Cumulative distance: 12,423 km

Christian, Yves and Frederique decided to make all the way to La Paz today, 110 km. More than 600 m in ascent meant I would have to spend my time walking up. To make the 110 km distance, it would require me to skate at least 15 km/h in order to reach La Paz before night fall. Skating 16 km/h on flat was a piece of cake but with elevation gain, I would be happy with my average speed 11 km/h. Therefore, reaching La Paz today was out of the question. I would have to skate halfway and camp somewhere.

I hate such 110 km distance. It was not close to skate within a day with such elevation yet it was too short to split into 2 days 80 km/30 km. With this elevation, I still could do 80 km and fall short of 30 km to La Paz. This was the case of so close yet so far. At least, with further distance of 140 km, I know it was definitely out of reach and be happy to split the distance into 2 days of 70 km.

Oceanie was not feeling well last night due to long exposure to hot desert sun yesterday. She didn't join us for dinner. Therefore, she and David would split the distance to La Paz as well and arrive in La paz the next day. At least I got company.

Had breakfast with the gang at restaurant Los Dolores where we camped. The owner made eggs with sausage and tortillas. Started late as I only need to do 50 - 60 km of uphill today. Through Google map, I analysed that the real descent starts after 55 km.

Today was unusually chilly. Had to put on my jacket, a rare occurrence in hot sunny Baja desert. The sky juice came dripping down. More like a drizzle but by Baja dry desert standard, it was pouring. Didn't bother to put on my rain pants as I predicted it would be just a tickle. However, the road surface was wet and as my wheels spun, the cold droplets sprinkled onto my legs. Horrible cold feeling.

As I passed through the 100 km marker, a couple of cyclists came by. I thought they were Oceanie and David. Instead it was another couple I had never met before. Where did all those cyclists come from? The gang mentioned that at least 20 cyclists apart from us, were currently on route but I have never seen them. By right, they were supposed to be faster than me and should have passed me by now.

At 100 km or El Cien village, 100 km away from La Paz, I stopped for photo and refilled my water. Then Oceanie and David arrived. Unwell Oceanie collapsed on the bus stop bench to rest. Looks like they were really not going to make it to La Paz today.

I pushed on, followed by Oceanie and David. It seemed Oceanie had recovered quickly. She mentioned that I am her motivation. When I get ahead of her, she would strive to pedal faster to catch up with me and pass me. No cyclists like to be slower than a longboarder. Therefore, I have become a motivator for cyclists now. When they see me, they have to speed up.

The terrain, as predicted was going up and down. More ascent than descent in fact. Still I could maintain average 12 km/h speed. On one of the upslopes, I spotted Oceanie and David waiting with a car parked aside. They turned out to be the couple we met in Mulege. They had to drive to meet their family and now driving back north. Gave me a bar of chocolate which would come in handy later.

As the hills got steeper, Oceanie and David started to pull ahead of me. Supposed to stop together for lunch but I couldn't find them as it had already passed lunch hour. I gave up searching for them as I saw incoming high hill waiting for me. Definitely I couldn't climb that steep hill with an empty stomach. Stopped before the climb and cooked my usual spaghetti and instant noodles.

Resumed at 1.30 pm. With Only 20 km to the top of the hill before the long 55 km descent, it gave me a slim hope of reaching La Paz today. If I could make it to the top by 3pm, that leaves me 3 hours to descend the last 55 km to La Paz, which suddenly become an attainable goal. The question was why do I want to rush to La Paz so early. Well the answer was ego and pride. To show off to the cyclists, I am equal or stronger than them. But nah, I have already proven myself. Don't need that ego boost. As I pushed on or walked up, the goal slowly get further, thus I have to content with camping somewhere in the desert tonight before descending to La Paz real early tomorrow.

As the day faded to an end, I began searching for a camp spot. Settled at 60 km of skate at the 49 km marker. With descent most of the way, I should arrive at La Paz before afternoon. Tonight, I shall enjoy my last night camping in the desert, sleeping among the cactus with stars in view.

Day 312: Peace be with you in La Paz
Mexico: Km 49 marker to La Paz
Distance: 55 km
Time on board: 4 hours 40 mins
Average speed: 12 km/h
Cumulative distance: 12,479 km

The last day skating to a milestone never fail to present me a final hurdle. After finishing most of the climb yesterday, I expect today to be plain sailing. Somehow, nature would deal me another blow. Really a huge blow from the wind. Last night, the signs were already ominous. The wind kept harassing my tent the entire night. Woke up to a freezing biting cold morning. According to Google map, I would have a bit of climb before descending to La Paz. Well, never trust Google Map on this. Even after 7 km of slight climb, where the downhill was supposed to start, the road continued to be rolling hill up and down. Or maybe there was a downhill but I just couldn't feel it as the wind acts as a natural brake, making any downhill feel like pushing on a flat land.

The wind continued to intensify, though not as horrible as the day to Vizcanio, putting a damper on my spirit. I predicted my arrival time to La Paz to early morning, expecting to make 55 km in 3 hours. Instead the wind decided to change its course today, just to play a fool on me.

I sluggishly pushed against the wind and hills, faring not too bad at 12 km/h average speed. At 17 km, I was expecting the hills to come to an end. It turned out to be a short disappointing foreplay. There was a sharp curve down into a road construction section where I had to walk. A driver then passed me a bottle of water to cheer me on. What followed were more rolling hills. Google map really played a cruel joke on me. Promising a nice smooth descent, gets my hopes up, only to dash it. The cruelest torture on a man. To promise hope and take it away.

Regardless. I cannot change the wind, nor the hills or the road. I could only change my mindset. Therefore, I kept pushing on. Daydreaming while I am on the road was a skill I acquired since young. I daydream and fantasize all the time to keep me sane in this seemingly insane world.

Gradually, after 32 km, the sea of Cortes appeared in front of my eyes, bringing hope to an end to my struggle. La Paz was still quite a distance away though. At least another 20 km away. La Paz was a large city, from the outskirts to the centre was pretty far. I stopped for Super Burros. Super Burros indeed lives to its name, energizing me for the final push. A km after, a car slowed down. I saw my camelbak hydration pack. Oh, I left my hydration pack in the restaurant. One patron chased me on his car to return me my hydration pack. What a blessing!

The traffic increasingly intensified with the widening of two lanes and a shoulder. I pushed to Malecon to have a landmark photo with The Sign La PAZ. There I spotted my warmshower host Tuly Arce. She was a popular warmshower host, nearly all the cyclists on route would stay with her. Yesterday, she hosted 16 cyclists. Today, I am her first longboard tourer.

A month in Baja California, 1400 km from Tijuana, finally arrived in La Paz, the capital of southern Baja California. Could be faster if I didn't take any rest days. In all, I rested 10 days and skated 20 days. 70 km in average for skating days. Here, I would rest many days to celebrate Christmas. Probably continue south to Los Cabos by bus or skate before returning to La Paz to take the ferry to Mainland Mexico. For now, merry Christmas.

CHAPTER 7

MAINLAND MEXICO

Day 326: First ride of 2018 into Mainland Mexico
Mexico: Mazatlan to Escuinapa
Distance: 92 km
Time on board: 6 hours 54 mins
Average speed: 13.4 km/h
Cumulative distance: 12, 592 km

Countless Wonderful memories spent in Tuly Arce's home, my warmshower host together with the Los Coyotes, my cyclists gang, the name we decided to name our squad and hordes of cyclists and travelers of all sorts staying with her. In fact, on Christmas Eve, a total of 22 travelers celebrated and stayed in her house. Some set up tents in her garage, some slept in living room including me and few lucky enough to get a room. Tuly was gracious to welcome all travelers, cyclists, skateboarders, hitchhikers and those who drive their van. Her house was equivalent of the united nations for travelers; Asia, Europe and the Americas, of course mainly dominated by the French. Almost half of them were from France. We each prepared a dish from our country. I made fried rice though it was not really authentic Singapore dish, but it was close enough and they couldn't tell the difference. The highlight of the party was the Pinata. We took turns to bash the Pinata while blindfolded.

Spent another week in Tuly's house to usher in the New year. All good time must come to an end. Los Coyote had to disband as we all went our separate ways. Christian, Yves, Frederique continued to finish Los Cabos loop before returning to La Paz to catch a ferry to Mazatlan. Oceanie and David hitched a sailboat ride to Mazatlan. While I chilled in Tuly's house and waited for 2018 before crossing the Sea of Cortes to Mazatlan via Ferry. Prior to that, I took a short bus trip to Cabo San Lucas, the southern tip of Baja California to signify the end of Baja skate. San Lucas was a hedonistic paradise for Americans to get drunk and party. I didn't like the place. Returned to La Paz on New Year's Eve to celebrate it with Tuly and rest of the cyclists. Much cozier that way. New Year's Eve was a much quieter affair with most of the cyclists already left. Only a handful of cyclists arrived after Christmas. To usher in the new year, I shaved my long curly hair kept since the beginning of my journey. Thanks to Nuno for providing the barber shaver and Jacob for shaving my hair. New year, new hair, new beginning.

It was time to leave Tuly's house on the 2nd day of 2018. Couldn't get the cheaper ferry fare on TMC cargo ship, had to settle for the more luxurious Baja Ferries. Stav from Israel, one of the travelers on car, sold his car to continue his way in Mexico, got a free ticket on Baja Ferry when he met the owner of Baja Ferry in a Jewish Centre in La Paz. The owner was a Jew as well. Therefore, he managed to get a cabin as well. I happened to travel with him on the same day so I shared the cabin with himl. What luck. Otherwise, I would be sleeping on the ferry floor as my ticket was the cheapest fare.

Arrived in Mazatlan next morning after 12-hour crossing. Slept in Hostal Mazatlan for 150 pesos as they had special price for cyclists and travellers like me. Ready to set off on day 325, but my valve on my water bank broke. Without it, I have no water and all the shops weren't open that early yet. Stayed another day to fix the issue. In the end I discarded my water bank and bought 2 bottles of 5 litres of water. Though it was against my environmental principles of buying plastic but I had little choice.

Finally set off on day 326. Leaving the huge city was a tedious affair. Mainland Mexico was a stark contrast to dry terrain of Baja Desert. For the first time in months, I got to see so much greenery and trees. There was water flowing in rivers. Baja's rivers were just a dry bed. Nevertheless, Baja was a much pleasant riding experience compared to here mainland Mexico. I don't fear the traffic behind me nor the enormous trailers incoming towards me but the vehicles overtaking in the opposite lane. Whenever the cars behind overtake the vehicle and cuts into my lane, my balls shrunk. Just an inch away from heaven. There was no shoulders for me to ride on thus I have to risk occupying half the lane.

By noon, I hit 50 km and stopped to cook lunch at a bus stop. Resumed my way to El Rosario. This was the umpteen times I passed a town called Rosario. Mexico loves Rosario so much. Since there were 2 hours of daylight for me, I pushed on another 23 km to Escuniapa. About to arrive at my destination, two cyclists sneaked behind me. It was Marge and Jacob, whom I stayed with in Tuly's house. Marge found a warmshower host Bruno in Escuinapa. He welcomed us with Hamburgers. Food for the strong before bringing us to the fire station to camp. Looks like I won't be alone again.

Date of entry: 6 Jan 2018
Day 327: Sweat gets in your eyes
Mexico: Escuinapa to San Miguel, Nayarit
Distance: 87 km
Time on board: 5 hours 52 mins
Average speed: 15 km/h
Cumulative distance: 12,679 km

Lesson learnt. Never put your dishwashing detergent together with your food sack cos when it leaks, your stuff gets soapy. The firemen shared with us that they seldom dealt with fire hazards, instead often they have to deal with accidents on the road caused by reckless drivers.

Woke up early to set the day before it gets too hot. Jacob and Marge arranged with me to meet for lunch in La Concha 56 km away. I set off an hour before them. Mainland Mexico was more humid than Baja. Resembled my home Singapore and SouthEast Asia. Just 5 km, I was sweating buckets. Salty Sweat kept getting into my eyes, burning my eyes. At times I had to skate with my eyes closed.

Soon after, the highway 15 merged with the Toll road. Best thing happened to me. The toll road provided me a wide shoulder and way smoother than the free highway. I was pushing at 20 km/h for 6 km. All good things must come to an end. I had to make decision either to continue onto toll road or free highway. At the split, the free highway was freshly paved. Therefore, I took the free highway. I was cheated. The fresh paved road only lasted for a short distance however the rest of the road was relatively smooth. Continued pushing at 16 km/h. Stopped at Ojo de Agua, tiny town for soda break. Just 10 km before the destined lunch place, the police stopped me. They warned me about the dangerous traffic and hot weather. They seemed worried about me. I had to assure them that I know what I am doing. After all I have already skated 15 countries in 3 continents, been through all sorts of insane traffic. The officer happened to be Adrian, my namesake. What a coincidence. They let me off with a caution to be careful. The heat was getting to me. By 11 am, I was consuming close to 5 litres of water and still dehydrated. Losing sugar as well, I had to snack on my crackers for last 10 km as I skated. By 11.30 am, arrived at La Concha. Half hour later, the duo arrived. Lunch at a restaurant, fried beef with tortilla. Mexicans served every dish with tortilla. Don't worry about going hungry. For the first time in Mexico, I had a siesta since we had only 32 km left. Napped till 2.15 pm.

Refreshing siesta rejuvenate me, resumed my previous pace of 18 km/h, keeping pace with the duo. The heat persisted to affect us. Had to pause at Acaponte to get drinks. Last 22 km was a chore due to the scorching heat. Pushing slowly to conserve energy and water loss. By 5 pm, arrived at San Miguel, however couldn't find the duo. Apparently, they were chilling in the plaza, not expecting me to arrive that quick. We found a restaurant at the roadside and asked whether we could camp. They were closing soon but the owner Veronica invited us to her home to sleep and have dinner with her family. Another amazing Mexican hospitality. Touring makes the world seem smaller and closer. Never regret quitting my job for this. Best decision ever.

Day 328: Mexico Hospitality
Mexico: San Miguel to San Blas
Distance: 77 km (30 km skate/ 47 hitchhike)
Time on board: 5 hours 31 mins
Average speed: 14 km/h
Cumulative distance: 12,756 km

Veronica offered us her store room. Jacob opted to sleep outside in his tent while I and Marge shared the mattress. The engine-like fan in the room kept the mosquitoes and other bugs away from us. Wanted to leave early in the morning but the house's gate was locked and Veronica's family was still asleep. Of course, it was a Sunday. Returned back to bed until the family was awake. Veronica made us breakfast, fried eggs, Fijoles (Black beans) with tortillas. By the time we finished, it was already 8.30 am and I had 80 km with lots of ascent to do today. I gave Veronica cans of tuna and Fijoles, her daughter my cap as gestures of goodwill for hosting us. Jacob, Marge and I decided to give her some money. Knowing she would refuse; we hid 200 pesos in an envelope we wrote to thank her. The money and gifts were never enough to pay for her hospitality towards us.

We set off at the same time. This time, they were ahead of me. We arranged to meet up for lunch in Lad Peñitas 44 km away. Leaving so late left me little time to skate there but I tried my best. The road was relatively smooth but the skating 180 km in 2 days took a toll on my sore legs. Still Skating 14 km/h wasn't that bad. 26 km to Rosamorada, it was already 11 pm. Couldn't reach las Peñitas 20 km away by lunch. Therefore, I hitchhiked at Rosamorada. It doesn't take long for a pickup to give me a ride. Juan helped me to load my pushcart at the back. However, he was going to drive on the toll road to Tepic, missing the Las Peñitas. Anyway, I received from Marge that they too got a ride. They found an injured Falcon on the roadside. Marge almost wanted to kill it to alleviate its suffering. After giving it some water, it started to be more alive. Thus, they hitch a ride as well to find a veterinarian for the bird. Meanwhile, the pickup dropped me off at El Jicote. I arranged with Marge and Jacob to meet at La Huerta Restaurant 4 km after El Jicote. I cooked lunch at El Jicote and had my siesta while waiting for them since it was still a long way for them.

Jacob arrived first. Marge was ahead of him but must have missed me at El Jicote. Jacob had his ceviche break while I skated to catch Marge. The road merged into the toll road again. Found Marge at La Huerta Restaurant. It was bustling full of Mexican drivers stopping for beer and ceviche and famous speciality shrimps. I have never seen a Mexican restaurant that crowded. Usually it was just us cyclist. Jacob soon arrived just to bid us farewell. He was heading to the coast toward Oaxaca, splitting ways from us. The trio was now left to Marge and me. Marge and I would ride together to Guadalajara. For now, we decided to stop here for it was going to ascend 1000 m over 40 km to Tepic. Save the climb for tomorrow.

There was a still constructed petrol station beside la Huerta, it was empty and clean. Good camping place for us. We had drinks at La Huerta first. We sat down on the floor, having our sodas. Omar and his friends invited us to join them for food and drinks. Another incredible Mexican hospitality. They wanted to give us a ride to Tepic but there wasn't space for my pushcart and Marge's bike. So they invited us to their house in Tepic tomorrow. For tonight, we had to settle camping in the restaurant. First time since France last July, I set up my hammock in the restaurant to sleep. Huge climb tomorrow to Tepic

Day 329: Epic with T
Mexico: San Blas to Tepic
Distance: 33 km
Time on board: 4 hours 12 mins
Average speed: 7.9 km/h
Ascent: 974 m
Descent: 203 m
Cumulative distance: 12,789 km

As the city Tepic suggests, you know it was going to be an epic climb today. Epic with capital T. I was reminded why I don't sleep in my hammock anymore. Cos getting in and out to pee during the night was a gymnastic exercise.

Surprisingly, Marge woke up earlier than me. After breakfast, we started off together. One of the conversations we had was that we grew up on our tour. I don't see much growth in me since my tour cos I am still who I am. It was my personality and thinking that prompted me to do this trip. We agreed that the journey was the continuation of who we were.

Decided on the toll road as it was usually flatter with shoulder lane. Marge rode ahead of me while I struggled with the mountain pass. Walking up and skating whenever possible. Walking up takes 4.3 km/h and skating up at 8 km/h. Occasionally flat and downhill boost my average speed to 8 km/h. Luckily, Tepic was only 33 km away.

Hour by hour, I slowly made my way through the hills. By 10.30 am, I passed through a toll booth. They let me through and I stopped at the convenience store for sugar break. Powerade and crackers cost me 40 pesos. My God! That was expensive as it was the only store in the toll booth and vicinity.

By 12 pm as targeted, I arrived at Tepic. Tepic was the state capital of Nayarit, thus it was a huge city with lots of traffic. Yesterday, met Omar, Mich and Stephanie at la Huerta Restaurant, they invited us to their house in Tepic today. With the given address, I navigated my way through the busy streets. Had a minor accident at the traffic. Crossing the road, I had to skate through wide railing. I don't know what was their purpose except to trip me. My wheels got stuck and I fell forward in the middle of the junction with cars passing me. I quickly got up and moved out for safety. Marge messaged me and she was waiting for Omar at his house. We reunited outside his house but he was not around so we had lunch, sharing a roast chicken meal. The owners at fruit stall saw us and gave us each an orange. Marge called Omar again and he answered. Apparently, we got the wrong address. It was still nearby. Arrived at Omar's house and welcomed us with open arms. They drove us to sightsee Tepic and brought us to ice skating. Who would have thought we could ice skate for free in Mexico. Free for 10 mins. Walked around the night bazaar. Nice to have locals bringing us around to see how locals live their lives. It was universal around the world. We all know how to have fun.

Day 330: Angeles Verde (Green Angels)
Mexico: Tepic to Ixtlan Del Rio
Distance: 82 km (13 km skate/69 km hitch hike)

Last few days of skating up mountains put a strain on my sore legs and plus last night's ice skating was tougher than skateboarding. I fell on my butt many times. Better stick to skateboarding. Decided this morning to take a train since I needed a rest yet I don't want to stop and miss my partner Marge. We have been a great pair. The Miami Ultraskate was 1.5 weeks away and couldn't afford to overstrain my body. I have enough training through this. One year of touring already. I needed at least a week break before ultraskate to be in good shape. Taking a train was definitely a must. However, Mich advised not to as there were incidents of Salvadoran robbing passengers in the train. Therefore, I still had to skate today.

In the morning, Marge prepared Crepes breakfast for us and Mich as gratitude for hosting us. Too bad, Omar couldn't wake up early to join us for breakfast. Mich showed us the news from last night. In Tepic, there was a gang war which an innocent passerby was caught in the crossfire and was killed. We cannot be complacent about our safety in Mexico despite the wonderful people here. We left their house at 8.30 am. Together we rode to the toll road before Marge sped off. Arranged to meet at Ixtlan Del Rio.

The mountains still continue and never stop after Tepic. I was having a hard time skating. As usual walking and skating. 13 km after, a pickup pulled over. It was Miguel from the Angeles Verde. Los Angeles Verde patrol the highway throughout, to offer assistance to vehicles needing repair or any mechanic aid. As well, they aided cyclists on the road. This time, Miguel offered me a ride. Just what I wanted badly. However, his pickup was full of tools, leaving no space for my pushcart. Still with Mexican resourcefulness, he managed to squeeze in my pushcart though it was left hanging. We had to tightly secure it. Anyway, he was going to drive slowly.

It was an interesting ride, I got to witness a Mexican at work. We patrol the highway. In the opposite lane, a vehicle suffered a breakdown and he fixed the engine for them in no time. Best of all, it was a free service, paid by the government. I didn't know Mexico got such service. In America, if your vehicle breaks down, you have to pay for a tow. Next, we saw an elderly gentleman needing help to load some logs up his truck. I lent a helping hand as well to carry the logs. I guess I am a Green Angel too. While chatting with Miguel, I learned that he was also a lawyer. This was kind of his sideline. Mexicans were truly Jack of all trades.

We stopped at Jala, to have a snack. I paid for our Elotes or corn as my way of saying thanks. Though I hated to eat corn but I don't want to appear rude. Surprisingly the corn was really good. Smeared with lime and chilli, it doesn't have the sweet taste which I dislike.

By 1pm, he dropped me at Ixtlan del Rio. At the entrance of the city, lies a toll booth. The toll booth was unmanned and closed, only leaving a security guard to man the place. Arturo the guard invited me to sleep in the office for the night. It was the perfect location as tomorrow we needed to head straight back into the toll road. By 3pm, Marge arrived. We left our stuff in the toll booth and explored the town. We walked 3km of cobblestone path to an archeological site similar to Aztec ruins. However, the entry fee was 55 pesos and half hour only to explore as it was closing at 5 pm. From what I could see, it doesn't look impressive, not worth 55 pesos. We headed back to town, hitching a ride, holding onto the back of the pickup. At the cathedral, a guy invited us to stay in his albergue, but we already had a place at the toll booth. Mexicans were truly angels.

Day 334: Drinking Tequila in Tequila
Mexico: Magdalena to Tequila
Distance: 18 km
Time on board: 1 hour 13 mins
Average speed: 14.5 km/h
Cumulative distance: 12,940 km

Arturo offered us a ride for 30 km as he thought it would be dangerous for us to ride through 12 km of curvy road. However, when we woke up at 7 am, he was long gone as his shift was over at 6 am. His colleague tried to help us but to no avail. We walked out to the crossroad of Ixtlan and toll road to see if we could hitch a ride. Marge did her magic trick. She pulled down her long blonde hair to look more feminine. It always works when you have a female companion. Maybe I shouldn't cut my hair and keep it shoulder length.

Instantly, a van pulled over. He was on his way to deliver some equipment to Mexico City. The van interior was locked shut with strong cable lock that he had to cut it open for us to enter. We managed to squeeze Marge's bike and my pushcart into what was left in the van. He drove us to Magdalena. Google map doesn't tell us the elevation of the 12 km curvy road as it was illegal for bicycles to ride on it. I could assume it was 12 km of super steep hairpin uphill climb. Actually, it wasn't. It was mostly downhill and few uphill. Screw our luck. We could enjoy the long downhill. Marge was too tired from yesterday ride. That was why she really wanted the hitch. Of course, I am happy to join in.

The driver dropped us off at the exit of the toll road where we could connect back to free highway 15. From there, it was only 18 km left to Tequila and most of it was downhill. It was a relaxing ride. We arrived at Tequila at noon where we could enjoy the afternoon off drowning ourselves in what else, Tequila.

Tequila was best known as being the birthplace of the drink that bears its name, "tequila," which was made from the blue agave plant, native to this area. The heart of the plant contains sugars and had been used by native people here to make a fermented drink. After the Spanish arrived, they took this fermented beverage and distilled it, producing the tequila known today. The popularity of the drink and the history behind it has made the town and the area surrounding it a World Heritage Site. It was also named a "Pueblo Mágico" (Magical Town) by the Mexican federal government to promote tourism.

We had pollo asado for lunch. Marge was so craving for it all day. It wasn't as good as the one we had in Tepic. The one we had in Tepic was super juicy and greasy. This one was rather dry. After that, we visited the museum of Tequila and dropped in Arrette factory, one of the many tequila distilleries in Tequila. We asked if we could walk around the distillery. Ramon gave us a tour for free. Ask and you shall receive. Ramon then brought us to the showroom where we had shots of Arette tequila, again free. We were drunk from trying shots of various tequilas from different years. We tipped Ramon 40 pesos.

Always useful to have a beautiful blonde companion with you. You get to enjoy lots of privileges as well. However, her blondeness come with a price. She garnered lots of male attention in Mexico. Mexican men would stare at her as if she was a piece of delicious meat. Mexico, though friendly, was primarily a masochist society. At one point, she lost her cool. On the way back, a man whistled at her and she lashed out at him, berating him. Never to piss a french lady off. Tomorrow would be our final ride together to Guadalajara where I would fly to Miami for ultraskate. But first, we have to drown ourselves in Tequila.

Day 335: Guapa Guadalajara!
Mexico: Tequila to Guadalajara
Distance: 65 km
Time on board: 5 hours 32 mins
Average speed: 11.7 km/h
Ascent: 619 m
Descent: 234 m
Cumulative distance: 13,005 km

The morning when we were about to leave the Red Cross where we spent the night, we found a red cross flag signed by the medics and doctors on my pushcart and Marge's bike. A pleasant surprise. Had to have a photo with them before leaving. These 7 days throughout Mainland Mexico, Marge and I experienced all kinds of hospitality. We slept in fire stations, red cross, a stranger's house, toll booths. Regardless where, Mexicans would welcome us with open arms.

Guadalajara was located 1600 m and we had to climb above 500 m today. Marge rode ahead of me once more. The road wasn't that steep except few occasions and I could skate up comfortably most of the time.

By 12 pm, I stopped for lunch at a petrol station and received a message from Marge that she was just 3 km ahead of me. She too was taking her time. I suppose the high altitude was taking a toll on us. Less oxygen to breath. I myself was trying to catch every breath as I skate.

After 42 km, I arrived at Guadalajara outskirt. Guadalajara was Mexico's 2nd largest city after

Mexico City. Not surprising, I still have a long way to go to reach the city centre. As expected for any major city, the traffic got a lot more chaotic with cars and trucks dashing past me. Marge messaged me, warning me about the crazy traffic but it was too late, I was already on the outskirts. I kept my nerves and skate straight. I couldn't control what was moving behind me but I could only control myself to keep calm and continue on skating. You know you were in Guadalajara when you started to see Western fast Foods, McDonald's, KFC and so.

At 50 km, Google map directed me to cross the bridge and led me to a bike lane. First time I saw a bike lane in Mexico. It was passable attempt at making a bike lane. The bike lane was laden with potholes and humps. Navigated into city centre in one piece and headed to the famed Guadalajara Cathedral first, considered as one of the most sacred sites in Christianity. As tradition, I have to take a picture of the city name in a colourful sign.

Made my way to the Casa Ciclistas which was a co-operative for hosting cyclists. Of course, I was the first longboarder to arrive. Marge was there, anticipating my arrival. The casa ciclistas, like Tuly's home, was already full of cyclists. There, I met Paul, the German who I rode with in USA. He had been staying there for 2 weeks. Oceanie and David soon arrived after. Oh my god, it was becoming another big reunion. I would have a week of rest before Miami Ultraskate on 19 January. Just in time to rest my body to prepare for gruelling Ultraskate. Would fly off from Guadalajara on 15 January to Miami. Hope to catch a Mexico football / soccer match in Guadalajara before leaving. After ultraskate, I would fly back to Mexico, Cancun and continue my way to Argentina.

Day 354: Post Ultraskate skate
Mexico: Cancun to Playa Del Carmen
Distance: 71 km
Time on board: 4 hours 55 mins
Average speed: 14.5 km/h
Cumulative distance: 13,529 km

Had to take a break after skating 254 miles / 408 km in Miami Ultraskate 24 hours. As expected, the wind conditions played a crucial role. The headwind on the back section aka the wall of pee really take a toll on our bodies. Luckily, I was prepared in the headwind of Vizcanio in Baja California, Mexico. Never fight against the wind, conserve my energy going slow in that section. Another routine I changed was adjusting my Garmin GPS fenix 3 watch to time every lap instead of per km as the readings would go off after a while. Therefore, timing each lap was more accurate this way. Target to reach the end of Wind tunnel section by 4 minutes 45 seconds before speeding up on the downhill section to finish each lap at 7 minutes 30 seconds to 8 minutes. This gave me 19-17 km/h more than sufficient to hit my 250 milestones. As the race goes on, we form alliances, draft trains to pace each other. Miguel, Calleigh and Ryan Villa combined forces with me to achieve our goals. As clock ticked away, they were exhausted and dropped off except for Miguel who actually sped up to join the lead draft led by Kyle Yan when the wind died off during the night. Felipe in the lead draft train for 300 miles had to quit the race after 180 miles due to knee injury. Kyle slowed down as well as the wind took a toll. Knowing he was not going to achieve his previous record 300 miles this time, he relaxed and went for 270 miles for first place. While I slowed down significantly after my 200 miles. From 7-8 minutes lap, I was reduced to 9-10 minutes per lap for last 50 miles, just enough to achieve my 2nd 250 miles and 4th place overall. After the race, I simply collapsed from exhaustion and Brooks Miller, my kind host and dearest supporter, had to carry me to his home to comatose for 2 days.

Another surprise at the prize ceremony was that I was champion for my 30-39 age IDSA Tour for 2017. Not that I won any race in my age category. Happened to be in the right place at the right time for Pacific Northwest race series and accumulated lots of points through finishing 2nd or 3rd places in my age group. But still, I am happy with it. 1st place in open Division for Miami Ultraskate, 4th overall, 250 miles club and IDSA tour champion for 30s age. What a way to end my USA tour.

After resting in Brooks' home for 3 days, time for me to continue my world Tour. Flew back to Mexico, Cancun, recuperating for a week and waited for the rain spell to be over. Took an organized group tour to Ancient Mayan city Chichen Itza as I calculated DIY by bus would cost as much as a group. The tour includes a buffet lunch. Good deal.

As I read that Russ McCoy, the Admin of the Bicycle touring Facebook group, was heading to Cancun after touring around Mexico, Belize and Guatemala, I decided to extend my stay in Cancun to wait for the rain spell to be over as well. Meanwhile I upgraded my pushcart tyres to Schwable Marathon tyres. It was said to be puncture resistant. I would see about that.

After 19 days since Guadalajara, I am finally back on the road, on route to Belize, my first central America country. I could see clearly now the rain was gone. Tailwind pushing me, was time to fly. However, I was met with much rolling resistance. Was it that I still am not fully rested or maybe i rested too much, or could be the new tyres. For first 7 km, I was slugging at 12 km/h with tailwind pushing me. Stopped at the roadside to figure what was wrong.

My backpack was rubbing against my front wheel, providing lots of resistance. Once I readjusted my backpack, I was flying, harnessing the power of tailwind. For the next 30 km, I was going at 18 km/h. Soon enough, I could enjoy myself in the sunny white sand beach in Playa Del Carmen by noon. However, good things must end. The road after 37 km was outrageously rough, could only manage 13 km/h speed. There goes my target to reach the beach by noon. The highway 307 was dominated by grandiose resorts along the way. Truly a place for rich tourists. After 42 km at 11am, stopped at the roadside to cook my lunch, I thought I could arrive early to have lunch at the beach. Mustered my newfound energy to skate against the rough road after lunch. Even with the strong tailwind, I couldn't harness its power to go fast. With rough roads, even tailwind couldn't save me. I rather have smooth roads with headwind then.

By 60 km, I have arrived at the city's outskirts and traffic increasingly becomes hectic. For the first time in Mexico, a police car stopped me and ordered me to walk. I have skated through the traffic of Mexico's 2nd largest city Guadalajara, Bangkok, Vietnam. Traffic here was considered only a trickle to what I have skated before. No point arguing with the police. I pretended not to understand Spanish and waited for him to drive on. Took the opportunity to take a 15 minutes break to wait for the coast to clear before riding off again.

Headed to the beach first to chill as I knew my hostel was pretty far from the beach area. For US$5, I shouldn't complain. As long as it provides a hot shower and good wifi connection, I am happy. Unlike the first hostel I stayed in Cancun, La Morena that had poor wifi connection and worse of all, no hot shower and I paid US$9 per night. The second hostel Mundo Maya, which I stayed with Russ was much cheaper and comes with hot shower and good wifi. Paying more doesn't mean you would get better quality.

Only left 300 km to Belize, in less than 4 days reach my new frontier.

Mexico: Playa Del Carmen to Tulum
Distance: 70 km
Time on board: 4 hours 40 mins
Average speed: 15 km/h
Cumulative distance: 13,599 km

There was something about Mexico that keeps me bewitched. I have been staying in Playa Del Carmen for 6 days. I am certain that Mexico doesn't want me to leave. Every morning, I woke up and went straight to bed and extend my stay. It doesn't help when the Hostel Punto Rojo was so cheap. By now, I should be in Belize but somehow, I kept delaying. Maybe I am getting too comfortable in Mexico. Good food like pozoles, caldo des res, ceviche and so many foods to taste. The Mexicans were warm and friendly despite the warning from my American friends. There were just so much more to Mexico that captivates me. The scenery, deserts, oceans and the ancient civilizations ruins. I could just stay in Mexico eternally.

There was another reason that kept me not wanting to leave Mexico. After Mexico, it would be new countries for me. I haven't set foot in Central America and South America. It would be entirely new frontiers for me. That scares me.

It was not that I have never backpacked to new foreign grounds before. I backpacked through Uganda, East Africa many years ago and I enjoyed it. However, now skating through foreign grounds, I questioned my sanity. Would the road be smooth or rough? Would the people there welcome me? These questions kept playing on my mind. As quoted from Victor, whom I stayed with in Cancun:

"Courage was a love affair with the unknown"

After 6 days of procrastinating, I finally mustered the courage to leave the hostel and set off for Tulum. I hope to arrive by noon to explore the ancient Mayan ruins in Tulum. Getting out was smooth. The highway 307 was smooth for me to ride at 16 km/h average speed. Being a Sunday today, I would expect the traffic to be light. But Sunday traffic was equally as hectic as on weekdays. Tourist vans made up the majority. Good thing about the highway 307, it has a wide shoulder. Despite the hectic traffic, I was never fazed by it, I wrapped myself in a bubble of safety surrounded by the wide shoulders. For 32km or 2 hours, the road was smooth. I could expect to arrive before noon. As previously to Playa Del Carmen, the road doesn't stay smooth for long. At 30 km, the road roughens up, still I could skate at 14-15 km/h. Hence not too bad.

However, the heat from the scorching sun dehydrated me, even though I drank 3 litres in 2 hours, my pee still came out dark yellow. Despite hailing from Sunny Singapore, the heat here was getting to me. By noon, already 60 km, 2 km away from Tulum ruins, I stopped at an abandoned building to cook my lunch and resumed to Tulum ruins at 1 pm.

Tulum archeological site offer parking space for bicycles but I couldn't find my Abus lock to secure my pushcart and longboard. I had to rely on faith in Mexicans not to steal my pushcart which was left unlocked. I believed that they were nice people. Took all my valuables including passport, phones, and longboard and power banks along with me. The queue for tickets was long, as expected from the weekend crowd. I took the shorter queue which was to pay through automated machine by Visa card. However, the automated counter left out the ticket for me which means I couldn't enter at the entrance. Tulan (pissed in Hokkien Dialect), I requeue and paid another 70 pesos at the ticket counter. They won't let me in with my longboard, have to leave it at the entrance. The Mayan ruins in Tulum wasn't as impressive as Chichen Itza but still it was worth seeing. The ancient Tulum city was right next to the turquoise sea and white sandy beach. No wonder, the Mayans chose here. I couldn't stay here longer as my pushcart was left unsecured. My faith in Mexicans was left intact. My pushcart was still untouched. Left the ruins and skated another 2 km to town.

Approached the Red Cross first for camping, they had to turn me down as their place was too small. Headed to the Fire station. Fire station never disappointed me and gave me a spot to pitch my bivy tent. This was the first time that I would be camping in my bivy since La Paz last December. There was no need to camp in Mainland Mexico. This fire station was absolutely perfect. Complete with Wifi and shower and it was free. No need to pay $10 for dorm bed in Tulum hostels. I got everything I needed.

Day 337: Road to Ruins
Mexico: Tulum to Felipe Carrilo Puerto
Distance: 97 km
Time on board: 6 hours 42 mins
Average speed: 14.4 km/h
Cumulative distance: 13,696 km

One tip in Mexico was always to go for Chinese food. Not that I am a fan of my Chinese cuisine. But Chinese eateries here gave an enormous portion of food for an affordable price. 2 dishes and a large serving of rice for just 60 pesos. Ideal for those touring after a hard day's ride, loads of calories for the journey. Another advice was always check if your bottled water was gaseous or not. I accidentally bought the sparkling type and refilled on my hydration bag and water bottle. As a result, the gas bloated my hydration bag, making it uncomfortable for me to wear on my back.

Started off from the fire station on the mark 8 am. Humidity here was very high, similar to levels in Singapore. Massive condensation on my bivy tent and laundry. The highway 307 was smooth again, pacing at average speed of 16 km/h. At 23 km, passed by Muyil Archeological ruins, one of countless Mayan ruins along the way. Seeing that it isn't manned by anyone, I did my cheapskate mode and sneaked in. The site was comparably small to ones in Tulum and Chichen Itza. I brisk walked the entire circuit in 15 minutes. Upon exiting, the staff spotted me, I had to pay 40 pesos, like 2 US.

Pushed on, and increasing my pace to average speed of 16.2 km/h. Continuing on this way, I could reach Felipe Carrilo Puerto 97 km from Tulum by 3pm. I thought I could reach 70 km by lunch and have a relaxing 27 km skate afterwards. However, it wasn't meant to be. At 52 km, Heaven's road turned to Hell's road like Mayan ruins. Dropped speed to 13 km/h. My lunch target of 70 km was immediately reduced to 57 km outside an abandoned ranch. The remaining 40 km was a torturing hell. 40 km of rough road! I noticed a trend since Cancun. The first half of the day was always fast, smooth heaven. Then second half would be a living hell. Figured even at 13 km/h average speed for next 40 km would take me 3 hours or so after resuming at 1.30 pm. Just 5 km after lunch break, unable to take the heat, I paused at a bus shelter to take a 45 mins nap. The nap didn't help much. I was still struggling.

As I predicted, at 5.30 pm, I arrived at Felipe Carrilo Puerto. The last 3 km was much smoother. Through Google map researched days earlier, I found Hostel Las Suenas. Dorm bed for 170 pesos. Pretty expensive but after skating 97 km in tough conditions, all I wanted was a comfortable bed and shower.

The remaining road to Belize border and Central America, I had to expect for the worse. Or it could be even worse for central America. I might have to settle for 60-70 km skate days. No more 100 km days if the road persist this way. Couldn't find a Chinese eatery so I had to settle for Domino pizza to replenish my calories.

<73. resting in hammock>

<74. Tulum Sign>

Day 339: Sleeping among chickens
Date of entry: 7 February 2018
Mexico: Felipe Carrilo Puerto to Pedro Antonio Santos
Distance: 75 km
Time on board: 4 hours 48 mins
Average speed: 15.8 km/h
Cumulative distance: 13,771 km

I was completely shagged by the 40 km of rough road that on the morning of day 338, I was impeded by my soreness, unable to move. Had to extend my stay in Felipe Carrilo for another day. Slept and watched YouTube video channel Film Theory the entire day.

The next morning Day 339, my body was totally rested well. Back on the road. Before leaving town, I had to stop by a gas station to fill MSR fuel bottle. The primus gas canister that Russ left me was almost empty after 3 days.

The road was back to its pristine smoothness. I was hoping the road would be rough for the first half for a change. With rough road in the first half, my expectations would be lowered, thus when the smooth road returns on second half, I could finish on a high. With smooth road on first half, I would be devastated to transit to rough road. Giving hope to a man, and then to dash it right in front of him was the greatest torture a man could execute onto.

The day rest rejuvenated me; my average speed was much faster than previous days on smooth roads. I was pushing average speed close to 17 km/h and rolling speed at 18-19 km/h. It was pure exhilarating. By 11 am at 45 km, stopped by restaurant Pollos a las Lena's. It was reviewed on Google map by travellers that the owner welcomed cyclists and likes of me to camp there. I had to drop by and take a look. This time, I had lunch at the restaurant. The restaurant owner Lena made me a hearty meal of Pollo Asado with Rice and Spaghetti. With time to spare, I took a siesta at the hammock provided till 1.30 pm. One thing I learnt was to never eat spicy during lunch on skate days. Your stomach would thank you for it. However, I ignored my own rule and went for the Jalapeño chili. Ended up I had to u turn back 1 km to the restaurant to execute my big business.

The road was smooth for 51 km, as expected, but the 2nd half was rough. Luckily, I I only targeted 75 km to Pedro Antonio Santos town. Only remaining 24 km of rough surface isn't so bad as the previous day of 40 km of hell. I could cope with 24 km of rough road; it only takes me at most 1 hour 45 minutes at 13 km/h. At Limones, passed a tiny Mayan ruin by the highway. It was fenced up and unattended. Supposed that no tourists visit this one, as there were bigger and more attractive Mayan ruins in Tulum and Chichen Itza. For the first time, I could go up close and took a selfie with my longboard.

By 3.45 pm I arrived at Pedro Antonio Santos 75 km. With 3 hours of daylight, theoretically I could do another 40 km to Bacalar, making 114 km distance. My body was still energetic, I could attempt to further on. However, the road ahead was unpredictable. If the surface worsens, I could be stuck in nowhere and not made it. I thought why not take a bus from Pedro or hitchhike a ride. After 2 hours of waiting, buses had to repeatedly turn me down due to lack of space for my pushcart. Supposed that I had to camp at Pedro Antonio Santos. Approached a restaurant and they were surprised, so no. Then I approached a church but it was empty. I walked around the perimeter in search for the priest. Encountered the neighbour and asked her if I could camp behind the church. She couldn't decide on behalf of the church because she doesn't own the church but she offered me her backyard to camp if I don't mind the chickens wandering around. Why not? They were better companions than dogs. After all, it was the year of chicken for one more week before ushering the lunar new year of the dog.

The family were harvesting their star fruits and gave me a couple. They also gave me a pineapple and some bananas. I don't know how to refuse them. I don't have the tools to slice the pineapple and also the lack of space on my pushcart. At night, while cooking my dinner in the dark, I couldn't see or smell that the egg was rotten after keeping them for days under the tropical climate of Mexico. A part of the rotten egg spilled onto my dinner when I cracked it before I realized it had already gone bad. I threw the portion contaminated by the rotten egg. Let's hope I would survive the night and tomorrow.

Day 340: Viva La Mexico
Mexico: Pedro Antonio Santos to Chetumal
Distance: 82 km
Time on board: 5 hours 49 mins
Average speed: 14.1 km/h
Cumulative distance: 13,853 km

Survived last night's scare with rotten egg contaminating my dinner but sleeping with chickens near me wasn't fun though less irksome with dogs. The cocks crow in the wee morning at 5am while I am still in my dream land, awaking me from slumber. Got up at 6 am and pack up my belongings while waiting for the sun to rise from the horizon. Thanked the homeowner for letting me camp and set off at the crack of dawn 7.30 am.

The highway wasn't the pristine smoothness I loved to have, but smooth enough to push at my comfortable pace, hitting 15 km/h average speed. There were sections of road construction but I couldn't see why they couldn't improve the smoothness of the road for me. If any consolation, the clouds blocked out the sun for me.

As planned, I arrived at Bacalar at 10.30 am. Bacalar was the last of the Magic Towns in Mexico I would visit before exiting. Bacalar was located right beside a lake by its namesake. I searched for the Bacalar Town's colourful sign as a part of photo collection for every major towns or cities I visited in Mexico. Usually, it was situated at the main plaza. Therefore, I looked for the main plaza with the Cathedral on Google map. Beside the sign, lies a fortress Fuerte San Felipe. The question puzzled me, Bacalar was located beside the lake, why did they build a fortress beside it. Don't they realise it was not a sea or ocean where enemies sail across.

Ran out of water as I didn't refill my water supply last night. 2.5 litres should suffice till Bacalar, 40 km away. Upon exiting Bacalar, I realised that there wasn't any store in the vicinity. In search of water to cook lunch, I had to U-turn back to the nearest store. Bought 5 litres, sufficient to cook lunch and refilled my water supply for next 38 km to Chetumal.

At 45 km, I spotted Cenote Azul. A cenote is a natural pit, or sinkhole resulting from the collapse of limestone bedrock that exposes groundwater underneath. Especially associated with the Yucatán Peninsula of Mexico, cenotes were sometimes used by the ancient Maya for sacrificial offerings. This Cenote wasn't inside a cave, it was located outdoors. Paid 25 pesos for entrance to soak myself in the cool clear water and escape from unbearable scorching heat. The Cenote look very deep, couldn't see the bottom, therefore I never venture further out of the rock platforms, in fear of sinking to the depths of the sinkhole, never to be found ever. Relaxed and napped for an hour before resuming my way.

The highway 307 wasn't pleasant. With 33 km remaining, I endured and push on. Seeing the traffic lane was smoother than the shoulder lane, I threw caution out of the wind and venture on to the main traffic lane. There were two lanes, therefore vehicles would just divert on to the fast lane to overtake me. I would soon miss Mexico's drivers. There were instances where I was on the shoulder lane and cars would drive on the opposite lane just to avoid me. They don't have to give me that much space. As long they don't enter into my shoulder lane, I am actually quite happy. Continuing on, I formulated a challenge. Chasing clouds. I had to skate fast enough to get into the shade provided by clouds blocking the sun as the clouds were moving in the same direction as I am. This has become the race with the clouds. The shade from the sun was at stake.

Highway 307 had come to an end; I entered a new highway 186 from the west Yucatan. Initially it brought me hope of a new paved road. That only lasted for a few km. The rest of it was much worse than 307. How I miss 307 right now. Heading eastward, I entered into headwind territory. Total goner. My speed drastically reduced to 11 km/h. A motorcycle tailed me. I wondered how he maintained that slow tortoise pace to follow me on his motorcycle. He should have just towed me along, saving me the energy.

I stopped at a store to replenish my energy. Apparently, the motorcyclist was the staff at the store. Pointing at my legs to others to signal that I have iron legs. I deserved a treat from the store but nah. Replenished my energy with snacks. Last 12 km to go. How tough could this be.

Chetumal was at the frontier of the Belize border. I could have headed to Belize today but I needed to stock up my food supply and buy new shoes. My Walmart shoes retrofitted with footbraking soles was wearing off. Not the sole, but the shoe itself. Better to get spare shoes in case. The fact that this pair lasted from Washington state to end of Mexico was remarkable given the fact it was bought cheaply from Walmart.

By 5pm, I arrived at Casa Anaya, and got myself a dorm bed for US $6 per night. The skate isn't over yet. There was a final task I needed to accomplish. That was to take a selfie with the Chetumal city sign. Skated along the malecon. There read the sign 'Aqui Incia Mexico'.

Here was where Mexico begins yet it was where it signifies the end of Mexico for me. I would stay another day in Chetumal. Day after tomorrow, I have to bid farewell to Mexico. What touched me the most here was the people. Mexicans never refuse to help me and treat me with amazing hospitality. I never had the problem of finding a place to camp or sleep. Thank you, Mexico, for the amazing adventure. Central America here I come. Viva la Mexico!

To end the night, I encountered upon a carnival at the plaza. Children dressed up in costumes were up on-stage dancing. Mexico just know how to have fun.

CHAPTER 8

BELIZE-GUATEMALA

Day 365: Happy Year One and Goodbye Mexico Hello Country no. 16 Belize
Chetumal, Mexico to Corozal, Belize
Distance: 29 km
Time on board: 2 hours 2 mins
Average speed: 14.5 km/h
Cumulative distance: 14,013 km

On 11 February 2017, I set off on my journey to Skateboard around the world.

Exactly, a year later, I have travelled across 3 continents and 16 countries, 14,000 km and meeting countless people, both strangers and friends. Best life decision I've made. News media has been portraying the world as dark and gloomy with stories of bombings, mass shootings and tragic crimes. Therefore, I embarked on this arduous journey to experience real humanity.

I was not disappointed. In fact, I kept encountering kindness bestowed upon me by everyone. Borders were just imaginary line drawn to divide yet we were united by our DNA as we were all one Human race.

Extended my stay in Chetumal, Mexico longer than I expected as I got lazy and Chinese New year was approaching in a few days. I needed a cheap place with excellent Wifi to video chat and wish my family a blessed new year. Hostel Casa Anaya in Chetumal was the best option for me since Belize would be too expensive. In 35 years, this would be the first time that I missed my family's reunion dinner, the most important meal in Chinese custom. On the eve of the lunar new year, families would gather to have a feast together as a symbol of unity. Through Facebook messenger, I chatted with my family during the reunion dinner. Though thousands of miles apart, the distance was diminished with the help of technology.

Since the Marvel movie Black Panther premiered in Chetumal, I had to catch the movie as well. After settling all my tasks to accomplish, it was finally time to leave Mexico for good and enter new frontier Central America.

Belize was my first stop. Exited Mexico after paying 533 pesos, or 30 US. My visa- free entry to Mexico was not entirely true. They entice us with free visa entry but earn back the money by making me pay exit fee. Having spent all my remaining Mexican pesos, I had to resort to paying in Belize dollars.

I crossed the bridge into Belize. Entering Belize immigration was a breeze. After spending 3 months in Mexico, Spanish language was literally the only language that I had to read and speak. It was refreshing to see Belizean signs in English. Like Singapore, Belize used to be a British colony. From their currency, it was evident they were part of the Commonwealth with Queen Elizabeth on their currency. In a sense, we were brothers and sisters, united by our former colonial masters. At last, I could communicate with locals in properly spoken English in this part of the world. However, this would be the last country I could get to do that. Onwards, it would be back to Spanish.

The Belizean highway was literally a narrow road with two lanes without any shoulders. The condition of the road was roughly similar to Mexico roads. I probably have to expect this kind of road conditions throughout Central America. Belize scenery was basically roads cutting through forests and sugar cane plantations. Reminded me of my time in Cuba.

Arrived at a junction with paved road on one side and pure dirt road on the other. Without hesitation, I continued on skating on the paved road, not knowing the dirt road was the way to Orange Walk, my destination for today. The paved road led me to Corozal, 26 km from Chetumal. After confirming with my Google map, I had little alternative but to continue to Corozal. My friend, Ilham, who used to stay in Belize for some time, mentioned that the northern highway that I was on, wasn't really suitable for me to skate. The highway from Belize City to Guatemala was much better. Therefore, I had to take his word and take the chance on the Western Highway.

Upon arriving at Corozal, I took the bus to Belize City, another 100 km away. While waiting for the bus, I took the opportunity to explore Corozal. In the town, I saw something utterly familiar to me. A lion dance procession as part of the Lunar New Year celebration. Firecrackers burst the tranquility of the seaside town with the roar of drums. It was really heartwarming to see this in this part of the world, thousands of miles away from Asia.

I also found out that most businesses in Belize were owned by Chinese. The Chinese opened supermarkets, shops and restaurants that sprouted all over Belize. There was a sizeable Chinese community living in Belize. Brought over by British during colonial times, and recent wave of immigration from Hong Kong during the 1997 British handover to China, the Chinese settled and assimilated into Belize society. With English speaking population and sizeable Chinese culture, I don't feel that alienated here and could actually migrate and settle here comfortably. Another food for thought. But first, skate the world.

The bus to Belize city was a retrofitted old American school bus, with little storage for luggage let alone, space for my pushcart. With ingenuity from the drivers, they opened the back door and stuffed my pushcart at the back of the bus. For this, I had to pay extra 5 Belize dollars which totalled to 15 Belize dollars. By the way, 1 US equals 2 Belize dollars. Definitely simpler for me to convert the currency in my head now.

The 100 km road to Belize took three and a half hours with the highway sections laden with potholes and dirt road. I was correct to take the bus to Belize city. Upon arriving at Belize city, I skated in search for a cheap guest house. I witnessed more Chinese stores and Chinese New Year processions with Lion dance troupes parading around.

Belize city was reputed to be not so safe for single, lonesome travellers. I was shouted at by several drunk locals. Not a good option to camp. First guesthouse was full. They were left only with rooms that goes for 50 Belize dollars. However, Wifi wasn't working. Moving on, the other guesthouses was also completely full. Maybe it was the Chinese New Year celebrations and weekend. Settled for a US $50 guesthouse, expensive for a solo traveller but if you were traveling with 2-3 travellers, it was pretty cheap. It came with 2 double beds and Netflix. Not wanting to camp out in Belize city, I had to settle for this.

Good thing was that Belize was the second smallest nation in Central America. From Belize city, it only takes me 2 days or 120 km to more affordable Guatemala. I would have to balance these 2 days of expensive travelling in Belize with cheaper Guatemala.

Day 366: Belize Blitz
Belize: Belize City to San Ignacio
Distance: 116 km (70 km skate / 46 km hitchhike)
Time on board: 7 hours 13 mins
Average speed: 16 km/h
Cumulative distance: 14,129 km

You may have thought that Belize city was the capital of Belize. Though it was the largest and most important city in Belize, on the contrary, Belmopan was the Capital. The same case with many other countries, where their largest city was not the capital. For example, the capital of Turkey was not Istanbul but Ankara. Tanzania's capital isn't Dar Es Salaam but Dodoma and Kazakhstan's capital was not Almaty, Instead Astana. You get the drift. The reason for countries to shift their capital to somewhere quiet was mainly to control the main population from afar. Any disruption or coup attempt in the main city would not affect political stability in the country. For Belize's case, it was because Belize city was prone to hurricanes and flooding.

Yesterday, as I was just about to leave, it rained so I went back to bed. Later on, in the day, I switched to a much cheaper guesthouse for $30 US. Belize was really expensive, even for take-away street food, it would cost me $5 US. In Mexico, it cost next to nothing. Damn, I miss Mexico.

Today when I was about to set off early, it rained again. Usually, I would just return to bed but I couldn't afford to spend another $30 in Belize. If it was in Mexico, I could afford to go back to bed and stay for another week. So, I waited for the rain to stop, which only took 30 minutes. A short huge shower and that was it. I am off at 8 am.

Skated through streets of Belize city and found the Western Highway, leading to Belmopan. The highway was just a narrow road without any shoulders. I am pushing at 13 km/h or so. The longboard was jerking so much from rolling on the surface. Felt needles in my foot after 3 hours of hard skating. Don't know if I could make it to Belmopan with my legs intact. Have to take several short breaks to rest my feet. After 42 km and nearing lunch hour, a pickup truck pulled over to offer me a lift. I grabbed the offer with no hesitation.

Hector from Guatemala was on a business trip in Belize. He was in the furniture business. He was on the way back to Guatemala and offered to drive me all the way to Flores. But I only spent like 3 days in Belize and 2 short skating days. I'd like to spend more days in Belize, at least another 1 day before crossing to Guatemala. He dropped me off at Belmopan after 40 km in the car. It was only noon and lots of time to skate further to San Ignacio, 2nd largest city in Belize, another 30 km away.

Stopped at a makeshift shelter to cook my lunch and 2 guys on their lunch break dropped in to chat with me. Saw two Mennonites on horse wagons. They came over to Belize from Germany centuries ago. Till today, they lived simply and mostly in isolation. They still speak German rather than English or Spanish. They were similar to Amish community in the USA.

I assumed Belize was really flat but the highway to San Ignacio was getting hillier as it approaches Guatemala. More hills to expect from Guatemala. By 4pm, I arrived at San Ignacio. Searched for a hostel. There were 2 attractive Asian ladies that caught my attention in the dormitory at the first hostel I came to, D's hostel. Without any hesitation, I decided to stay here for $15 US. Only to find out later there were slightly cheaper hostels around. Oh well, here I met Michelle from Canada and Hsien Low, a Malaysian lady who was raised in London. Hsien Low could recognize my Singaporean accent. I felt so much relief, able to speak in my Singlish accent again. We hiked to a Mayan ruin to watch the sunset and explored the town. The last day spent in Belize was memorable.

Tomorrow I will be in Guatemala for country no. 17. Belize is a tiny country; I could easily cover Belize in 3-4 days. That was why I called it the Belize Blitz. And it was expensive so I have to Blitz through it fast to save cost. Goodbye Belize, hello Spanish speaking Guatemala tomorrow.

Day 367: Goodbye Belize Hello Guatemala, Country no. 17
San Ignacio, Belize to Tikal, Guatemala
Distance: 35km
Time on board: 3 hours 34 mins
Average speed: 10 km/h
Cumulative distance: 14, 165 km

I was all set to go for my 17th country Guatemala. Except I forgot to inform Rafeal, the hostel owner that I would be leaving early in the morning. My pushcart and longboard was locked up in his garage. He lived in another town and so I was unable to contact him. By 9 am, he arrived at the hostel. Great, finally I could have my peanut butter breakfast as my food was also kept in the pushcart. The Malaysian lady, Hsien, was heading to Guatemala today as well. Rafeal kindly offered us a ride to the border. At last, I could make up for lost time.

Crossing the border was a simple affair. No queue. Paid BZD$40 for Belize exit fee, just sufficient cash for me to leave Belize and then enter Guatemala. At Guatemala immigration, I just left my pushcart outside. Well, the counter was barely inside a building. No questions asked and the officer stamped my passport without any hesitation. Another simple border crossing.

Hsien was heading to Tikal today and invited me to share a taxi ride with her. I have to admire Guatemalans' ingenuity. The taxi driver managed to squeeze my pushcart and longboard into his tiny bonnet. It was a good decision to share a ride with Hsien. Shortly, we drove onto a road construction section lasting for a couple of miles. I have to walk that long section if I had chosen to skate.

The taxi dropped me off at El Rameta where I would continue skating 35 km to Tikal and then drop her at Flores, where she would leave her luggage at the hostel and take another bus to Tikal. We arranged to meet in Tikal. I stopped for lunch in El Rameta. Chose a fairly expensive restaurant so that I could have Wifi.

By 12.30 pm, I was all set to go. The skate to Tikal, another well-known Mayan ruin, would be a hilly terrain. In fact, the journey throughout Central America was expected to be extremely hilly. My daily mileage would be toned down to perhaps 60 -70 km. First 2 km was an extremely steep climb. As usual, I walked up the hill. After 2 km of steep climb, the terrain was rolling hills. Along the way, local kids spotted me and was excited to see me. Waved and chased after me.

After 18 km, arrived at Tikal ticket checkpoint. Paid entry fee for 150 Q or US$20 and additional 100 Q for 2 nights of camping. Upon passing the checkpoint, Hsien now in a bus, waved at me. Another 17 km to go. Some sections of the road was newly paved and smooth. On the opposite end of the spectrum, some sections were dilapidated. Spotted signs of different animals expected in this region. Panther, snakes, deer and turkey. I sure hope to see a turkey at night. Early Thanksgiving dinner, I hope. I have phobias of snakes. I rather have a panther than those slimy snakes. I skated with caution, for fear of running into snakes. These really terrified me. The nut on my longboard went loose, and kept scraping the ground. I had to stop and replace it with brand new infinity bolts.

At 4.30 pm, arrived at Tikal and the camping ground was next to the ruins. But Hsien was nowhere to be seen. She probably chose to sleep in a hotel. The locals in Tikal were about to play football in the camping ground and invited me to join in. Haven't played football in a long time. Playing football with locals was another authentic way of bonding with them while traveling. I had a couple of chances to score a goal. We won 4-0.

Tomorrow I will have a full day to explore Tikal Mayan ruins.

Day 368: Tiko Tikal
Guatemala: Tikal to Flores
Distance: 65 km
Time on board: 5 hours 29 mins
Average speed: 11.8km/h
Cumulative distance: 14,230 km

What makes Tikal stands out from other Mayan ruins in Mexico and elsewhere was that you could climb on top of specific pyramids for panoramic views over the vast city. Plus, most structures were well preserved.

I woke up real early yesterday on day 353 to meet Hsien for the sunrise view in Tikal. The spectacular view of the orange sun partially covered by the misty clouds alluded the golden rays on the horizon. We climbed onto the top of temple 4 for the viewing and indeed, it was a spectacular show of nature. There, I met 2 German couples with bicycle panniers and chatted with them. Like me, they were on their way south to Argentina. More company on the road.

Spent the entire day exploring the vast Tikal temples enveloped by the jungle, as it was left untouched over the centuries. After exploring the ruins, I sat at the top of Temple 2, admiring the plaza down below, imagining what it was like to live during Mayan era.

Experimented using a pee bottle last night so that I don't have to leave my bivy tent to pee. This was so that I won't have insects creeping into my tent during the night. It works. Just remind myself not to drink from that bottle. Woke up early at 6.15 am upon sunrise to start the day. Have to make a quick dash to the toilet, but it was locked. Another few hundred metres sprint to the nearest toilet while trying to hold my poo in. Unfortunately, a small amount of poo managed to escape before I could reach the toilet. Enough of the shitty talk. Back to business.

Had a light breakfast with two packets of snacks. Should have bought more food before camping in Tikal as the place was purely a tourist area. No locals stay there therefore there wasn't any grocery store to buy food.

I skated back the 35 km, the same way I did to Tikal. I am well aware of road conditions and elevation profile now. That terrified me, knowing I would encounter rough patches with rolling hills and super steep downhill at the last section. I fared slightly faster on today return journey, averaging 11 km/h. By 9 am, I reached at Tikal ticket checkpoint 17 km. The staff were simply amazed at what I am doing.

Continued on the next 18 km, paused for a short break, watching a school-organised football tournament for its students. Next, comes the moment of truth. The outrageously steep downhill for 2 km. Recently, I replaced my old shoes retrofitted with footbraking soles with new sports shoes without any proper footbraking soles. Couldn't footbrake in these new shoes. The only reason I got them was because they were in my favourite colour, green. Have to rely on my braking system on my pushcart. However, this downhill was too steep to solely brake on my pushcart. So, back to walking down the hill once again.

When it wasn't so steep anymore, I went back to skating once more. My stomach began growling since I only filled up with tiny portions of snacks. Had to stop at a store to fill my empty stomach before riding down another 6 km for lunch. Settled at a bus stop and cooked my lunch. The bus stop was next to a school. At 12 noon when school ended, the children were picked up by parents and a crowd rushed to the bus stop, only to watch me having my lunch.

One of the parents handed me a bag of oranges. Another moment where everyone shares their love and kindness for each other. After everyone had boarded the bus, it was back to just me. As I was about to leave, the German couple came cycling. Been waiting for them the entire day. Finally, they caught up with me. They were heading to Flores today and have arranged for a Warmshower host. I haven't got internet access over the past weeks since Mexico, so was unable to check Warmshower spots. Anyway, I have already booked a hostel stay for tonight.

We rode off together but the rolling hills proved to be too daunting for me to catch up with them on two wheels. Made one final stop at a small town for a break before pushing the last 15 km to Flores. As Flores approached, the road observably turned smoother and flatter, thus accounts for faster pace. Flores was a town in Petén, Guatemala. The town proper was an island in Lago Petén Itzá, connected to land by a causeway. By 4pm, I checked into my hostel, Green World. A fitting name for hosting the famous World on Board. Evidently from its name, it was decorated in green paint. That was why I chose this hostel. Walked around the island, cobblestoned streets with houses lining along its side. The island was partially flooded along its banks during low tide. It was like the marriage of Cuba and Venice. Bumped into the German cyclists once more. Their Warmshower host, Tree, was across another island. I would head there tomorrow.

Spent the last few days in Tree's House in San Miguel, on the other side of the lake from Flores. Met with my Warmshower host and other cyclists on tour as well. One interesting character was Adam from Hungary. He was a movie-maker and on this journey to make a documentary on bicycle touring, in which I would be featured in his film. Oswaldo, an Ecuadorian, travelling with Adam as well, invited me to his home in Cuenca, Ecuador, definitely along my route. I had learnt that Oswaldo's previous cycling partner had taken away their 2-man tent when he quit the tour and returning home, leaving Oswaldo without any tent. Hence, he had to use Adam's hammock when they met. Since Oswaldo offered me a place to stay in Ecuador, and plus, I had a spare hammock tent currently not in use, which was a dead weight to me. Therefore, as a gesture of goodwill, I gave him my Hennessy Hyperlite Hammock tent. Finally, I got rid of my dead weight since Canada. The hammock tent was useful in Asia and Europe, where the climate was somewhere between tropical and temperate. In the desert of Baja California, it was rendered useless as there weren't any trees in the barren landscape to hang my hammock unless I want to poke myself with cactus.

Decided to take a bus to Guatemala City after hearing the roads there was treacherous and steep. Took a night bus and met Tang Yi, a lady from China at the hostel I was staying in. Prior to this, we had bumped into each other in Flores. Tang Yi couldn't speak a word of Spanish and could barely speak English. I was astonished how she could travel around without Basic English. I suppose that travelling is another form of language. Since I could speak Mandarin and Spanish, I acted as her translator for the duration of our travel in Guatemala City. As an exchange, she cooked meals for me. Fair exchange, I supposed.

I am going back to my backpacking roots and leave my pushcart in the hostel while I travel to Antigua over the week and hike up the Volcano Fuego. How often do you get to witness a volcano eruption?

Day 360: Downtown Guatemala City

Walked down downtown and Financial district of the Capital. Found their mass public transport interesting. It was similar to tram systems but without the tram lines. Buses run down the middle of the street, separated from other traffic, and stop at stations approximately every kilometre. The stations were in the middle of the street, located near areas of heavy pedestrian activity. Platforms were elevated so as to be level with the floor of the bus. Passengers may access the station via stairways, street crossings, or, in some places, underground tunnels. I must say it was cost effective as they don't have to build new infrastructure. I found it much more efficient than the public transport in most cities in the USA. USA was really too reliant on cars and without a proper mass transportation system.

The downtown was filled with mega shopping malls. You could find almost everything you want in Guatemala. Of course, like any country, there were the rich and the very poor. The gap between the classes was widening.

Who says Guatemala was a shithole now? That was in reference to Donald Trump's speech, referring to Central America and Africa as shithole countries.

Day 362-363: Eternal Eruption of Volcano Fuego

I took a break from skating and took a shuttle to Antigua with Tang Yi, the Chinese lady I met in the hostel. Stayed in Ox Expedition, another Warmshower, which allowed me to stay for a night for free as part of the Warmshower hospitality. There, I met Antoine and his family.

Antoine was cycling from France all the way to South America with his wife and his 3 young children; from 8 to 13 years old. They have already been on this trip for 6 months and the children were being home-schooled on this trip. In Singapore, the parents would be branded as irresponsible, taking children out of the school system. On the contrary, education doesn't just lie within school. Education could happen everywhere. Nothing beats real life experience being on the road, travelling through countries, experiencing different cultures and learning to respect them. That was something you couldn't replicate in school.

Anyway, they invited me to join an organized hike tour to Volcano Acatengo. It's an overnight camp to view the eruption of its sister volcano Fuego. Since Ox Expedition only offers hikes on Wednesday and Saturday, we went for other agency Aproder for US$50 inclusive of 4 meals and a guide. As I wasn't prepared for the hike, I never bought any warm clothes for the high altitude. I had to rent the warm jacket and gloves from Aproder.

At 6.30 am, the owner picked us up and drove us to his house near the entrance of the hike. Had breakfast at his house before commencing the treacherous hike up Acatengo, the 3rd highest mountain in Central America standing at 3975m high. The climb was incredibly steep and the path was slippery with pulverized soils, making my sport shoes ill equipped for this type of activity. I was prepared for freezing conditions at night but I forgot about proper shoes for hiking.

Climbing up was tedious but easy in my current physical condition. However, my shoes were unable to grip properly on the sandy path. Kept slipping on the steep, treacherous path. Thankfully the porters pulled me and kept me from falling. Antoine's youngest child was struggling and it was heartening to see the other siblings cooperating to help carry her on a stick. That was what travelling could do; build characters. As we got higher above the cloud lines at 3000m above sea level, it almost seems that we were in Heaven.

By 1.30 pm, we arrived and camped at base camp, located directly opposite Volcano Fuego. "Fuego" is famous for being almost constantly active. Literally an eruption at 15-minute interval. Sometimes, the eruption doesn't arrive sooner as anticipated. We know the upcoming eruption was going to be a big one. Good things come to those who wait. Large ash cloud erupted from Fuego. But the real magic show began at night. Red lava burst out from Fuego. Truly a spectacular show. It was like being live on National Geographic, you couldn't get any closer to an eruption than this.

Though the campsite provides tents, I insisted on sleeping in my bivy tent. My black diamond spotlight bivy tent was meant for Alpine, suitable for high altitude, keeping me warm throughout the night. Best part was, I could view the eruptions directly as I lie down on my bivy. Every roar from the eruption kept me awake throughout the night.

I finally woke up at 4.30 am for the sunrise summit climb. Almost made it to the summit, just 200 m short, when my shoes stopped me in my tracks. I stopped at a clear spot to view the glorious sun rising above the mountain. The next challenge was to descend down. Descending down the slippery slopes was much more challenging. The porter had to accompany me down, holding my backpack to keep me from falling. At last, I made it down in one piece. However, the knees were seriously tested from the descent. I must say hiking was way more challenging than skating 100 km. But it was totally worth it.

Day 389: Antique Antigua

After climbing gruelling Volcano Acatengo, my calf muscles were seriously strained. Had to take another stretch of rest day in Antigua. Just as I was ready to leave and return to skating, I was hit with a bout of diarrhea. I literally camped in my hostel's toilet for days.

Antigua was formerly Guatemala's capital until the 18th century when an earthquake devastated the city and forced the Spanish to move its capital to current location Guatemala City, 40km away. Since then, it hasn't really recovered from the devastation, many of its ruins still remain as tourist attractions. Most were church ruins, kept as remainder of its past. Pretty much like Pompeii. That was how Antigua got its name. Old or Antique in Spanish.

Antigua was designated as a UNESCO World Heritage site. If you read my post in Hoi An, Vietnam, I actually loath the term UNESCO heritage, which meant Disneyland for tourists. In Hoi An, big businesses rushed in and bought over the town to develop hotels, restaurants, bars for tourists, forcing locals to relocate elsewhere. Preserving its body yet losing its soul. Surprisingly, Antigua doesn't give me this touristy vibe. No doubt, there were hotels, hostels, fancy restaurants, and bars, but they seemingly co-exist with the locals. Antigua wasn't too overrun by tourists, making it my favorite UNESCO WORLD heritage city. Even McDonald's restaurant was in an old building, giving McDonald's an authentic look.

The roads were paved in cobblestone, that was one of the important safety features for road users. Cars cannot travel beyond 20km/h, otherwise the drivers would feel a sharp pain in their ass. If you sprint, you might actually overtake a car. The same cobblestoned road inhibited me from skating. Imagine doing an Ultraskate in Antigua.

Attractions in Antigua were everywhere. Spent my days just walking and exploring every corner of Antigua. I wanted to try Guatemala's famed chicken bus or transportation for locals. Much adventurous of course but in my current state, I couldn't risk having to stop the driver on the road to purge my watery poo. Settled for the tourist shuttle at $10 to deliver me directly to my hostel in Guatemala City. My pushcart was still in the hostel as I left it there a week ago.

Back in Guatemala City, I wanted to send postcards to my sponsors and family. Strangely, I couldn't post them overseas. Great. Guatemalans sold me postcards which I couldn't post abroad. At the post office, the staff was explaining to me that they do not sell stamps. What was the purpose of a post office? It's like going to a restaurant that doesn't sell any food. After further digging, I discovered that the national post system was on transition, being nationalized from previous private ownership. However, the transition has been going on for months. How hard was it to sell stamps? I found this very amusing. Anyway, I would post my postcards from El Salvador. If you were the recipients of my postcard, don't be surprised to see Guatemala postcard with Salvadoran stamps. That, of course, if El Salvador even has a post office. But of course, they sure do. It isn't reclusive as Wakanda, the fictional country in Marvel Cinematic Universe.

Another oddity I have to mention while walking in Guatemala City was the security. Even a small pharmacy was fenced up and guarded by a shot-gun trotting security guard. Yes, security was serious business in Guatemala, providing employment to young males. Along the streets, you won't see any cars parked anywhere open. Cars would be parked in private car parks, walled up and guarded by guards 24/7. If you leave your car outside overnight, you could kiss it goodbye.

Supermarkets were heavily guarded as expected, I found it amusing to find shampoos, and toiletries being locked up in a shelf. You have to indicate your interest in buying one to a staff then the staff would open up and give you a number card to pay in the cashier before going back to collect your toiletries. Toiletries must be really valuable in Guatemala and everyone was trying to steal one. I could imagine when I am being held at gunpoint, the first thing the robber would ask for would be my soap and toothpaste.

"Shampoo or your Life!"

Don't get me wrong, I felt absolutely safe in Guatemala City with all the amount of security in place. But don't be foolhardy to walk around during late night. Usually, in other places, you would meet young hot-blooded backpackers hanging out outside of hostels to get drunk and laid. Here, everyone was back hanging out in the hostel by 7 pm.

That was my observations on Guatemala so far. Once I recover and get back to full health in a couple of days, I would be back on the road. By the way, I have recalibrated my number of days on the road as I have miscalculated somehow.

Day 395: Goodbye Theatre Hostel!
Guatemala: Guatemala City to Los Esclavos
Distance: 47 km
Time on board: 4 hours 15 mins
Average speed: 11 km/h
Cumulative distance: 14,279 km

After recovering from my diarrhoea, I sort of got lazy and comfortable in Theatre Hostel in Guatemala City. I must say, this was one of the best hostels I have ever stayed in. The breakfast was the highlight. Unlimited amount of freshly cooked pancakes paired with fresh fruits, pineapples, strawberries, papaya, watermelon and bananas. The raspberry jam was freshly home made in the kitchen. Every morning, I saw the staff boiling a pot of raspberry to make into jam. So fresh I could taste the seeds in it. I could eat 5-7 pancakes for a heavy breakfast and save my stomach till dinner. It was budget saving. I just have to spend $6 on hostel stay and $4 McDonald's dinner daily. Adding to the hostel's splendour, it has a tiny pool to soak my body in this hot climate and an outdoor lounge to chill with the other travellers. Hot showers and fast WiFi, what more could I ask. If you drop by Guatemala City, Theatre Hostel was a must stay.

Extended my stay there by many more days as I got too comfortable. I also received a message from Michelle that she was arriving on Sunday. Might as well stay longer and meet her. I met Michelle earlier in San Ignacio, Belize.

Theatre Hostel indeed lived up to its name. Another interesting character was Mike from Belize. He owns several restaurants and farms all over Central America. He was a loud character but extremely friendly. You could see that he really owns restaurant chains when he cooked for us lunch and dinner. Mike fed the whole hostel with his cooking. Daily, he would buy loads of groceries and cook a storm for us. Chicken curry and rice with lots of vegetables. Good food daily, tempting me to extend my stay every single day. I never needed to spend money on food whenever Mike was around.

There were many other interesting travellers in Theatre hostel as well. Such as the South African lady who was there on a volunteer trip, Tom from Guadeloupe and many more. I earned a nickname there as well, Green Man. If I stay any longer, I might as well buy over this hostel and stay forever.

On 13 March 2018, I finally mustered my will to leave and resume my skate towards Argentina. Guatemala City traffic was one not to be messed with. Hectic traffic from morning to afternoon. I could survive through Bangkok, Saigon, Guadalajara 's chaotic traffic yet Guatemala City just adds to my no skate list, together with Paris. Narrow lanes with impatient drivers leave me no room to manoeuvre. Therefore, I had to Uber to the outskirts where I could skate safely. Before getting in the Uber, I simply had to enjoy my last breakfast, having 7 pancakes before bidding farewell. Dropped off Michelle and Tom at the Indigenous museum since it was along the way. The Uber driver then drove me with lots of detours, avoiding the traffic jam. It was so out of the way, I thought he was bringing me somewhere to rob me.

After an hour, we arrived at Plaza Madero where I could start skating. Next 24 km was on downhill. However, Guatemala 's engineers were too lazy to build any switchback to reduce steep gradient. Instead, they just cut the road straight down the hills, making it extremely steep. Throughout the entire downhill, I was clutching my brake lever. My left hand did more work than my legs today. Once, I lost control of my pushcart and dived into the drain. No injuries or damage whatsoever. Picked myself up and continue skating down with extreme caution. Kept my downhill speed to mere 15km/h.

Since I had super heavy breakfast, I skipped my lunch and skated without much break. Felt the sky juice aka rain coming down. Looked like I picked the wrong day to resume. It turned out to be mere droplets as the rain clouds had already passed me. Guatemala highway diverted to new roads which were not on the Google map. I am supposed to pass Cernial and Barberena town. I had to cross the dividers, back onto original Pan America highway. Now the uphill climb began. A series of steep climb to Barberena before descending down to Los Esclavos. In Cuilapa, a couple of ladies selling food waved me to come over, I was too lazy to go over and interact. Ignored them and continue my way.

At Los Esclavos, approached the first restaurant to camp but was refused for unknown reasons. Thought of getting a hotel since the cloud look ominous for the night but it was 175 Q, US $23 for a single room. I took a chance with another restaurant. This time, they allowed me to camp. Tomorrow, I would cross over to El Salvador, reputed as having the country with the Most Homicide cases and the most dangerous countries, together with Honduras. Wish me luck.

CHAPTER 9

EL SALVADOR - HONDURAS

Day 396: Adios Guatemala! Hola El Salvador Country no. 18
Los Esclavos, Guatemala to Ahuachapan, El Salvador.
Distance: 71 km
Time: 7.03 am - 3.31 pm
Cumulative distance: 14, 350 km

Cuilapa was the middle line of the America Continent, therefore, I have passed the halfway mark. After dinner, Eva and her husband, Alejandro, the restaurant owners, invited me to have dessert with them for free. We chatted throughout the evening. Alejandro was 3rd Generation Guatemalan Chinese. His grandparents migrated from Canton, China to here Guatemala to seek a better life. Alejandro has already completely assimilated into Guatemala culture and was more Guatemalan than Chinese. He completely couldn't speak Mandarin or any dialect and doesn't observe any Chinese tradition. One thing I admire about our Chinese gene was that we could migrate anywhere in the world and adapt to the host's culture, forsaking the Chinese tradition. In many cases like the Indonesian Chinese and Thai Chinese, they even adopt the names in accordance to the nation. The ability to assimilate and integrate into any society provide us, Chinese, the edge to prosper.

Turning in for the night, only to realise my Garmin Fenix 3 doesn't charge at all. I don't know whether it was the charging point on the charging cable being corroded or my watch has issue with charging. That meant my Fenix 3 would die a slow death without power. Without my Fenix 3, I couldn't track my distance, average speed anymore. This poses a lot of inconvenience to me as I wouldn't know how far and fast, I have travelled during my day skate. Therefore, I am unable to gauge whether I could reach my destination in time or not or when to stop for lunch. No point waiting in Guatemala to wait for replacement to arrive as Guatemala doesn't have any postal system since 2016. I have to continue on without tracking my daily journey. Hopefully, in San Salvador, I could get a new Garmin GPS tool. For now, I would be skating blind. Therefore, I could only post my daily updates in the new format.

I set off at 7.03 am, pushing uphill. The next 2 hours was simply uphill. Without the Fenix, I couldn't gauge how far I have travelled. Regardless, I just continued on, alternated between skating and walking up the hill. Roughly before Jalapagua, a pickup truck pulled over to offer me a ride. Since I had finished the hard part, might as well accept the ride going down. My last Guatemalan angels. They dropped me about a few km before El Salvador border where I resumed skating. The ride gave me the chance to gain back the time lost on the hills. Looking at Google map, I assumed the straight road leading to the border was flat. I was wrong.

As I approached the Guatemala exit, the money changers swarmed onto me, offering to change 7.40 Guatemala Q to 1 US. Yes, El Salvador adopted the US as their official currency after their economy collapsed and suffered massive inflation. I thought the exchange rate offered by the money changers looks alright, I don't mind losing a bit. Changed 700 Q to US $52. When I got wifi in my destination Ahuachapan, I realised I was totally ripped off. Changing 700 Q, I am supposed to get at least 90 US. Got scammed of 40 US, feeling really bummed. Another lesson learnt, always get the conversion rate before going to a new country. I took it as I donated US $40 to their poor family to make myself feel better.

Exiting Guatemala in a matter of minutes. The officer stamped my exit and I was off to El Salvador. Crossing El Salvador was even easier. After crossing the bridge, the El Salvador immigration officer just checked my passport and waved me off. What, not even an entry stamp? They explained they don't stamp passport anymore as long I got Guatemala exit as proof. I travelled all the way to El Salvador so I could get a stamp on my passport to boast that I have been to the most dangerous country in the world. Totally bummed and I don't get to collect their local currency at all.

From the border to Ahuachapan was a 12 km pure ascent. What makes matters worse was that the road was completely chipseal. I could walk up faster than I could actually skate on these roads. Stopped at an empty hut to cook lunch. Resumed skating after 1.30 pm, alternating between walking and skating actually. On the opposite lane, the road was in a better condition so I risked my safety skating against the flow of traffic. By 3.30 pm, I arrived at Ahuachapan.

Approached the fire station to camp for the night. Of course, they never refuse any traveller in need. I don't know how I am going to cope with Salvador 's atrocious roads if it stays this way. I might have to take the bus and hitch hike more than I could skate through Central America. Hopefully, I won't have to resort to these.

Day 398: Pan America
El Salvador: Santa Ana to San Salvador
Distance: 64 km
Time: 7.30 am to 4 pm
Cumulative distance: 14, 450 km

Had pupusa for dinner. Pupusa was traditional Salvadoran dish of a thick corn tortilla stuffed with a savory filling; like cheese, pork or chicken. It was typically accompanied by Curtido (a spicy cabbage slaw), and tomato salsa. A piece costs $0.50 and four of those could easily fill my stomach. After the cheap and tasty dinner, hung out with guys from another hostel, Casa Verde, one of the best rated hostels in Central America. Tried to book it but it was fully occupied so I went for the 2nd best, Santa Ana Pool House, opened by a Canadian-Salvadoran couple.

Today, I was expecting another rough day on the road but surprisingly, it was pretty smooth. Yesterday, it took me 5 hours to cover 35 km. But today, it took me less than 3 hours to cover 40 km. Quality in road conditions could make or break my skate. Huge difference to my timing. As usual, there were ups and downs. But the long descent makes up for rapid gain in speed, lasting for several kilometres.

By 11.30 am, I was already 40 km and 2/3 way done. Stopped by a food mart in Texco petrol station for lunch. Couldn't resist splurging on Caldo de Res, beef stew and rice with mashed potatoes. Since tonight, I got a Warmshower host, Thomas Fay, I could afford to splurge on lunch and still keep my daily expenses under budget. Rested in the food mart for 1.5 hours. I could afford to nap in the air-conditioned area, chilling myself away from the burning afternoon heat.

As I approached San Salvador, the capital, traffic gets hectic and lanes widen to 3. Still, vehicles tried to squeeze me out off the road. I drowsed in black fumes emitted from these ancient American yellow school buses. I could have gotten lung cancer in a day. By Colon, the climb began. Long, ascending road with heavy vehicles threatening to crush me. I simply walked most of the time till I reached Santa Tecla, the outskirts of the capital. Entering into any major city and capital was expected to be nightmarish. Stopped for orange juice, supporting local businesses before making my way down to San Salvador. Friday's rush hour traffic came to a halt. That was when I could weave around the traffic and snigger at them, being faster than the slow-moving traffic. Passed by an area with political party supporters at the side of the road. Recently, Salvador held an election. Now they were cheering for my arrival.

Reached Thomas 's apartment which was located in an affluent neighbourhood. His wife, Kira, was working for an NGO promoting safety in not-so-safe zones. That was why they get to travel to all sorts of undesirable places. They welcomed me with beer and nachos. Hopefully, tomorrow I could find a place to fix my Garmin Fenix 3 watch or buy a new one to track my distance and speed.

Day 400: Team Los Coyotes Reunion
El Salvador: San Salvador to Zacatecoluca
Distance: 63 km
Time : 5.49 am to 3.10 pm
Cumulative distance: 14, 513 km

Day 399

Thomas brought me around San Salvador in search of a place to repair my Garmin Fenix 3 watch. Prior to that, he demonstrated how to maintain my brakes. We walked around the affluent safer areas, avoiding the ghettos. First, we entered a phone repair cum bicycle store. We asked them if they could fix my Fenix 3 charger, the first thing was they enquired about my age. Things got stranger when the lady took out the weighing scale to take my weight. What has that to do with fixing my watch? We realized that they misunderstood us, they thought we asked them to configure my watch. Anyway, I weighed 55 kg, no difference from a year ago.

San Salvador has all the major stores and American brands like Nike and Adidas, but no Garmin store here. I guess no one bicycle tour here and the market was too small and expensive for local Salvadoran. Looks like I have to forgo tracking my distance for now. All I bought in San Salvador was a pair of cheap US $10 shoes meant for footbraking from a makeshift stall. I love to support local businesses.

Day 400

Thomas and Kira made me lunch and dinner. Delicious nachos and burgers. Today, I had to start real early as Thomas and Kira had a hike at 5.30 am. So, I had to wake up early and leave at the same time as them. It was not a bad thing, as today was Sunday, traffic was supposed to be much calmer. Leaving during the wee hours of the morning made it even quieter. I started skating before dawn. Still the traffic was pretty busy for a Sunday morning. Spotted a few road cyclists. They had cars escorting them, an essential safety measure. Road cyclists replaced the golf as a sport for rich middle-aged men. Could see from their expensive road bikes.

Climbed up the ridge before descending down all the way. I had to alternate wearing my left shoe between my new footbraking one and the current one. Whenever, I encountered a long descent, I stopped to change into the shoe meant for braking and switched back when I needed to push again. My footbraking shoes were typical skating shoes, with narrow feet, causing me discomfort. Therefore, I only use it for braking.

With long descent and early start time, I did roughly 40 km by 10 am. Paused at a petrol station food mart. They were broadcasting La Liga football match between Barcelona and Bilbao. Might as well take a long break and watch the match. Continued watching the subsequent match and had lunch there.

Left the petrol station only after the 2nd match at 1.30 pm. It was a short and flat 22 km to Zacatecoluca. Reached the fire station at Zacatecoluca. They welcomed me to camp for the night. There was another Argentinian cyclist heading northwards. The fire men took down my passport particulars for security measures. Then, I got a pleasant surprise; Yves, Frederique, Oceanie and David arrived shortly. Team Los Coyotes was finally reunited. Now Team Los Coyotes were back together except for Christian who was still stuck in Mexico due to bike issue.

Day 401: Heat was on
El Salvador: Zacatecoluca to Usulutan
Distance: 55 km
Time: 7.54 am to 2.55 pm
Cumulative distance: 14, 568 km

After a brief reunion with our Team Los Coyotes, we have to split once again. Yves and Frederique left their bikes at the fire station and departed for Antigua, Guatemala to hike and witness the nature's fury, Volcano Fuego's eruption. They would return and resume after a week or so. I doubt so cos Antigua would seduce them to stay longer like she did to me.

Last night, another french family with 3 young children arrived in a campervan and were parked at the fire station. They have been traveling around the world in their campervan for 4 years. Similar to Antoine's family on bicycles. Likewise, they withdrew their children from the traditional school setting and educated them in the world of cultures and differences. Most of the bicycle tourers I met on the road were French. I suppose that the desire to see the world was part of the French DNA.

Last night, was a sauna. Camping outdoors, I was perspiring profusely and couldn't sleep even with my bivy completely open. There wasn't any wind circulating around to cool me down. I resorted to sleeping in the kitchen under the fan. Totally different from the nights sleeping in the higher altitudes. I am back on the coast so the temperature would get hotter.

Woke up at 6 am and leisurely packed my stuff since today's destination was only 55 km. With unpredictability in road conditions and steep climbs, I could only plan 50 km - 80 km at most, and seeking accommodation in fire stations. Just so happened that most fire stations were roughly 50-60 km apart. Bid farewell to everyone seeing me off at the entrance.

At the crossroads, a shabby man dressed in dirty, torn clothes approached me while I stopped to orientate my way. I chatted with him in my broken Spanish. No matter who the person was, I would attempt to entertain them. Of course, at times, I got tired of interaction with locals and skated off, giving them the cold shoulder. During my interaction with that man, I was rather wary of him, maybe he tried to beg money off me. I don't know. Just that my judgemental instinct kicked in. I shunned him by skating off. Yes, even after travelling through countless countries, I still would judge and stereotype people just as the locals would stereotype me as Chino.

The locals in Central America took rather odd interest in me being Asian rather than my Gringo (white Caucasian) friends. They have seen gringos here but not many oriental Asians or maybe none. Everywhere, they would shout "Chino" when I passed by. They barely encounter an Asian in their daily lives. They couldn't distinguish from Chinese and Korean or Japanese, just as I couldn't distinguish Central Americans or Germans from French. We all just look the same whatever region we came from.

Once, I chatted with Kira, my Warmshower host in San Salvador, about stereotypes of different Central Americans. Salvadorans and Hondurans were drug dealers, Costa Ricans and Panamanians were rich snobs. Nicaraguans were poor. We all have some stereotypical image of others as it was embedded in our human genome. No one was entirely non-judgemental no matter how well travelled he was. They would be less judgemental than those who don't travel and experience different cultures. Travelling could and does narrow this tendency to stereotype.

I have to take back my words saying El Salvador's roads were Shithole. The Shithole roads only applied to Santa Ana and Guatemala border. Now the road was really smooth. There was hope for me, even the poorest country in Central America could have good roads, so others could have better ones. At least, I hope.

Flat and smooth roads make today's skate a breeze. Except for the heat. As the day approached to noon, the mercury in the thermometer soared as well. Hailing from Equatorial island of Singapore, I could cope with heat better than the French. Still, I had to take frequent breaks and seek solace in shade provided by the trees. The shoulder lane on the highway was smooth as well, however, littered with debris which I had to avoid.

During one of my breaks, I took a look at the front of my pushcart and realized I was pushing with resistance for 3/4 of the way. My backpack was rubbing against the front wheel. You mean I could have skated faster and reach my destination by now!! I couldn't tell whether I am struggling or not without my Garmin watch telling me how fast I was going. 12 km/h on a smooth road could feel like 15 km/h, it was hard for me to gauge now. I really need to get my Garmin fixed soon. Just as I reorganized and arranged my pushcart, Oceanie and David arrived over the horizon. Now with their cycle computer, I knew how long to go now. Another 15 km left. That was quick, looking at how fast time goes by when I am not calculating how long more to my destination.

Sometimes, it was good to enjoy the process without looking at the progress.

We stopped at a petrol station for respite from the scorching heat and continuing on in search for lunch. I found a makeshift stall selling cooked food beside a factory. It has been a long time since I had food in such settings. I ordered rice with stewed pork while the French couple had chicken with rice.

At 2 pm, we resumed to finish the last 10 km to Usulutan. Another welcoming fire station for the night. Today was also the last day we get to ride together. They would head to the coast and grab a ferry to Nicaragua, bypassing Honduras. While I would continue to cross into Honduras cos, I want my World's most Dangerous Country stamp on my passport since El Salvador denied me that prestige. I would be a week behind them, but we would reunite once again like we always do.

Day 402: I survived El Salvador
El Salvador: Usulutan to San Miguel
Distance: 53 km
Time: 7.26 am to 1.13 pm
Cumulative distance: 14, 621 km

Slept in the store room in the fire station last night. Sprayed insect repellent onto myself in order to sleep well. Woke up early to hug Oceanie and David farewell as they left for Playa El Cuoco and onwards to La Union to catch a ferry to Nicaragua. We braved through tough times, strong winds in Vizcaino and through Baja California. Such bonds were forged through braving difficult conditions together.

I left the fire station shortly after the French couple. Once again, the road condition was smooth and flat. I checked everything before setting off. The wind blowing against me provided cool respite from the sun. An hour later, Oceanie and David caught up with me, while I was trying to take a selfie against the backdrop of San Miguel Volcano. Apparently, they stopped for breakfast. We rode together till the junction where we had to split. At the final stop at the petrol station, we took a long break from the sun since we were left with only a short distance to cover. After napping for a while, I recalled I needed to post my Guatemalan postcards here in San Miguel, last major city in El Salvador before Honduras. Another farewell then I rushed off to San Miguel.

Along the way, in one of the many stalls on the road, I saw a toddler in a wooden cage. By Western standards, this would tantamount to child abuse. However, looking at the context here, the parents had to mind their stall to make a living while having to keep an eye on the child. The stall was right beside the busy highway, any distraction and the child might cross paths into fast-moving vehicles. Therefore, that was the only safe option they had.

Another km, I passed by a stand selling iguanas. They simply tied up the live iguanas and hung them by a branch, waiting for hungry customers. Yes, iguanas were a local delicacy in Central America. It was a good source of protein. I wonder if I could find a restaurant to taste iguanas. How would it taste like?

Before entering San Miguel, I had lunch at a local stall. Rice with beef stew for US $2. I don't have to cook lunch and dinner here anymore. The cheap cost of eating out beats having the hassle to cook along the way. I resumed my way to San Miguel. It was the last major city before entering Honduras. You know San Miguel was a large city when you see a Walmart. I went straight to the post office to buy stamps. The queue was long but luckily the office was air conditioned so I didn't mind waiting any longer inside.

Approached the fire station in San Miguel, as usual. Surprisingly, for the first time, they denied me permission to camp in the station. The reason was that they had a horrible experience with cycle tourer once last year. The cycle tourer actually stole their phones and stuff. My god, who would steal from those poor firemen who fed and provided lodging for us in times of need. Now the experience left them to be wary of travellers. I didn't ask where that cyclist came from or where he was headed to. I hope he doesn't go on my route, spoiling my further experience with the firemen. Without them, I wouldn't have any sanctuary to rest after a hard day's ride. One bad egg could spoil it for the rest of the good ones like us. May that cyclist face eternal headwind, eternal steepest of uphill and punctures wherever he goes.

Luckily, I had a backup plan. Europa Guesthouse was nearby though I never saved it in my Google map. Asked a kid on the street and he directed me to the guest house. Normally, if I book through booking.com, I would have to pay $12 with tax. For walk in, I only need to pay $10. Well, good reason to pamper myself for probably my last night in El Salvador.

57km to Honduras border. I could say I have survived the 2nd most dangerous country. So far, I felt completely safe in El Salvador, as long I don't stay out late in the night. The locals were genuinely friendly. All these hype over the security was over exaggerated. The homicides cases were only limited to gang fights over the drug trade. The gangs wouldn't touch us, if we were careful to not cross into their line of fire. Now I am going to the most dangerous country, Honduras.

Day 403: One more night
El Salvador: San Miguel to Santa Rosa de Lima
Distance: 41 km
Time: 7.15 am to 12.24 pm
Cumulative distance: 14,662 km

Thought today's route was fairly simple, and I could reach Nacaome, Honduras, 92 km away. Went on the Ruta Militar road. To my horror, it wasn't the flat smooth CA 2 highway I have been riding for days. It was back to a condition similar to Santa Ana's road. Immediately, my hope of crossing into Honduras was dashed. I could still cross into Honduras border but probably could only make it to border town instead of Nacaome where I could camp in the fire station, if they still had the trust in us travellers.

Ruta Militar was hilly and rough. Didn't recall that I had any flat road before. It was just up and down the whole time with patches of smooth tarmac and pure roughness. Like they ran out of budget and decided to patch bit by bit. Passed by several village schools, in time when classes ended. Hordes of school children came chasing on to me like I was their candy. It was an exaggeration no doubt.

Threw in the towel after 41 km, decided to stay one more night in El Salvador in the border town called Santa Rosa de Lima. As I rode past Texco, petrol station, the attendant waved and invited me to have some water. Sure, of course, I wouldn't refuse freebies. He passed me two bags of water. I had to bite through the plastic to create an opening for me to suck the water. Interesting concept, different from traditional plastic bottles. To my surprise, he then passed me another bottle of Gatorade. I sat on the petrol station bench and chatted with the drivers resting on route. One of them bought me a subway sandwich for lunch. Salvadorans were so hospitable to me.

As I always had a backup plan, in case I couldn't make it to my planned destination, I marked out Hospedeje Gomez in Santa Rosa on Google map. Easy to find my way. Hospedeje was a cheap, no-frills basic accommodation for weary travellers who just wanted a resting place, nothing much. It was cheaper than a $10 dorm bed I had been paying in El Salvador. US $6 for a room with a fan but no bathroom, and US $8 for room with a fan and a bathroom. Bathroom was a shower pipe to bath and a toilet bowl. It had a hammock and Wifi too. It looked grimm but for the price, it would do for me.

Left 16 km to Honduras border, 51 km to Nacaome or 79 km to San Lorenzo.

Day 404: Adios El Salvador! Hola Honduras! Country 19
Santa Rosa, El Salvador to Nacaome, Honduras
Distance: 51 km
Time: 7.07 am to 3 pm
Cumulative distance: 14,713 km

Realised there was a tear on my left shoe but it was too late to replace as shops closes early before sunset. I believed it could last till Choluteca in Honduras, the next major city.

The road I was on was called Ruta Militar. It made sense to me as this was the road used by El Salvadorans to invade Honduras in 1969. The war was termed as Football war. El Salvador was the smallest nation in Central America and yet, it had the balls to invade its larger neighbor. Size doesn't matter in this case. Israel and Singapore were examples of small nations with powerful military. The war was ignited by Honduras evicting Salvadorans from Honduras soil. I skated on this piece of history.

By 9.30 am, I approached the Honduras border. You know you were approaching a border when you see long lines of trailer trucks queuing to deliver their goods across the border and steady stream of moneychangers waving their cash. This time, I was prepared and had the conversion in my head. One US converts to 23 Honduras Lempiras. The moneychanger offered me US $1 to 22 Lempiras. The rate was not bad, money changer could earn few dollars from me which I don't mind. Not like the Guatemalan changers who ripped me off 40 US. I would only spend 3 days in Honduras; hence I change US $40. US $20 to buy new shoes.

The El Salvadoran police stopped me when I was skating. They were intrigued by me. Checking my passport exit date from Guatemala, they were surprised it took me 8 days including 1 day of rest in San Salvador to cross the whole country. In fact, I could easily complete in 5-6 days if not for rough roads in Santa Ana and the Ruta Militar and overwhelming heat wave. The police took turns to try my board which I had to oblige, of course I didn't mind.

Exiting El Salvador was simple, the officer issued me a tiny piece of paper indicating I exited El Salvador. Crossed the bridge into Honduras. Paid US 3 for entry fee and that was it. I earned my Honduras stamp, the world's most dangerous country. It doesn't feel dangerous to me. Everyone was friendly and cheering me on.

Honduras greeted me with freshly paved road. Smooth heaven, I am starting to love Honduras now. Black-like hair asphalt gave me pure skating orgasm. For the first time, I actually welcomed headwind. The wind acted like a fan, cooling me off from the scorching heat. Going slow wasn't an issue, the heat was. Now I wanted the headwind to blow onto me. Looks like Honduras was upgrading their infrastructure in this region. Bus shelters, bridges and paved road. Stopped at a constructed bus shelter to cook my lunch. Lunch was 2 packets of instant noodles with egg and tuna, I wasn't that hungry. Bought a bottle of coke to quench my thirst from nearby store for 20 Lempiras before taking a nap.

By 3pm, I entered Nacaome, where there lies another fire station waiting for me. Asked a local where the fire station was and he cycled to direct me the way. The street road in Nacaome was cobblestoned like in Antigua but in dirt. The local patiently cycled with me to the fire station where the firemen immediately greeted me with packets of water. They sure knew what I needed the most. Realised I had a large blister on my left heel. I knew it was the footbraking shoe as the blister was on my footbraking leg. I have to leave it till I get to Granada where I could get a long rest. After all, it doesn't really cause me much discomfort. I survived skating with it for 4 days already. Nacaome was a small town but it has free Wi-Fi in the town square. I love Honduras. It was dangerously seducing me.

Day 405: Last Night in Honduras

Honduras: Nacaome to Choluteca
Distance: 55 km
Time on board: 7.06 am to 3.47 pm
Cumulative distance: 14,768 km

Honestly, I was a little hesitant coming into Honduras for its recent riots and protests over the presidential election last November. The Constitution only states a single term limit for president. The leader amended the Constitution so that he could run for another term or even longer. Not surprising who won the election. The incumbent won over his rival, a TV talk show host, by controversial razor margin. Was there a trend of celebrities running for office and gaining popularity? A trend that citizens were probably getting sick of mainstream establishment and went for alternative populist figures. For months, protests sprawled over Honduras. However, in the days when I was here, everything seemed calm. Everyone in the south Honduras just continued their normal lives. I could say It was safe to pass over this stretch of Honduras.

The stretch from El Salvador border to Nicaragua border was only a mere 150 km. I could easily cross it in 2 days and for hardcore tourers, they could do it in a day. Though it was a tiny stretch, I love its freshly paved road and affordable cost of living. Simple lunch or dinner cost about 70 L or US $3 and soft drinks only 10-20 L or $0.50 to $1. No wonder I observed people ordering 1.5 litres of cola for lunch. The hot weather makes it tempting to keep drinking cola to quench thirst. Instead, it just keeps you addicted for more like drugs. In Central America, drugs were not the issue but cola was! There should be a war on Coke!

The smooth paved highway continued. Took my first break at San Lorenzo, where I detoured for malecon. However, it was under construction. Had a glimpse of islands across the malecon. Headed back on highway to Choluteca.

The headwind, though cooling me down, was also slowing me down as well. If only I could control the intensity like a fan, that would be awesome. Not too strong to slow me but sufficient to cool me. At 11 am, I stopped for lunch at a roadside stall and break from the heat. The TV was showing Dodgeball and Big Mama house in Spanish. I watched through the shows while seeking refuge from the fiery blazing ball of sun.

Realised the tear on my shoe had already propagated past its half way mark. My shoe would not survive past today's skate. I better hurry to Choluteca where I could replace a pair. My shoes lasted me a month since Chetumal, Mexico and cost $20. I probably have to set aside US $20 monthly for replacing shoes. My gregarious blister was causing me discomfort as well. I had to wear my left shoe without heels on. With these ongoing issues, it was a miracle that I made it to Choluteca in one piece.

Approaching the fire station was my protocol now, the fireman asked me to wait for his superior. After checking and filling in my passport particulars, they led me to their garage to sleep. Nowadays, the night was too warm for me to sleep in my bivy, I simply laid my sleeping pad and put on my insect repellant to repeal the bugs from having me as their meal during the night.

After a good shower, I left for Unimall, Choluteca's largest mall for my new shoes. While trying on my new shoes, my blister popped. I felt a sensation and liquid goo flowed out. I got my new shoes and my blister popped. Killed two birds with one stone. Selected the cheapest comfortable shoes for 400 L or US $18. I don't know how long it would last. I simply chose the cheapest one.

From Choluteca to the border, the road was still under construction. After verifying with the firemen, it was true, I would have a tough 40 km to the border. Since the fire station was next to the bus station, I might as well take the bus tomorrow to Nicaragua. Since Marge was there in Leon, Nicaragua, I would have to rush there and take a break.

CHAPTER 10

NICARAGUA

Day 410: Adios Honduras, Hola Nicaragua country 20
Nicaragua: Leon to Managua
Distance: 90 km
Time: 7.20 am to 6.47 pm
Cumulative distance: 17, 858 km

Day 405 - 409

Took a bus from Choluteca, Honduras to Nicaragua border as my popped blisters was causing me discomfort and I didn't want to risk further infection. Now the issue was which bus would take my pushcart. The transport to Guasaule, the border, was a minivan since the distance was a short 40 km. But Hondurans want your business, so they would demonstrate all sorts of ingenious resourceful ways to fix the problem. They lifted and tied my folded pushcart on to the top of the van and surprisingly, it stayed secure throughout the journey. At the border, I skated to the Honduras exit.

By now, I would expect central America immigration to be settled in a matter of seconds. This time, I had to queue for an hour to get my exit stamp and had to put faith in honest Honduran as I had to leave my pushcart outside the office during that time. The queue was mixed with people entering and exiting Honduras. No wonder the queue was so long. After an hour or so, I got my exit stamp and my pushcart was left intact. Honduras might be the most dangerous country but its people were generally honest.

I crossed the bridge over to Nicaragua, the border guard directed me to the immigration office. I had to pay US $12 for entry and weirdly, they did not accept their own Nicaraguan currency Cordoban. I gave them US $15 but they don't have the change. They asked me to go out and find a money changer to change my Cordoban back to US $2 to get exact change. What a red tape! Hopefully it doesn't illustrate the culture of Nicaragua.

Skated to the bus station to catch a bus to Leon. The chicken / ex American school bus only leaves when it was full. After lifting and securing my pushcart on top of the bus, I went for lunch since I was the first to arrive. Lunch was cheap. Rice with beef for 70 C / US $2.30. I am loving Nicaragua again. I entertained the kids at the comedor. They probably find me interesting as they never interacted with an Asian guy. I translated whatever Spanish words they wanted to in English.

At 12.40 pm, I boarded the bus for Leon. There, I got reunited with Marge 'magic hair'. She was with two female companions, Alana Conner from USA and Laura from Spain. Looks like I am the odd male here. However, they made a move towards Granada the next day while I had to stay in Leon for a few days to recuperate from my blisters. During my stay in Leon, I binge watched three movies; Tomb Raider, Pacific Rim 2 and Mary Magdalene since each movie cost US $4 only. On the last day in Leon, I signed up for volcano boarding at nearby Cerro Negro. This was the only place where you could slide down a volcano on a wooden plank. The slope of the volcano was fine volcanic debris, suitable for sliding down a roller coaster speed. But first, we have to hike for 45 minutes to get to the top in order to slide down the 500 metres slope. Speed could go up to 90 km/h, however, I prefer to slide at a comfortable speed of 50 km/h, not risking further injury. Sliding down at 50 km/h was very different from skating down at that similar speed. I must say skating down was much more exhilarating.

Day 410

At last, I had fully recovered from my blisters and my heel had regrow new skin. And I had gotten used to my new shoes bought in Honduras. I realized I always have to get shoes larger than my normal size as my feet were wider at the front. Skated out of Leon without any hinge.

According to my Intel from Anthony Chamssy and family who were ahead of me, the roads were very smooth and I am going to love it. Followed their recommendation, Highway 12 followed by Highway 28. Somehow, they forgot to mention the headwind. Headwind provided a catch 22. Headwind slowed me down with much resistance but cooled me down. Without headwind, I could go much faster, but I have to take frequent longer breaks from the heat, which turned out to be slow as well. The highway provided a wide shoulder but it was riddled with horse shit. Instead of looking out for cars, I have to dodge from lumps of shit on the road.

By noon, I arrived at Nagote, 50 km into my skate. Good time for lunch. There, I bumped into my hostel mate in Leon. Now he had to believe that I really skated all the way.

After lunch, my legs felt jelly, from pushing hard through the headwind. Took a nap at a bus stop for 30 minutes before stopping shortly after to admire the scenery. It was a volcano on a lake. Bought a soft drink to sit down and enjoy the view while catching a breather. A local approached me. I was too tired from the wind to entertain. I pretended not to understand Spanish but he could speak English. Damn, I couldn't escape this time. Answered his questions grumpily, and I left after 5 minutes to get back on the road.

Arrived at Managua at 4.30 pm and tried finding my hostel, Cesar Roof. Google map pointed the place inside an oil refinery. I tried to enter the premises but of course the guards stopped me. Apparently, there wasn't any hostel inside the oil refinery. I read that Managua address was based on geographical landmarks, street names don't exist. An example was Calle 2, 2 blocks north from Parque Central.

Failing to find a cheap hostel, I continued skating further into the city in search of a hostel. Hostal Las Palma's was another wrongly pinned address. Luckily a local directed me further down the road. The hostel was more like a cheap guesthouse. US $15 for a private room. I don't need a room; I want to save money. I further skated on, the next one was a hotel, US $40 for a room. No way. By then, it was getting dark. Skating on unfamiliar places in the dark wouldn't be a wise choice. The cheapest bed in a hostel here would cost US $10, not much of a saving from Las Palma's US $15 room. So, I returned to Las Palma's and settled for a room. In the end instead of skating 85 km today, I probably ended up skating 90 km in circles in search for a hostel.

Famished after my shower, I went for dinner. Settled for a Chinese eatery, knowing they would satisfy my enormous appetite after a tough 90 km skate. I got more than I asked for. I ordered a US $5 fried rice, thinking it was rather an expensive meal. It turned out to be a gigantic plate of fried rice meant for a family. It was the Mount Everest of fried rice. Even a famished me had a tough time finishing a quarter of it. Next time I would bring 3-4 famished cyclists. I had to pack it away for my next days meal. I could save money, not having to buy food for next 3 meals. Breakfast, lunch and dinner worth of fried rice. US $5 for 4 meals, now that makes a cheap meal. Tomorrow I would reach Granada and prepare for the holy week Easter Sunday. Another long break for me.

Day 411: Semana Santa in Granada
Nicaragua: Managua to Granada
Distance: 54 km
Time: 7.39 am to 3.07 pm
Cumulative distance: 14,912 km

Another exhausting morning. I woke up to an aching body. Since Granada was only 50 km away, I could afford to sleep in. Had my fried rice leftovers for breakfast. I portioned the Mt Everest's mountain load for lunch and dinner. Saving money was my top priority.

It did not take long for me to pack up and prepare. In the end, I still managed to set off around my usual time 7 am albeit 40 minutes later. Found the streets to be deserted on a weekday. Oh, it was the eve of the holy week, where Christ died and was resurrected. Nicaragua being a Catholic country, so it was not surprising that it was a holiday for the entire weekend, since Easter was the most important festival of the year. That was why I was scheduled to arrive in Granada, the crown jewel of Central America, to celebrate the holy week. Of course, Antigua, Guatemala might dispute this.

The deserted roads played to my benefit. No cars to worry about as I skated out of the capital. It was only when I was moving out of the city that the traffic got busier.

Managua was founded on hills, thus naturally the road wasn't flat for me today. Lots of climbing to do. Took breaks hourly to rest from the heat. At one of the bus shelters, an elderly lady chatted with me. This time, I was more enthusiastic in chatting in Spanish than yesterday when I was totally zonked.

Stopped by the entrance to Masaya volcano. It was the place to visit if you like to see lava in the crater. It was best to do at night, when you could see red hot birthing lava. However, they only allow motorised vehicles to enter. You were only allowed 15 minutes at the crater and if the volcano suddenly turns active, you need to evacuate fast. Walking or skating isn't the best option. I might have to go on tour to do this.

Since I got my fried rice ration for lunch, I sat down at the petrol kiosk to finish my fried rice and enjoy the gassing sensation of coke down my throat. Continued on quickly to the next bus stop where I could take my nap till 1.30 pm.

The last 10 km on Nic-4 highway deteriorated. It wasn't that rough, still skateable but I was pampered by high quality roads in central America. I used to worry about the road condition in Central America prior to entering. I thought I was going to have a tough time. Thinking Central America region was impoverished, I thought they would not have the funds to maintain the roads.

On the contrary, 80% of the PanAmerican highway here were of excellent or good condition. Only a few stretches of rough roads like the one from Guatemala border to Santa Ana in Salvador. Other than that, Central America could be a skate touring haven. Guatemala road was good except crazy steep roads, El Salvador was not bad, Honduras was simply heaven till the Nicaragua border and Nicaragua was great. Worst on the average, I would say it was Belize. Luckily Belize was a short stretch, doable in 4 days.

So now 10 km of rough road to Granada, I could accept that. Jesus suffered and died under the cross. What was suffering 10 km of roughness for him. By 2pm, I approached Granada and reached the main cathedral first for photo taking. The baroque-styled cathedral stuck me as golden rich extravaganza. Granada was named by Hernández de Córdoba after the ancient Spanish city of Granada. This was done in honour of the defeat of the last Moorish stronghold, which had been Spanish Granada, by the Catholic King and Queen of Spain. Granada, Nicaragua was historically the sister capital in Central America to Antigua, Guatemala. During the colonial period, Granada maintained a flourishing level of commerce with ports on the Atlantic Ocean, through Lake Nicaragua (also known as Cocibolca) and the San Juan River. Quoted from Wiki travel.

I noticed Nicaraguan revered Che Guevera, the famous revolutionary as statues bearing his image were all over town. Another striking similarity between Cuba and Nicaragua was that locals love to have rocking chairs and sat outside their houses to chat with neighbors. This explains why they have such strong ties. After the successful socalist revolution in Cuba, Che then fought in Nicaragua's civil war, supporting the Sandinista Socialist revolution.

Another long break for me over the weekend as I celebrate holy week. Last year, I celebrated Easter in Ho Chi Min City, Vietnam. This year, I would be celebrating across the Pacific Ocean in Nicaragua. I wonder where would I celebrate my next Easter. Singapore, probably, or my mother would come chasing after me with a broomstick. Have a blessed Easter.

Day 415: No Soy Chino! Soy Singaporean

Nicaragua: Granada to Rivas
Distance: 68 km
Time: 7.05 am to 2.31 pm
Cumulative distance: 14,980 km

Day 411-414

Good Friday procession was indeed an eye opener for me. Hundreds of devotees followed the statue of Christ being crucified and Mother Mary and a Roman Soldier carried by more than 20 devotees on a fiery day through the streets of Granada. We did the 14 stations of the cross as we walked around, chanting the Lord's prayer and hail Mary. Of course, I did mine in English. In Singapore, we never did such procession, everything was done within the confines of the church. And here, streets were closed. No cars were allowed on the streets at this hour. Therefore, it was an experience for me, my first holy week in Latin America where everyone was Catholic.

On Saturday evening, Yves and Fed arrived in Granada, staying in the fire station which was right opposite my hostel. We gathered for an expensive pizza dinner. They left for Rivas. Throughout the holy week mass, I made friends with a homeless guy, who also begged for money. Instead of giving alms to the church, I gave it to him. Catholic Church has billions of dollars already. Why not give it to the poor. Nothing much, just sufficient for him to get a cheap meal.

Throughout Central America, everyone on the streets have been shouting Chino, whenever they saw me. Sometimes, it turns to racial slur like Ching Chong Chang. Though my ethnicity was Chinese, I don't really identify as Chinese, I see myself as Singaporean. No Chinese or whatever. I always replied back "No Soy Chino, Soy Singaporean". But Singapore being a tiny island nation, nobody here has ever heard of it. I have to explain to them that it was near Malaysia and Thailand.

Finally, once a guy actually guessed I was from Thailand. I was so glad cos it was a close answer. My sunburnt dark complexion distinguished me as Thai, no longer as the typical Chinese. Now, I would probably pass off as Filipino even.

Day 415

Leaving Granada was a small hill which I have to climb. The temperature, by 8 am, began to soar. Without my Garmin GPS watch, I couldn't gauge how fast and far I am going. But luckily, there were the milestone markers indicating the distance to Costa Rica border. From the marker, I could calculate how many km left to Rivas.

As usual, the highway was smooth. The wind was keeping me cool and slowing me as well. On Nadame, I left highway 4 and switched to Nic-2. Everything remained the same. At 11 am, stopped at a Comedor for lunch. Best lunch for a long time. Chicken stew with rice. It was only 60 C or US $2. Must enjoy these cheap meals while I am still in Nicaragua. Once at Costa Rica and Panama, things get really expensive. Almost western Europe standard. Then again, when it comes to expensive countries, I tend to spend less.

From the lunch place to Rivas was only 26 km more. I took a short nap at a bus shelter but it was crowded. Resumed at 12.30 pm to finish the last 26 km. At 2.30 pm, I arrived at Rivas Fire station. It was a 3-storey building. I had the whole 2nd floor to myself for tonight. There were two kids, Jeffery and Lucia. They tried to communicate with me in English they learnt in school but it wasn't sufficient. Being a former teacher, my teaching instincts kicked in. Taught them a few basic English phrases and corrected their homework.

Tomorrow, I would try to leave my pushcart in the station, as I would be going to Playa Gigante to meet up with Marge Magic Hair to celebrate her upcoming birthday on the 4th. Playa Gigante was another detour off the pan American highway. Not wanting to skate the same way, I would try to hitchhike or get Magic Hair to transport me there. Gawd, I am never going to reach Argentina at this pace.

Day 419: Adios Nicaragua! Hola Costa Rica, Country 21
Rivas, Nicaragua to La Cruz, Costa Rica
Distance: 55 km
Time: 9.45 am to 5.18 pm
Cumulative distance: 15,035 km

Day 416-418

Took a taxi to Rivas since I couldn't find a bus to Gigante at the bus station. The driver first quoted me $15, but during the ride, he begged for another US $5, I then bargained down to $3. I hate people who agreed with initial price then increased the price afterwards. They should quote me that price, I still would have taken it. At Gigante, Marge's host was already hosting 10 surfers at his place, couldn't accommodate me anymore. I went over to Warmshower host, John, where Yves and Fed were there. John works for Camino Hostel beside it. His boss gave the house to accommodate John and other volunteers at the hostel. For us skate tourers and Cyclotravellers, we could stay there for 2 nights. Together, we celebrated Marge "Magic Hair" 27th birthday the next day. I bought her a LED hair band with Minnie Mouse on it as her present. I made Piña Cola with Alana as contribution to the potluck birthday dinner. Alana used her pretty dress as a filter for the coconut and she was going to wear it again after laundry. That's how rugged female cyclists could be.

Gigante lived to its namesake. Gigante refers to the Gigantic waves. No wonder so many surfers settled here to surf their hearts out. From a tiny village, it rose to be a surfer's paradise. Still unknown to the outside world.

On 5th April, after Marge's birthday, I headed back to Rivas on a chicken bus that was way cheaper than a taxi. Less than US $2. The road to Rivas was built on tiles making my skate difficult, hence I opted for a bus back. I stayed in Hospedeje Coco for US $8. Planned to stay one night, waiting for Laura, Marge and Alana to set off from Gigante the next day. We could travel together once more as a group to Panama City. 3 attractive ladies riding with me. I'm a lucky guy. The next morning, I heard from Marge that they too were taking the chicken bus back to Rivas. I figured that they would arrive 9-ish am. I set off from my Hospedeje at 8.30 am and skated to the outskirts on the main road to wait for them. By 9.40 am, Marge arrived first, followed by Alana and Laura. Yeah, the gang was formed. We would ride together all the way to Panama City for the next 2 weeks, except for Alana. She has to fly off from San Jose back to California, home.

Naturally, being on bicycle, they rode faster than me. Laura and Marge sped off. Except Alana, she rode behind me. For the first time, I got someone to accompany me during the ride. The wind and hills made it tough for me to really go fast. Especially, when I see rows of wind turbines along Playa Virgen, generating renewable energy. That meant there was significant intensity of wind in this area, that was why Nicaraguans placed them here. Either I got strong tailwind working for me or headwind working against me. Unfortunately, it was the latter. Along the way, a polish couple in tandem bike sped past me. Shortly, they stopped on the road with Marge on the road for a chat. Joined by Argentinian cyclist traveling on the opposite direction. He was heading to Mexico before heading to Europe and cycle to Russia for the World Cup. Left 10 km to Costa Rica border, they went ahead of me, waiting for me at Penas Blanca, the border town. Before the town, I stopped to buy a drink, spending my last Nicaragua Corboda.

At the border, the polish couple and my trio ladies waited for me. I went straight to the money changer to change my US to Costa Rica Colon. US $1 for 550 colon. I changed US $100; in turn I got a huge denomination of colones. Had our last meal in Nicaragua before entering the expensive Costa Rica. Having spent all my Cordoban, Alana offered to treat me for lunch. After lunch, the polish couple had to break away from us, as they have a large distance to cover today. We only had 20 km remaining.

We entered the border control where I saw the most beautiful Nicaraguan lady. She was the border guard. In my mind, please arrest me, I am an illegal immigrant. Please detain me for life. Haha of course I didn't say that to her. I shared this with Alana. Even she agreed with me that she was so hot. At the immigration office, we couldn't bring my pushcart and their bikes in. Therefore, we left them outside and split into pairs to guard our stuff. Alana and I entered the immigration first. I simply couldn't comprehend the process involved in exiting Nicaragua. First, I have to pay 1 US to a counter and go over to the actual custom and pay another US $4 for my exit stamp. Couldn't they just set it for us to pay US $5 all together at the custom? Then it was Marge and Laura's turn. The immigration only wanted US dollars, not their local currency. I lent them my US to pay the immigration. Finally, we got out of Nicaragua.

We rode to Costa Rica customs, but not before taking group pictures at the 'Welcome to Costa Rica' sign. Marge carried the Petite Alana on her shoulders. To complement the pose, Laura carried me on her shoulders, since obviously I was the lighter one. That was Gender Equality.

At Costa Rica customs, it was a straightforward affair, no entrance fee or whatever. They just asked us a few questions and we were off. Once we've crossed the border, immediately the terrain changed as we crossed the imaginary line. Costa Rica was filled with greenery, lush thick forest greeted us. A stark contrast to the barren Nicaragua farm lands. Costa Rica was one of the countries with the most biodiversity in the world and they sought to protect nature. Almost 40% of the land was designated as a nature reserve. Way to go, Costa Rica. Being that said, it was one of the more affluent nations in Central America besides Panama. We could expect living costs to be much more expensive here. Luckily, I stocked up on my food supply before leaving Nicaragua.

I had to walk on gravel side to avoid getting hit from traffic coming towards me. As usual, Marge and Laura sped off while I rode together with Alana, who was the same age as me. No wonder we could click so well. Caught up with Marge and Laura as they sat by the roadside to fix Marge's punctured tyre. Good time to have a break. We rested for 40 minutes till Marge fixed her punctures. Last 8 km to go. We rode together as a group as only I had the online map of Costa Rica and knew the location of the fire station in La Cruz. Last big hill to climb, I resorted to running and walking briskly. Running and walking briskly seemed to be a faster option than skating up. I somehow managed to keep pace with Alana's climbing speed. In the end, she too gave in and pushed her bike with me.

At La Cruz, we saw the bomberos or fire station. You could tell Costa Rica was a really developed country. The fire station was the most modern that I have ever seen so far in Central America. However, it was closed for unknown reasons. We rode further to the Red Cross in the city centre to try our luck. However, they had to turn us down as well. Third time lucky, we found a church willing to accommodate us for the night. We camped in their backyard.

While shopping at a nearby supermarket, I was shocked to see the astronomical prices. My 6 litres of water cost me US $5 and my loaf of bread cost US $2. In all, just 2 items cost me US $7. Laura from Spain gruntled that it was more expensive than in Spain. It was close to Northern Europe cost of living. Indeed, Costa Rica and Panama would burn a hole in my budget. Gone was the cheaper Central America's way of living. No more eating out or sleeping in hostels like I used to do in Central America. Here, it was back to Europe way of touring.

CHAPTER 11

COSTA RICA

Day 420: Liberty Liberia
Costa Rica: La Cruz to Liberia
Distance: 60 km
Time: 7.30 am to 12.08 pm
Cumulative distance: 15, 095 km

We shared our poo story last night over dinner and this morning. There wasn't any toilet at the church, so I had to poop somewhere in the backyard. While cleaning my butt, my hand was dirtied by my poo, exactly what happened last year in Thailand. Good thing there were 3 ladies with me. I got to clean my hand with soap. First time since Guatemala, I felt chilly during the night. Had to put on my hoodie and sweatpants to sleep.

The benefits of travelling with others was we get to share resources. They made tea and oatmeal for me; I shared my bread. Best of both worlds. Noticed I wrote 'we' more often than the usual 'I'. Now as a group, we collectively made decisions on what to eat, where to sleep and how far to travel for the day. We decided on a short 60 km ride to Liberia instead of opting for a longer 80 km to Bageces which we would end up riding longer distances over the next day.

While having breakfast, we chatted. Alana, like me, had her own downhill song. Song to sing when riding a long downhill. Hers was 'Naked and Free' by Sabana. My downhill song was 'Country Road' by John Denver. Thought I was the only weird one, found someone as quirky.

Left la Cruz to get on highway 1. Costa Rica 's road was well paved and smooth for me. However, they left me without any shoulders. I had to jostle with cars and trucks over the tiny pathetic road space. There was a reason why Costa Rican drivers were known for their crazy insane driving. They overtake vehicles in front whenever they felt like it. Today, I was much faster than I was in Nicaragua. Costa Rica has more trees, blocking the wind whereas wind in Nicaragua was almost unstoppable by the barren lands. Once the variable of wind was removed, my speed improved. Alana rode together with me again.

At the uphill, I discovered that rapid, shorter strides helped in me skating uphill. Was like bicycle on lower gear, more cadence for the hills. There was a section where I rolled down and the momentum was enough to continue finishing the next up slope and down. I didn't have to kick once for a few km.

At 30 km, halfway to Liberia, the 3 ladies and I took a break. My pushcart was just off the road as I forgot to put on the parking brakes. When a huge truck came zooming across, the force from draft wind came pushing my pushcart down into the forest. Nothing was damaged or lost. It was only 9.30 am and 30 km to go. We decided to ride all the way to Liberia without any breaks. At this pace, it was projected that I could reach Liberia before noon. Yeah, I could wash my clothes.

Laura and Marge rode ahead while Alana and I rode on together. The wind intensified when we entered into farmlands. Without any trees slowing down the wind, it was back to Nicaragua's slow speed. Just as I was cursing the wind, a pickup truck pulled over in front of me. The driver, with his children, came out, saying 'Liberia'.

I replied, 'Si'.

Instantly, he opened his back of pickup and signalled for me to get on. Alana was thinking she could ride the last 20 km but nah, we could have a longer day of rest. Why not. The driver helped us load my pushcart and her bicycle and drove us 20 km or less to Liberia. Apparently, the driver used to tour the world on his bicycle too. He toured around the USA once, and his children were also avid cyclists. When he spotted the two of us, he was happy and stopped for us. He gave me a Costa Rican flag to put on my pushcart. Finally, my first flag.

While waiting for Marge and Laura, Alana did her yoga under the bridge. We waited 45 minutes for Marge and Laura at the roadside. Alana bought a honey melon for us to enjoy, which cost her US $4. That was one expensive melon. The Rica in Costa Rica was really living to its name. It meant Rich. Indeed, it was rich and expensive.

We rode to the fire station but they had to turn us down as the alarm system would sound off during the night if we walked in the fire station. Didn't know the fire station in Costa Rica was so high tech. Then we tried the Red Cross, and it was successful this time round. They held on to our passports till the next morning. Showered and washed my clothes, after which we had lunch at a Chinese restaurant. I shared a huge plate of rice with curry chicken. Costa Rica was lovely except it's really expensive. Luckily, we discovered the tap water was safe to drink, therefore I don't have to spend US $5 on water every day.

Day 421: The bomb at Bomberos
Costa Rica: Liberia to Canada
Distance: 55 km
Time: 8.38 am to 3.19 pm
Cumulative distance: 15, 090 km

A little background on my 2 new companions. I already introduced Marge "Magic Hair". She and Laura were lesbian couple. They met in Guatemala and fell in love almost immediately. I must say theirs was rather a love-hate relationship. One moment, they were bickering over something every day, then the next they were lovely dovey couple. As for Alana, she met Marge in California while on a weekend bike trip. They only knew each other for a night and Alana asked Marge if she could join her in Mexico when her vacation was approved. By the way, she was an architect. Alana acts as a mediator between the couple whenever they were having fights. Now I came along to ease the tension. I wonder what would happen when Alana splits from us in few days to return home and left me alone to be a go between. Alana had a crazy idea. When the two were having arguments again, we went up to them and pulled down our pants to show them our naked butts. This worked, immediately we laughed and forget what they were arguing. It was Laura's brother birthday today. Thus, we made a birthday video for him. Inspired by Alana's antics, we pulled our pants to show him our naked butts. This must be most fun group I ever had since my tour. As you could see that I got 3 quirky companions to compliment me on this leg.

We were abruptly awakened by the alarm at 6 am. We were supposed to leave the Red Cross by 7 am. At full speed, we packed our stuff to make space for ambulances. We still could have our breakfast in the red Cross. Upon leaving, the staff returned us our passports at 9 am. Instead of heading out on the road, we headed for central park to connect to WiFi. There wasn't wifi at the Red Cross for us. Today's destination was Canas, 50 km away. Marge discovered a waterfall midway on Google map. Decided to head there first for a swim since it was only a short day. Today, I was much slower. Alana sort of abandoned me and rode ahead. The highway 1 road was concrete with grooves. As I mentioned before, I hated this type of surface. Not as bad as the Santa Ana, that I would still prefer the concrete type. Another reason why I was so slow was that my backpack was rubbing on my front wheel again. Once I adjusted my backpack on my pushcart, I am back to my usual speed.

At midway, before turning into the entrance to waterfall, we stopped at a fruit stall for thirst quenching coconuts. The owner warned us that there was an entrance fee to waterfall and it was 7 US per person. Daylight robbery! Just to swim in the waterfall. We were not ready to pay exhortation. He then suggested there was a river down 2 km. Not the nicest, but it was free. Free was good for us. We rode down to Rio Pierdas and asked the house owner if we could park our bikes here while we went for a swim. No issues. We gathered our lunch and swimming gears. The river was below the highway bridge and there was already a local family having their weekend picnic. Our swim was short-lived as the ladies couldn't stand the fish nibbling their bodies in the river. I am from Asia, we pay for fish spa, for fish to nibble our dead skins. It was spa therapy for us Asians. Of course, I dipped long in the river to enjoy the free fish spa. Simple lunch of sandwiches and long siesta break. Life! While I was napping, Laura and Marge broke into argument again. Laura steamed off and left. The remaining 3 of us left the place at 1 pm after 3 hours. Marge sped off to catch up with Laura for the last 27 km. Alana and I just took our time to enjoy the ride. It was great weather today, not sunny thanks to the clouds.

Bicycle touring was like being in a relationship. We collectively set a destination for the end of the day to sleep. Everyone has their own comfortable pace. Therefore, we all rode separately, but at the end of the day, we still would gather together. In a relationship, everyone has their own pace. As long as we set our common goals together, going at our own pace and achieving the goals together was perfect. Everyone would have their own breathing space to explore and do the things what they want to do. Laura and Marge rode separately but they would meet each other at the destination. This allowed them breathing space to cool down.

At the entrance to Canas, Marge waited for Alana and me. Marge was worried that Laura really decided to break up and goes separate ways. Her fears were unfounded. Then just up ahead lied Laura. We were back to our group once more. We rode to the Red Cross but 2 months, they already stopped accommodating cyclotravellers. That was the last entry on ioverlander app that a cyclist once stayed there at the red Cross 2 months. Something must have happened between them and the cyclist that they decided not to welcome us anymore. We then turned to the Fire station. The firemen welcomed us. Their fire station and facilities were indeed modern and professional looking compared to the rundown stations that I stayed before in Mexico and other central America countries. Their fire trucks were new and at the top of its game. While the fire equipment in El Salvador, Honduras and Nicaragua were mostly donated by Japan. Through this, you know Costa Rica was a developed country on par with USA. The firemen gave us a tour and showed us their equipment. We could sleep in their meeting room tonight. There was a pool table and gym equipment. Fire stations in Costa Rica was really world class.

What a coincidence! The female staff that worked at Liberia's Red Cross yesterday, was working today in Canas Fire station. She was working full-time in the Red Cross and volunteers at this fire station. She lives in Canas, that was why she wanted to get a job at this Fire station and so she was volunteering here first. We have a great time trying on fire suits and it weighed a ton. How these firemen survived wearing these thick suits. Kudos to them for saving lives.

Day 422: Rio of life
Costa Rica: Canas to Punta Arenal
Distance: 75 km
Time : 8.38 am to 6 pm
Cumulative distance: 15,165 km

Last night was the most luxurious fire station I have ever slept in. The staff turned on the air conditioner for us in the meeting room. So comfortable that we overslept, forgetting that we have to leave the fire station by 6 am. They were ok with us leaving at 8 am. We went to the supermarket to buy groceries for breakfast. Alana and I made pancakes for breakfast for the gang last night. After breakfast, we made our way to Punta Arenal. The road was never once flat. Constant going up and down. Even my female cyclists also struggled as well. In contrast to Nicaragua, Costa Rica highway was narrow without any shoulders. What makes it worse was that there seemed to have more large trucks passing through here. I don't give a damn, if they want, they have to overtake me on the other lane.

Had our first break at Limonal, where Alana bought Vino de Coyol.We had seen stalls selling the mysterious bottles in the hot sun along the highways of Costa Rica's Guanacaste Province. It was actually not a wine but fermented from sap of Coyol palms, native to Costa Rica. It does contain a small amount of alcohol, enough to give us a buzz for the ride.

We then rode on till 40 km where Marge had her punctures once more. I could no longer count the patch holes in her tube. It was a galaxy of patch holes. We settle for the river below a bridge for lunch and swim. Costa Rica has one of the highest number of rivers per sq km in the world. That means every few km we ride; we were bound to pass through a river. Cooked 2 packets of pasta with tomato sauce. Swam in the river. Since there was just us, ladies decided to go skinny dipping. The ladies were checking me out too. They admired my toned back and muscular legs. Next time when I want to impress the ladies, I would have to show them my back. I have to talk to them facing backwards. "Hey ladies, look at my back, not my face"

After 2 and a half hours on the river, we continued on. Laura let Marge charged on and followed Alana and me instead. Our next break was at a stall selling rambutan. I have not seen the red hairy fruit for a long time. I thought it was exclusively grown in South East Asian region. Costa Rica has a similar tropical climate to my region; therefore, I am likely to see more of my local fruits here.

By 5.30 pm we have reached at cross road between Punta Arenal and San Jose. We rode to the fire station. This time, fire station rejected us due to government policies. We got lucky at the previous fire station. Without any backup plan, we attempted to head to the beach for camping. Marge asked a local on where was a good place to camp. The local knew of a Warmshower host nearby. Many foreign cyclists passed by here, therefore Alex, the Warmshower host was well known by locals here. We expected to be hosted by fire station, that was why we never bothered to search for any Warmshower hosts. Alex and his family welcomed us even though we arrived at his doorstep unexpected.

The four of us have our last meal together as Alana would have to fly off from San Jose to San Francisco back home to return to her normal life after 2 months of nomadic lifestyle. Laura and Marge opted to head over to Caribbean coast which means if I want to follow them, I have to climb over a mountain range and back another mountain range to Panama Pacific coast. For me, all coast were the same, large bodies of water. I decided to stick to my plan of continuing on the Pacific coast. I would see how. Just follow through the river of life.

Day 424 : Crocs Ahead!
Costa Rica: Punta Arenal to Jaco
Distance: 64 km
Time: 7.10 am to 2.54 pm
Cumulative distance: 15,229 km

Day 423

The ladies have to split away from me. Alana have to get to San Jose to fly back home in San Francisco while Laura and magic Hair wanted to see Caribbean Sea on the other side of Costa Rica. For me, riding to San Jose, meant 1500 m elevation gain over 92 km. For sure, I am not going to make it in a day. After San Jose, would be a terrifying descent. Then in the end I would have to climb another mountain range in Panama to return to the pan American highway to Panama City. 2 mountain range would be too much for me to bear though eventually I have to do the Andes mountain soon. For now, I prefer to stick to the flatter coast which I am on right now. The ladies woke up early to prepare for daunting ride ahead. Alex allowed me to stay in his house for another night. Longer sleep for me.

Day 424

Had to wake up Alex from his sleep so that he could open the door for me. Surprisingly, no one in the house woke up early for work today. I wonder why. Thanked Alex for hosting us, the unexpected guests. We never planned to stay with him hence we never wrote a Warmshower request. Still, he welcomed us with open arms. I skated back to highway 27. All the road cyclists were out on the road and today wasn't a weekend, it was a Wednesday. Everyone else were on the beach as well. I did my investigation, today was a public holiday. Juan Santamaria day, commemorating the Battle of Rivas, made famous by their national hero Juan Santamaria who sacrifice himself in the battle against Nicaragua led by William Walker, an American who usurped Nicaragua.

Today' s weather was cloudy, I guess the Sun was taking his holiday as well. Ideal for my skating but not ideal for heading out to the beach which I planned to at my destination Jaco. Followed the Highway 27 enroute to San Jose, that meant more elevation until I split off from Highway 27 to get on highway 34 to Jaco. Had my first break after the split off. Spotted the sign Jugo de Cana. Sugar cane juice. I haven't had this green thirst-quenching drink since Vietnam a year ago. A must have for me even though it cost an arm and a leg, US $2. Been craving for this drink for so long, at last I am satisfied. I swore this drink was an addictive drug. A customer overheard my conversation with the stall owner that I am skating around the world. He asked me for photos and gave me a packet of local snacks.

Few kms after, I crossed into the crocodile bridge. Underneath the bridge, the river hosted a colony of crocodiles. The bridge was crowded with tourists trying to catch a glimpse of those 3 m reptiles. I cooked my lunch next to the bridge outside the rows of shops selling souvenirs and restaurant. A costa Rican of African ancestry, selling necklaces to tourists, came up to me while I was cooking pasta with instant noodles on my camp stove. He wanted to try some of my lunch, I obliged since he looked pitiful and I usually cooked a large portion. If only he had asked me earlier, I could have prepared a larger portion to share.

After lunch, I had a big hill to overcome. I thought the coast was supposed to be flat! I walked up for several km before descending all the way to Jaco, a beach and surfing Paradise. My foot braking shoe was put to use. Descending 5km, my foot braking shoe was Paramount to my safety. Arrived at my hostel Bed on Bohio by 2.50 pm. Without my female companions, I got lazy to search for camping, decided to pay for accommodation today. Since I arrived early, swam in the beach and swimming pool in my hostel. I last heard from my 3 amigas, that they have a hard time yesterday climbing that 1500 elevation to San Jose. They braved through the darkness and arrived late at night. Good thing I didn't follow them.

Day 425: Make love peace, not war
Costa Rica: Jaco to Quepos
Distance: 67 km
Time: 8.10 am to 3.38 pm
Cumulative distance: 15,296 km

One thing that was still cheap in Costa Rica was going to cinema. A movie costed 1800 Colons or US $3.50. Watched Steven Spielberg 's Ready Player One at a rather late timing 9 pm as that was the only session for English. I was hesitant to catch the movie at this timing, meaning I could go to bed at 11.30 pm. But if I don't catch it now, the movie might end its run by the time I reached Panama City. I overcame my sleepiness to catch the movie and slept later than usual 10 pm.

I had the whole dorm room to myself and all the fans were directed at me to keep me ventilated. Despite the late-night sleep, my biological clock woke me up at 5.45 am. But there lies the issue. The hostel reception only open at 8 am and I couldn't leave without retrieving my US $10 key deposit. Tried to go return to bed but couldn't. Had my breakfast and watched few more YouTube Documentaries. Once the hostel returned my deposit, I began my day skate. Today was a 67 km skate to Quepos. After overcoming a short hill, it was all flat road for me. Easy peasy day. The Sun returned from yesterday's vacation and it was back to work as normal. The usual hot day again.

An interesting fact about Costa Rica was that they didn't have any military forces. They abolished the army during 70s if I am correct. They sure had the balls to abolish their army amidst all the conflicts going on in Central America. Guatemala fighting with Belize, El Salvador at war with Honduras and not to mention drug cartels war. They cannot afford to be a dick to everyone especially their neighbours. Instead they have to make friends with everyone especially the powerful ones like USA. This was how the world should go. Don't be a dick and make peace with everyone. With savings from military budget, they invested the money into infrastructure, education and healthcare. No wonder, Costa Rica was a world apart from other central America countries. If a certain country could do the same, hint to the country with the largest military in the world, that country could really benefit and help the poor and homeless and those in need of universal healthcare, instead of spending on needless wars. That country doesn't have to abolish its entire army but only a budget cut to military spending. Same goes to my country Singapore. Do we actually need to spend so much of our budget on military? The world was rather different from the 1940s. A sufficient armed forces should be enough to deter aggressors. Besides, we got an American base in Singapore, they have to back us up. Make love peace, not war.

Despite the late start today, I still made pretty good progress before noon. At Parrita, dropped by Maxi Pali, budget mega supermarket for more groceries and enjoying the air conditioner inside. Skated further to a bus stop to cook my lunch. My lighter ran out of fuel. Oh damn. How am I going to lit my stove? Luckily, I had a spare lighter after searching through my backpack. Since only 23 km left to Quepos, took a siesta at bus shelter. 30 minutes, a bunch of police woke me up. They took down my particulars and explained my skate journey and convince them I am just taking a short nap, away from the heat with no intention of camping here. If I understood them correctly, they were trying to warn me that it was dangerous here. I could get robbed or shot down. I don't know if they were trying to scare me into leaving. I rather not take the risk and don't want the police to come on me the second time. I continued skating right away.

With the easy smooth flat road, I arrived at Quepos fresh. Approached the fire station as usual. They allowed me to stay with few conditions. If I understood their Spanish correctly, I have to be in the station by 7 pm and not leave after due to alarm system. I have to leave by 7 am the next morning. That isn't an issue. I start my day real early. I camped in their garden for the night. For the first time, I pitched my tent since El Salvador.

Day 426: Pura Vida
Costa Rica: Quepos to Dominical
Distance: 45 km
Time : 7.45 am to 12.10 pm
Cumulative distance: 15,341 km

Was bombarded with bird poops landing on my bivy tent. Only realised the carnage done on my tent. Never sleep under a tree full of birds. Washed up my tent and waited for the fireman to open the gates for me to leave. Sat at the central park for free Wi-Fi. Wifi has become a necessity in life. Millennials would die without it, so as I. Humans could go without water for days, food for weeks but we would not survive without WiFi for a day.

Another super short day for me. 45 km to Dominical beach. I like to take it easy nowadays and what's more, Dominical would be my last beach afterwards I would be heading inwards all the way to Panama City. Might do a short day to arrive early and enjoy the beach.

Making good pace since the road was flat. Had my first break in Maritima. Sat in the bus shelter outside a school. It happened to be a recess time for students. The young sprouts came up to the fence to chat with me. Found it easy to chat with these kids in Spanish. Last few days with my companions, I switched off my Spanish brain. Since Laura was a native Spanish speaker, all conversations were referred to her. I just gave a blank look and signalled them to speak to Laura. Furthermore, when locals were conversing with Laura and Marge, they were speaking rapidly like a machine gun firing millions of rounds. Now I am alone, have to switched on my Spanish brain to communicate. It was evident that I am obviously not a Spanish speaker, therefore they would mouth their words slowly for me to understand. A kid handed me their apples through the fences. Soon, everyone followed suit in handing me their apples. I ended up with a bag full of apples. I should visit every school in Costa Rica now to coax them into handing me their lunch box.

Encountered a road construction where one lane was left open. Both sides of traffic have to wait and take turns to use that one lane. The workers let me through first since my rig was tiny to pass through. As a result, I got the entire fresh paved road to myself at a point and rows of impatient drivers zooming at me at another point. Before noon, I arrived at the turn in to Dominical beach. Two ladies were at the side trying to hitchhike to the next town, Uvita. Chatted with one of them, they were camping on the beach and invited me to join them when they returned from Uvita later. Two attractive ladies at the beach, oh yea I am definitely camping.

At the beach, made my lunch and had a swim but the Pacific waves were too strong for me to handle. The sediments carried by waves filled up my underpants. Now my underpants were filled with sand. There were few campers around. Looked safe to camp for the night. But the universe has another plan. For the first time in central America, the sky started to unload its long-awaited juice, it has been holding on for too long. At last, it finally poured. Luckily, I ended my skate early before the rain. Alright, looked like it was a hostel for me tonight. Right opposite, lies Piramy hostel. A bed for $10. Anyway, I have been saving quite a bit of money in Costa Rica, cos it was too expensive to eat out and indulge in soft drinks. Hence, I have some budget for hostel tonight.

Day 427: Pura Vida Siempre
Costa Rica: Dominical to Palma
Distance: 61 km
Time : 7.31 am to 2.24 pm
Cumulative distance: 15, 402 km

The access road back to highway transformed into a mud fest after last night's heavy downpour. The mere 300 m road took me 10 minutes to navigate around the muddy potholes. Last night, met the two gorgeous ladies in my hostel, the German ladies too, were seeking refuge from the downpour. It could signal the beginning of the monsoon season.

The usual lush green forest greeted me with gusto. The sun returned to its full glory, after taking a break from yesterday. If only it could take a break when I am on the road, and worked when I am relaxing on the beach. This was not how life was supposed to go.

The road was never flat, going up and down. You think being next to the coast, the road must be flat. No, it isn't. Well, it isn't that hilly, but climbing up and down does tire me somehow. The heat drove me to crave for soft gassy drinks to soothe my throat. I succumbed to my craving. In Costa Rica, the cost of living was significantly higher than the rest of Central America. I tried to curb my craving in order to keep to my budget. A tiny could of 235 ml fresca cost me $0.90. Hopefully, Panama isn't that expensive.

On the road, there were several gangs of Harvey Davidson motorcyclists in their typical Leather jackets zooming past me. Was this a trend now In Costa Rica? By 10.45, I covered 37 km and spotted an access road to a beach. Opposite the beach was an island, helping to break the mighty Pacific waves. The water was unusually calm. Since it was only 27 km to Palma, decided to visit for swim and lunch. Over the 3-hour long break, I swam, napped and ate my lunch, rinse and repeat. 'Pura Vida' as local Costa Ricans (Ticos) termed it. It simply translated to Pure Life but the meaning goes beyond that.

Ticos use this term to say hello, to say goodbye, to say everything's great, to say everything's cool. Pura Vida was the way Ticos live. Not surprisingly, Costa Rica has been named one of the happiest countries in the world, mostly because its inhabitants don't stress about things the way most foreigners do. Ticos have a very relaxed, simple way of looking at life. No worries, no fuss, no stress—pura vida to them means being thankful for what they have and not dwelling on the negative.

Although many people love to use the phrase, not many know where the term actually originated. The most common explanation comes from a Mexican movie called ¡Pura vida! that came to Costa Rica 1956 (directed by Gilberto Martínez Solares). In the movie, 'pura vida' was the saying used by the main character who remains optimistic, despite the unfortunate circumstances that continue to surround him. Although it took a little while to catch on, the phrase pura vida was being used nationwide by 1970. Today, it was an inherent part of the culture.

Although many people use the saying 'pura vida', until you've been to Costa Rica, you would not truly know what pura vida feels like. It's an emotion, it's an attitude, it's happiness, and it's a way of life.

I thought of my fellow Singaporeans and everyone else in the rat race slogging their life away. Spending time in office wondering how to pass the time quickly, watching the clock ticking to 5 pm, then rushing off in crowded trains like zombies. Not my kind of life. I am glad that I did my journey.

In the beach, boats ferrying passengers to and fro the opposite island. One of the Ticos, Marcos came up to me and chatted. I was surprised that He knew where Singapore was as he had travelled to Southeast Asia. After 3-hour long break, I continued my skate. Last 15 km, a pickup truck drove next to me and it was Marcos. He offered me a ride to Palma, exactly where I was going today. Though it was short 15 km remaining, I accepted the ride. I like interacting with locals and hitchhiking was better way to interact with locals, as I got to chat with them during the ride. Marcos was an engineer, and happened to be working today on a Saturday. He lives in Neily, where I am going to tomorrow but he has to work somewhere today. He dropped me off at Palma. I headed straight to fire station but bomberos had to turn me away and suggested that I tried asking the Catholic Church nearby. Father obliged and showed me the place where I could sleep. Next to the church was a park with free Wi-Fi. Pura Vida Siempre! Pure Life Forever!

Day 428: Last night in Costly Rich
Costa Rica: Palma to Neily
Distance: 78 km
Time : 7.15 am to 4 pm
Cumulative distance: 15,480 km

"Ask and ye shall receive"

These words in the Bible resonated with my travel. Marge mentioned before, she never has to worry about where to sleep for the night. You have to ask around. Somehow, things would work out. Yesterday, I approached the church and Father welcomed me to sleep in his store room. He provided fan and brand-new mattress for me to sleep. You have to ask, and things would work it out. I left early before Father could wake up. Unable to find him, I left the keys to the store room on the fan left outside his home. Before setting off, I surfed the internet for the last time on the park. Today was 77 km to Neily, 17 km away from Panama border.

Though Costa Rica was much costly than another central America, but I somehow spent less here. In 9 days in Costa Rica, I only spent 40,000 Colons or US $27, which was US $8 per day. Whereas i spent US $100 in Nicaragua in 8 days. Because Nicaragua was much cheaper, I don't bother to cook my meals, and eat out all the time, hostels are cheap as well, I only slept free in fire station in Rivas once and 2 days in Gigante with Warmshower host. During my skate, I indulged in soft drinks to quench my thirst. Also, I paid $30 for Volcano Boarding in Leon. All these adds up. Whereas, Costa Rica was too costly for me to even consider buying soft drinks every day. Probably once daily. I almost cook all my meals. Approaching the end of my skate in Costa Rica, I realised I don't spend much here. Expensive equals to less temptation to splurge except for today.

Weather was exceptionally humid today. I drank 4.5 litres of water in 3 hours and still remain dehydrated. To conserve water consumption, I walked up some minor up slopes. I was literally drowning in my sweat. Though Maps.me, I knew there was a waterfall at 55 km. Sounds like a good lunch spot and cool swim for me. The motivation drove me to skate faster. Every hourly, I stopped to check my location, calculated roughly to skate 15-16 km in the last hour.

As Costa Rica doesn't have any military, they spent their savings into building better infrastructure. As a result, I could observe their roads to be consistently smooth. Of course, they would have constant road maintenance. At one of the road constructions, the workers dropped their work upon watching me skate upslope. They chatted with me and gave me cool drinking water from their cooler. This was much better than my water supply which was already heated to almost boiling point. I resisted the temptation to fill my entire 3.78 litre bottle. The workers needed it more than me. The perk of having construction workers supporting me was that they could stop the traffic for me to go unopposed on the road for several kilometres.

The waterfall was urging me to skate faster and I did. By noon, I arrived. There wasn't any sign leading to entrance to waterfall. I wouldn't know about the existence of this waterfall if I don't search my online maps. Only ticos would know of this place. Opposite the entrance was a restaurant. I asked the staff if I could park my pushcart and longboard outside while I headed to waterfall for a dip. I promised to patronize them after my dip. Crossed over a low-lying barb wire, there wasn't any clues leading to waterfall. Then I heard some screams and splashes and followed the noise. Finding waterfall was like searching for hidden treasure. There was a local family already dipping in the pool. I joined in for a dip to cool myself from the Sun. The waterfall was small and have a pool for us to swim around. After I have cooled myself, returned to Bar Cascada. Ordered Ceviche, first time I ate this since Mexico. I t was much disappointing. I would expect prawns and fish in it from my experience with it in Mexico. Mine here was a pathetic small bowl of fish Ceviche. Unable to fill my stomach, Ordered another hamburger. As I bit into my hamburger, the weather turned for the worse. The sky juice came pouring down. Since I have only 22 km left, I took my time to wait for the rain to stop before continuing.

I thought this would be the end of rain, it was just the appetizer. 6 km into Claro, the rain intensified into downpour. Sought refuge in a petrol station. Instead of being drenched by my sweat, I was soaked to the bone by downpour. The rain showed no signs of stopping, I braved through the rain when it slowed down, in hoping some driver would pity my poor soul or my crazy resolute to skate all the way in the rain and offered me a ride. Well, it didn't work. I am left to my own resolve. Funny thing was that whenever I don't need a ride or complete the peak of a big climb, someone would pull over to offer me a ride. But when I am in need of a ride, no one offered me until I finished my challenge. Was like God like to watch me suffer and then rewarded me with a driver when I finished the worst section.

The rain pushed me to skate faster to my destination. No sun or heat to slow me down. All in my thought, it was to reach Neily as soon as possible. Today was the first time I skate through the rain since USA. Mexico doesn't count as it was just droplets. I was lucky through Central America and Mexico to have good sunny weather for 5 months. My lucky streak had to come to an end as I am approaching May, the start of the rainy season. The last 16 km to Neily was a torture, I am just anticipating where was Neily as if it doesn't exist. Good thing was that the rain here was warm due to the tropical climate. If it was in Oregon, I would be wet and shivering cold.

At last, arrived in Neily soaking wet. Went to the fire station, they turned me away then I tried the Red Cross. Same result. Last resort, I tried the church. But the priest wasn't around. Was like all the stars turned against me today. Soaking wet and cold, I am really in need of warm shower and comfortable bed. Succumbed to my weakness and went for a hotel. Had to choose a more expensive hotel cos I could only pay using my debit card as I don't have enough colones to pay. Didn't expect that I would stay in hotel tonight. Paid 15,000 colones or US $27 for a room with hot shower. Thankfully, I received donations from my followers to indulge in comfort today. Thank you all for those have supported me. Today, your donation came into good use. Tomorrow I would cross into Panama, my 22th country and the last country on North America Continent. My Last night in Costa Rica or I should say Costly Rich.

CHAPTER 12

PANAMA

Day 429: Adios Costa Rica, Hola Panama, country 22! Possible end to my trip?
Neily, Costa Rica to David, Panama
Distance: 72 km
Time: 6.56 am to 1.30 pm
Cumulative distance: 15, 552 km

Glad that I stayed in the hotel last night, it was raining all night. However, my clothes were soaking wet from yesterday's rain and unable to dry in the room. As a result, I have to wear my wet clothes to skate. It was not a bad thing after all, the wet clothes helped to cool me in the immolating heat for a while. My clothes dried fast then soaked from my sweat moments later.

The border to Panama was only 17 km. By 8.15 am, I reached the border Paso Canoas. Queued up for exit stamp, midway into the queue, a traveller informed me that I have to cross the road and pay US $8 for exit tax. This was another unnecessary red tape process and there weren't any signs to inform the travellers on where to pay exit tax. The guy kept the queue for me while I went over to pay. Continued on to Panama checkpoint. I read on the internet from those travelling to Panama's first-hand experience. They must produce proof of exit from Panama, and proof of sufficient funds for travelling. I have prepared and screenshot my flight itinerary to Bogota, Colombia on 28 April and my bank statement. However, the immigration officer never asked me for all these. I wasted all my time and effort in preparing all these to enter Panama and they never bother to ask me for these. I could have booked my flight when I arrive in Panama City. Now I have to rush to Panama City by 26 April to catch my flight. I double check with the officer. "Are you sure that you don't want to check my flight out of here?" The lady simply shook her head and gave me the entry stamp. Furthermore, there isn't any entry fee though I remember reading that there was a US $3 fee. Well, I save US $3.

Panama uses US as their currency as El Salvador. Only the difference was that panama has their own coins which has the same value as USA ones. Back to using US, easier to budget now. Panama was my 22nd country on my World tour. With Panama, I have transversed through all the Countries on mainland North America Continent. And today could be the end of my North America leg as well.

By noon, I stopped at a bus shelter to cook my lunch and napped as usual. I left my pushcart and longboard at the bus stop. While dreaming, a crushing noise abruptly woke me up. The next thing I saw, horrified me. This was becoming my worst nightmare. Was it just a nightmare? No, I was truly awake. The driver failed to notice my pushcart and drove past it, crushing my left side wheel. The pushcart collapsed under its weight. My rim was completely bent and seemed unsalvageable. The driver immediately got out to assess the situation. Surprisingly I wasn't angry and actually showed little emotion as if I was calm about it. In my head, was just "now what". I wasn't mad at the driver; I could only put the blame on it. I shouldn't leave my pushcart and longboard on the side of road where drivers couldn't see. Should have lifted it up the kerbs but I was too lazy and too tired to do so. Unable to ride to David anymore, he offered me a ride and he knew a workshop to fix it. In the car, was two German hitchhikers whom he picked up at the border. He drove us to David, and dropped me off at a car workshop before driving the Germans to bus station. He paid for the repair and whatever needed it to fix. The mechanic took a glance at it and assured us that it could be fixed in no time. And so, the driver left me and my poor pushcart at workshop.

The mechanic then struggled to remove my rim from the pushcart. My pushcart was a pretty unique rig. The rim was welded to the cart. I had it for 7 months, I still couldn't figure out how to remove the wheel, let alone the mechanics who probably never fix a broken baby stroller. They were supposed to fix cars, not a baby stroller. After trying for hours, they gave up and refunded me the money the driver paid to them. Had to grab a taxi to my hostel to figure my next move. Could it be the End of my Round the World on Board? Well, at least I have crossed through 22 countries and 3 Continents including entire North America Continent. There were a few options left for me. Find another workshop to fix it or replace a new stroller but replacing it would be difficult. My pushcart had been a perfect companion to my longboard. It enabled me to carry large loads, exceeding the supposed weight limit. Most importantly, it has brakes for me to control my speed safely. Getting another one here would be mission impossible. Another option was to return to my original way of skating. Skating with my just my backpack on my back. Meant that I had to discard much of my stuff and go really minimal with only my essentials. But the climate was too humid for me to skate with my backpack. I consume at least 7 litres of water during my skate. My back could only carry a maximum of 4 litres of water with my tent, cooking stove, sleeping bag and food. Which remains an unlikely option. I would have to stay here for a while to figure out how now. My flight to Colombia was 12 days away. I have to figure out by then. Only God knows.

Day 433: Pushie's Revival
Panama: Santiago to Pilotos Truck Stop
Distance: 81 km
Time: 6.40 am to 3.33 pm
Cumulative distance: 15,633 km

My Saviour comes in the form of car mechanic. My hostel owner knew a workshop that could fix my pushcart and brought me to Taller Robinson. Taller was workshop in Spanish. At first, I thought the mechanic couldn't replace it as he too struggled to remove the axle until he stumbled upon a lever at the bottom which release the axle. For once, after 7 months skating with my pushie, I finally knew how to remove wheels. It was that simple. The mechanic subsequently straighten the bent axle and installed onto my rim. I replaced front rim with my new spare rim as spare rim was originally used to replace the front for braking. My pushie was Revived!! I could resume my World Tour on board. Upon pushing my pushie, it felt strange. Pushie kept steering to the left. Upon further investigation, my tire was damaged by the mishap. Woon from love cycling Singapore Facebook group, advised me to get soapy water and massaged the tire while it was deflated. Probably, I wasn't doing it right, so I spent another additional day to find a bicycle mechanic to fix the issue. The mechanic simply, with a wave of his hand, instantly fixed the problem. In all, I spent 3 days in David. Maybe the accident was meant for me to take a break before pushing on to Panama City.

The mishap caused me to lose a few days behind my schedule to reach Panama City by 23 April. Took a bus to Santiago, 200 km away and 250 km to Panama City to keep up with my schedule. The night before, there was Charles, an American Peace Corp volunteer in Panama. He brought his puppy along in the hostel. The puppy kept jumping onto my bed during the night. I argued with Charles to keep his puppy under control. I am not against dogs, but I paid so much for a good night's rest and expect a good rest. What an Inconsiderate dog owner. At least, keep your dog outside the room, not disturbing others. Enough ranting.

In Santiago, stayed in the fire station. Slept in the garage behind the fire truck. The siren woke me up at 5.40 am. Unable to sleep further for another mere minutes, I had an early start than usual. It worked well. I got to put in more mileage while the temperature was cooler, before the heat kicked in. Kept on skating without any breaks to capitalize on the cooler temperature till 9 am. By then I already covered 30 km. From then on, the heat kicked in and I switched to slower pace. At 11 am, upon approaching Agua Dulce for lunch, a car pulled in front of me and a lady waved me to pause. She handed me a packet of lunch, Chicken with rice and Spaghetti. Carbo loading for me. I explained to them my journey and thanked them. Saved a day's ration.

Not taking any chances, I lifted my pushcart up the kerb to the bus shelter which I did my usual routine, lunch and siesta. After a rejuvenating 2 hours break, I returned to the road. This time, I encountered an intense headwind. If this wind was prevalent, then tomorrow, I would have a fun ride, tailwind pushing me as I would be going back South. For the headwind, it was cooling and slowing me down. Looked like I am not going to make it to Penonome, a 100 km skate from Santiago. But I do have a backup destination. On ioverlander app, there was a truck stop where I could camp and eat. It wasn't well marked on Google map or map.me. All I knew was it was 81 km from Santiago. Hence, I had to keep looking at my phone to find the place as I was approaching. The Sign 'Pilotos Truck Stop' appeared on the horizon like an oasis. The truck stop was truly an Oasis in the long journey. There was Wifi, restaurant, gas station, convenience store. Behind the store, lies shower, laundry machine and rest area for weary travellers like me. 160 km to Panama City, finish line to my North America Leg.

Day 435: Panama Jinx

Panama: Pilotos Truck stop to Anton (bus to Chorrera after fall)
Distance: 44 km
Time : 6.58 am to 1.30 pm
Cumulative distance: 15,677 km

Day 434

About to set off early from the truck stop, immediately the sky showered. A calling to return to sleep. The truck stop has wifi, shower, restaurant to dine and a comfortable sofa to sleep. Most importantly it was Free. I could definitely stay another day.

Day 435

The weather looked ready for a great skate. Left the truck stop, if only it was located nearer to Panama City, then I could stay till the end. First 20 km to Penonome, I have to endure the headwind coming from North. But once after Penonome, I head south, that wind became Tailwind, a sail for me to skate faster. Indeed, my pace steadily rose after Penonome. A touring cyclist overtook me without saying hello or a simple wave. Most touring cyclists I encountered would either slow down to say hi or chat with me at least. He either assumed I am a local bum pushing his pushcart on a skateboard or just too unfriendly to say hi. I couldn't catch up with him anyway, with tailwind aiding him further.

Further on, a driver pulled over. He goes "loco loco" Loco was crazy in Spanish. I took that as a compliment of course. We took a selfie together before he presented me with a box of cologne from his car boot. His car boot was filled with newly wrapped items from shampoo to toys. I would assume that he works in a trading business. That box of cologne might come in handy, especially being stinky after days without showers. Probably, he could smell my stench, hence he gave a cologne to me. Maybe that was why I don't have any luck with the ladies cos I stink at the end of the day. Now with this cologne, Ladies couldn't resist me. Touring on a longboard with a wonderful smell, definitely irresistible.

I swore Panama doesn't like me or was a jinx to me. On the first day in Panama, a driver crushed my pushie. And today I got my first accident since Spain. I was going fast with the tailwind. All of a sudden, I tumbled and scraped my previously left knee. The culprit was a tiny pebble. I assumed that I was infallible now with my pushie providing stability and balance. I guessed I was wrong. The accident left my knee bleeding and tore off a layer of skin. Though it wasn't that horrific as the accident in Spain, which ripped the entire flesh to the bone. I recovered and poured water over my wound. Few minutes to recover from the shock. Tried to hitchhike a ride but traffic was moving too fast to stop for me. Anton, a town bearing the namesake of my dutch friend, was a km away. I skated slowly with caution not to have another fall. I tried a hospital first however it was crowded. The time to queue probably was longer than the time for my wound to heal. I moved on. Next was a pharmacy. I pointed my bleeding knee to the pharmacist and asked "Me puedes Ayudar" I wasn't sure if my sentence structure was correct but he got the drift. He cleaned and bandaged my wound. It costed me $16 for medication and treatment.

Unable to continue skating for the day, I had to take a bus to Chorrera. Chorrera located 40 km away from Panama City, the finish line to my North America leg. I didn't want to end my North

America leg with a bus. I have to cross across the Panama Canal to signify the end. Therefore, I settled for the nearest City to the capital. Hopefully, the next day I could recover well enough to do an easy short skate to Panama City for the finish. The bus dropped me off at the crossroad between Chorrera and the autopista/toll road to Panama. I looked at the massive 5 lanes highway, and I have to cut through 3 fast lanes in order to access the road to Chorrera. I am not going to risk that, especially with my current condition now.

After lunch at the bus shelter, I took the quiet village road beside. I couldn't push mongo, which required me to bend my left wounded knee. Could only push on my wounded leg as it doesn't require much bending motion. Fortunately, I only have to skate 5 km to Chorrera. Originally, planned to sleep in the fire station. With the accident, I would need a more comfortable rest. Another cheap hotel for me. Hospedeje Lamas quoted me US $30, which was still the cheapest in town. Too bad, had no choice but to go for it. Tomorrow to Panama, end of my North America leg

Date of entry: 23 April 2018
Day 436: Goodbye North America! Hola South America! Continent no.4
Panama: Chorrera to Panama City
Distance: 41 km
Time: 7.42 am to 3 pm
Cumulative distance: 15,718 km

Last September 2017, I first set foot on the North America Continent in Vancouver, Canada and 7 months later, I completed my North America leg in Panama City. Transversed through all the 10 countries in Mainland North America Continent on my trusty 1166 longboard. Skated along ocean roads, desert, thick forest, farmlands and mountains and all kinds of terrains that you could think of except for snow. Finally, today marked the finish to my North America Odyssey as I have to fly to Colombia cos there isn't any road for me to continue on to South America. Either you have to fly or sail to Colombia. Though the two countries were connected by a tiny strip of land, known as the Darien Gap. Impassable terrain marked by dense jungle, habituated by dangerous wildlife, like venomous snakes and man-eating Jaguars. Even if you managed to survive the wildlife, there was the drug cartels roaming and smuggling their drugs across here on route to USA. Chances were you might be kidnapped and murdered by them. There isn't any road connecting the two continents, leaving the pan American highway, the longest road in the world, separated by this tiny 90 km gap. Building a road to link the two continents would be costly and damaging to the fragile ecosystem. Therefore, travellers could only travel by air or sea to cross over to the next Continent. I prefer flying cos it was more affordable to sailing. Sailing could cost up to $500 whereas flying only cost $100. Only the foolish would attempt to cross the gap by land.

My knee recovered pretty well from yesterday's fall. Loco motion of my knee was just enough to skate. Since it was only 40 km away from Panama City, slept longer to enjoy my expensive room. Skipped my usual breakfast to begin the day cos I had only 4 slices of bread left, insufficient to fill my engine. I figured that I could find something to eat along the way.

Being so close to the Capital, naturally the traffic would be extremely hectic. That was why I always skated as close to the Capital the day before to have a less stressful skate, jousting against the raging traffic. 5 km away from Chorrera, found a Fonda, which was a small eatery stall and they had Empanadas, something similar to curry puffs, a taste from my home. The customer there warned me impending dangers I am about to face on the roads. Indeed, it was horrific hair-raising affairs. Clusters of mega shopping malls, apartments, office buildings were sprawling throughout the highway, there wasn't any space left for greenery. Signs that I was approaching a Colossal Concrete jungle. The terrain was unforgivingly hilly. I thought Panama Canal was supposed to be flat. In fact, the Americans have to spend tons of dynamite to blow up mountains in order to construct the Panama Canal.

The construction of the Panama Canal was first attempted by the French after their success in Suez Canal. The project fell apart due to bankruptcy and rough terrains. The project was then revived by USA president Roosevelt in 1904. However, Panama at that time, was part of Gran Colombia. What did the Americans do? They instigated a coup and Panama became an independent country. And so the construction of the canal began and opened the canal on August 15, 1914. One of the largest and most difficult engineering projects ever undertaken, the Panama Canal shortcut greatly reduced the time for ships to travel between the Atlantic and Pacific Oceans, enabling them to avoid the lengthy, hazardous Cape Horn route around the southernmost tip of South America via the Drake Passage or Strait of Magellan.

Needless to say, the raging traffic and hilly terrain made my progress slow on the road. In 3 hours, I only made 21 km. That was like 7 km per hour. Since I only had a light breakfast and my stomach rumbling for fuel, decided to stop at the bus shelter for lunch. By noon, I was back on the road. Noticeably, the traffic intensified, relegating me to the rough, rarely maintained shoulder Lane. Still had to push on. Entered San Juan hills. At least some greenery without any concrete building around. The dark clouds loomed over my head, hinting that it might rain anytime soon.

My excitement grew as I spotted the bridge of the Americas from afar. The bridge provided a crossing across the Panama Canal. It has to be high for ships to pass through. That meant I have to face my greatest fear of heights once more. Prior to crossing the bridge, a Chinese monument lied strangely across the highway. Chinese played a major part in constructing the canal. Large number of Chinese immigrants during the 1900s came over to construct this colossal engineering marvel. No wonder, I met many multiple generations of Chinese here.

Before crossing the bridge, the shoulder lane gradually vanished, leaving me no room to manoeuvre across the bridge. A local guy warned me not to cross the bridge as there isn't any room for me and vehicles might hit me. However, there wasn't any alternative route to Panama City. As far I checked on the map, this was only the road to the capital. After all, touring cyclists passed through here all the time, it must be safe for me to cross as well. I cautiously skated while traffic squeezed past me with the thinnest of margins. Until a police officer in motorcycle came to my rescue. At first, I thought he was going to arrest me for illegally skating across. Instead, he waved me to continue. He escorted me from behind and blocked one lane for me to skate through. At that moment, I felt like a star, having a personal escort. What a way to end my North America leg. After exiting the bridge and where more lanes were opened for traffic, I stopped by the shoulder to thank him. More selfies and he left me to myself as the road diversified and it would be less dangerous for me to skate. Just 500 metres to my hostel, the sky welcomed me with a pouring rain. As if the sky was celebrating my finish. I couldn't care less about the rain anymore. Anyway, I would not be skating anymore. This was the end to NORTH AMERICA!!

Through the 7 months here, I encountered all sorts of adventures and made many friends, some really close companions on the road. Met Yves, and Fred, and Marge 'magic Hair' in Baja California last December. Since then, we have been riding together, crossing through Central America. They have become family away from home to me. They have already arrived in Panama City yesterday by hitchhiking. Would meet up for another reunion and this certainly won't be the last as well. We were all going to ride through South America.

My North journey has been nothing short of amazing. From my American friends who hosted me throughout the Pacific West Coast, to strangers who supported me in one way or another. I cannot thank you enough for all the wonderful memories. Goodbye North America! South America awaits me!

APPENDIX

Camino Santiago – A pilgrimage is leading to the shrine of the apostle Saint James the Great in the cathedral of Santiago de Compostela in Galicia in northwestern Spain, where tradition has it that the remains of the saint are buried. Many follow its routes as a form of spiritual path or retreat for their spiritual growth.

Warmshower - An online hospitality exchange organisation for touring bicyclists or those on human-powered transport that want either indoor accommodation or just a break from cycling and a warm shower.

Bivy – A lightweight one or two person Shelter. They were first developed as solo shelters for mountaineering and climbing where participants were interested in a lightweight and highly compressible gear.

LDP – Long Distance Pumping or Pushing on a longboard
Westssup – 2 metres long Rattan pole developed by Deejay Pascua as means to propel longboard through paddling off the ground.
Bend - **A** city in, and the county seat of, Deschutes County, Oregon, United States

Chipseal - A pavement surface treatment that combines one or more layer(s) of asphalt with one or more layer(s) of fine aggregate. The rough surface causes noticeable increases in vibration and rolling resistance for bicyclists and Skateboarders — a harrowing ride.

REI store - **Recreational Equipment, Inc.**, commonly known as **REI**, is an American retail and outdoor recreation services corporation. It is organised as a consumers› co-operative. REI sells sporting goods, camping gear, travel equipment, and clothing. It also offers services such as outdoor-oriented vacations and courses.

IDSA – International Distance Skateboarding Association. Governing body for the sport of Long Distance Skateboarding.

Fatbike - an off-road bicycle with oversized tires, typically 3.8 in (97 mm) or larger and rims 2.16 in (55 mm) or wider, designed for low ground pressure to allow riding on soft, unstable terrain, such as snow, sand, bogs and mud.[1] Fatbikes are built around frames with wide forks and stays to accommodate the wide rims required to fit these tires. The wide tires can be used with inflation pressures as low as 340 hPa; 0.34 bar (5 psi) to allow for a smooth ride over rough obstacles. A rating of 550–690 hPa; 0.55–0.69 bar (8–10 psi) is suitable for the majority of riders.

UltraSkate – 24 hours endurance skateboarding event whereby the participants will test their body limits to skate laps around a track within the 24 hours time frame. Depending on their goals, they can rest to sleep and eat if they need. For the top racers, they will skate non-stop. Currently, there are 2 Ultraskate events held annually, one in Miami, USA and other in Netherlands.

iOverlander – a mobile app created to meet the primary needs travellers face every day: where to sleep, eat, get fuel, find a mechanic, or just help locating a pretty place to catch the sunset and snap off a few pics.

Camelbak – a water bladder carried inside a backpack with a tube sticking out for easy access to drinking water.

Steripen - a gadget designed to sterilize water, making it safe to drink and cook with. Resembling a large bottle of nasal spray, SteriPEN is a compact device which uses ultraviolet light to sterilize water and make it safe for drinking.

Mongo - A person skates mongo if they use their leading foot (the foot that is in the front while riding) to push. While they are pushing, their back foot stays near the rear of the board and they push with their front foot.

Tailwind Nurition – a powder mixture when mixed with water, designed to overcome the nutrition problems faced by endurance athletes in events like 50's, 100's, 24-hour, and multi-day epics. Tailwind combines complete fuel, hydration, and electrolytes in a tasty drink that won't turn your stomach into a brick.

SPECIAL THANKS

To My Support Crew and my Sponsors who assisted me throughout the Journey

Sponsors

Mark Groenenboom – G|Bomb
Martin Schumacher – 1166 Longboards
Dan Furrer – Don't Trip Longboards trucks
Orangatang Wheels

Support Crew

Uncle K.C Au Yeung
DeeJay Pascua
Clark Blumenstein
Andrew Andras
Nat Halliday
Panta Gruelon
Jack Smith
James Peter
Brooks Miller
Iris Eldelsmid
Cory Poole
Ted Bilderback
Calleigh Little
Raymond Tan

To those who supported me on Kickstarter

Ben Sadeghi
Henry Hemmerde
Dave Price
R. Merz
Kevin Mok
Colin Quek
Jaslyn
Bernard Ho You Kong
Matt
John Cheng
Florian Michl
Tan yun yan
Servien Kwan
Fugitive Bob
John tan
Niklas
Norita Mansor
Hey burt
Steven Yoon
Garry Kraft
Yvonne Yock
Luwynleo
Yvonne Yock
Cecilia Sim
Randy Chong
Elvin Goh
Adrian Lim
Nick
Chong Wei Sing
Heidi Lau
Ng Li Xi
Bob NLD
François Bardouil
Heng Mui Chu
Janice Cheong
Alexander Kruglov
Edmund Vong
Mathieu Bon
Raymond Tan
Ryan Chin
Juvena
Lars-Terje Lysemose
Jun Yuan
LEE JY
Travis Buck Kingsley

Milton Keynes UK
Ingram Content Group UK Ltd.
UKHW050423171123
432729UK00002B/49

* 9 7 8 1 5 4 3 7 5 3 1 3 4 *